THE NOTORIOUS RENO GANG

THE NOTORIOUS RENO GANG

*The Wild Story of the West's First Brotherhood
of Thieves, Assassins, and Train Robbers*

RACHEL DICKINSON

Guilford, Connecticut

An imprint of Globe Pequot
Distributed by NATIONAL BOOK NETWORK

British Library Cataloguing in Publication Information Available
Library of Congress Cataloging-in-Publication Data

ISBN 978-1-4930-2639-5 (hardcover)
ISBN 978-1-4930-2640-1 (e-book)

♾™ The paper used in this publication meets the minimum requirements of American National Standard for Information Sciences—Permanence of Paper for Printed Library Materials, ANSI/ NISO Z39.48-1992.

Printed in the United States of America

For my husband, Tim Gallagher,
and our children, Railey, Clara, Jack (d. 2012), and Gwendolyn

Contents

Prologue ix

Chapter One: Old Rockford. 1

Chapter Two: Meet the Players: John Reno and
Allan Pinkerton 10

Chapter Three: The Birth of Seymour 22

Chapter Four: The Reno Boys and the Civil War. 40

Chapter Five: Allan Pinkerton Goes to Washington 50

Chapter Six: Seymour Takes a Stand 66

Chapter Seven: Koniakers and Boodle 73

Chapter Eight: Incident at Pana, Illinois 80

Chapter Nine: The First Train Robbery 87

Chapter Ten: Talley and Brooks Meet the
Vigilance Committee 103

Chapter Eleven: The Second Train Robbery 108

Chapter Twelve: Vigilante Fever 114

Chapter Thirteen: Missouri Breaks John Reno 122

Chapter Fourteen: Iowa Raids 130

Chapter Fifteen: The Third Train Robbery. 137

Chapter Sixteen: The Fourth Train Robbery 144

Chapter Seventeen: Hanging, Redux. 155

Chapter Eighteen: Will and Simeon Reno's Day in Court . . . 160

Chapter Nineteen: Extradition from Canada. 168

Chapter Twenty: Cutting Off the Head of the Snake 179

Chapter Twenty-One: Fallout from the New
    Albany Hangings 190

Chapter Twenty-Two: Dr. Monroe Moves On 193

Chapter Twenty-Three: John Reno—Last Man Standing . . . 197

Chapter Twenty-Four: Allan Pinkerton Writes His Books . . . 205

Chapter Twenty-Five: Seymour after the Reno Gang 209

Chapter Twenty-Six: And in the End 213

Acknowledgments 217

Bibliographic Note. 218

Bibliography 221

Notes. 226

Index 237

About the Author 249

Prologue

We don't know exactly what happened that dark moonless night in early December of 1868. Newspapers all over the country picked up the same story, originated by the *New Albany Daily Ledger,* and ran it with embellishments. However, one central fact was clear. When the sun rose, four people were found murdered in the cavernous hall of the Floyd County Jail.

The incident started when sixty or so men of the Seymour Vigilance Committee began the three-block walk from the New Albany train depot to the jail. It was two in the morning, December 12, 1868. The tension was palpable. No one spoke. All wore the darkest clothing they owned, and most had stuffed a red bandanna partway into a jacket pocket. One man had a chisel and a mallet. A couple of them had neatly coiled ropes slung over their shoulders. Many carried wooden clubs. Most carried pistols, revolvers, or rifles. They all kept an eye on the large man at the front leading them through the dark side streets of town.

The jail in New Albany, Indiana, was a fortress-like stone building surrounded by a tall cast-iron fence. One guard, Luther Whitten, stood at the front gate. The night was cold, really cold. There was a light dusting of snow covering the ground and flakes rising and swirling on little gusts of wind. Whitten pulled his coat closer around him and warmed his hands in the small fire he had built in the gutter of the street. When he saw the large group of men coming toward him, emerging out of the black night, Whitten ran into the jail. About twenty men from the mob followed him in, funneling through the doorway, two by two. The rest stayed outside with their guns ready, prepared for any trouble that might arise.

Where's the sheriff? Bring us the sheriff! yelled the large man leading the invasion.

Sheriff Fullenlove was asleep in bed with his wife in their apartment on the first floor of the jail building. Hearing the commotion, he came out to the darkened entryway in his nightshirt and drawers and bolted down a stairway leading to the basement. The crowd surged forward and someone shot into the stairwell.

You know why we're here, shouted the leader. *Give us the keys to the cells and you won't get hurt!* But it was too late. The sheriff had managed to climb out through a basement window and was heading across the snowy lawn in his bare feet. One of the vigilantes standing lookout on the lawn shot at Fullenlove, who crumpled to the ground. The bullet entered his arm, right below the elbow. A red stain spread on his nightshirt. Several vigilantes ran up to the bleeding man, and one of them hit him on the head with the butt of his gun.

The sheriff wasn't going anywhere.

Inside the jail, men were yelling back and forth. The leader and some other vigilantes tried to get his agitated associates to calm down. When vigilantes started opening doors they found two men, Neal and Perrette, county commissioners who were there for the night. They were ordered into the hall, where their hands were tied, and they were motioned to sit in the corner. The leader barged into the room where the sheriff lived and found Mrs. Fullenlove in bed.

What have you done to my husband? she screamed.

Shut up and give me the keys, said the leader.

The woman refused. *Where's my husband?* she shouted over and over again.

Don't give them anything. It was the sheriff, yelling in a strained voice to his wife after the vigilantes had brought him into the jail and propped him in the corner of the hall with the county commissioners.

The leader ignored Mrs. Fullenlove, who at this point was wailing, and began rifling through the nightstand next to the bed, where he found a set of keys. This discovery sent the vigilantes scurrying from the bedroom.

Once more in the hallway, a dozen vigilantes trained their guns on an overweight young man. Thomas Matthews was standing guard in front of the locked door to the cell block, sweating profusely in spite of the cold air.

Open it, the vigilante leader demanded as he threw the keys.

The trembling Matthews refused, which prompted one of the vigilantes to knock him down with the butt of a gun. Stunned, the guard, who was really no more than a boy, slowly got to his feet and began to cry. He turned toward the door and, with shaking hands, tried to fit the key into the lock. After several attempts, he got the heavy wooden door open. Several of the armed men pushed past him and entered the main part of the jail.

The New Albany jail, a large two-story structure, was made from blocks of limestone cut from local quarries. It could hold dozens of prisoners in cells—solid, 6-foot-by-10-foot metal boxes painted gray—arranged on two floors. A narrow bed folded down from each cell's long side. A sink with a lid (a toilet really) stood in the corner. The only thing resembling a window—letting light in and also keeping it out because of its inadequacy—was a small metal grate about a foot square in the cell door.

Once inside the block, one of the committee men shouted, *Where are the Reno boys?*

Show us where the Reno boys are, and we also want Charlie Anderson, cried another, directing his words toward the quivering Matthews.

The cells were arranged on two tiers, the second-story cells opening onto a balcony. The arrangement allowed the guards to see all the cells at once, and the prisoners could see the guards if they pressed their faces against the door grate. That night, the only guard on cell-block duty was Matthews. He had proven he was no match for an angry mob of men with weapons. The vigilance committee leader demanded to know which cells needed to be unlocked. *Numbers 7, 11, and 24,* whispered Matthews.

Grabbing the keys, the leader barked out the order, *Take the guard and tie him up and put him with the others.* Then, seeing that the keys were numbered, he opened cell 24, the cell closest to him.

What do you want with me? A voice came from the darkness of the cell.

Step out and state your name, the leader demanded.

The prisoner stepped into the murky light cast by a few handheld lanterns.

He said his name in a low voice as one of the vigilantes stepped behind him and began tying his hands. *Frank Reno.*

Likely, Frank Reno had also stood quietly a dozen years earlier, not in a jail, but as an eighteen-year-old with his parents and siblings outside the family's farmhouse on the edge of Rockford, Indiana. On that occasion, he would have watched as the town's hotel burned, sending licks of flame high into the night.

He would have seen the fire move, roof to roof, engulfing other buildings, and sending sparks into the cold wintery air. He would have noticed his father, Wilkinson Reno, the family patriarch, staring at the crackling horizon, unconcerned with his neighbors' losses, considering, instead, the opportunities this disaster laid out before him.

CHAPTER ONE

Old Rockford

BETWEEN 1856 AND 1860, THE TOWN OF ROCKFORD, INDIANA, HOME OF Wilkinson Reno and his clan, was almost entirely destroyed by a series of mysterious fires. The first occurred late on a cold night at the end of November. A blaze broke out in a kitchen shed attached to the Rockford House hotel. Flames tore through the room, which was really no more than a shack tacked on to the back of the main building, and then made quick work of the hotel.

The acrid smell of the smoke, the roaring fire, and the sound of glass windows popping from the heat woke Rockford residents and brought them to the scene. They watched, almost helpless, as the flames leaped from building to building. People hurried from the scene, rushing into their homes and businesses attempting to save something, hauling furniture and goods into the packed-dirt streets. Total catastrophe was averted when a cold, soaking, steady rain arrived with the morning light and left smoldering piles of blackened rubble in its wake.

Miraculously, not one of the seven hundred people who lived in Rockford died in that first fire, but John Shmitt's cabinet shop and wareroom were lost, as was the large storehouse of Peter & Bro. The tin and hardware house of Mr. E. Moore also burned, as well as a number of homes. Mr. Henry Peter lost "a choice selection of valuable books," while Mr. Harding, the keeper of the Rockford House, saved nothing above the ground floor.

The night of that first fire, Rockford was a thriving river town, its main products being pork packed in barrels and corn. Yet, just thirty years earlier, when pioneers arrived in this part of eastern Indiana, the land was covered with a thick and heavy hardwood forest. Settlers wanted to make homes for themselves on this kind of land, believing that where trees grew in abundance, so would crops.

In a wry observation, Indianan Ebenezer Tucker wrote in 1882: "A few years ago timber stood on the ground a burden and a nuisance costing untold labor and toil to clear its bulk from the face of the land and make ready the soil to receive the precious seed for the hoped-for crop . . . Now the value of the timber alone far exceeds that of the land itself."

Trees weren't the only draw to Rockford. The White River also influenced the growth of the settlement, providing a ready source of power for gristmills. Once mills were established, homesteaders soon carved out the forests to make way for pastures and fields. In those first years, corn was planted around the stumps left after cutting the trees. Over time axes, chains, and strong horses tugged and pulled out the reminders of the earth's previous inhabitants. Pig farming flourished. Hogs were a particularly good choice for they could be let loose into the still vast forests surrounding the little farms to root and forage in the mast for acorns, walnuts, and other fruits from the trees. As winter approached, farmers rounded up the animals, feeding them corn harvested from the fields to fatten the hogs up before they were herded to the Rockford slaughter yards. It was a sight that rivaled a cattle drive.

Dr. Parsons, an easterner on tour through Indiana in 1840, then considered part of the West, witnessed one of these hog drives in Terre Haute. "We stood at attention on the sidewalk, watching the surging mass of porkers go by, a sight well worth the seeing. First went a man on horseback, scattering corn and uttering at intervals in a minor key the cry 'Pig-oo-ee! Pig-oo-ee!' All along the sidewalk, at street crossings and at alleyways helpers were stationed to keep in line the pigs that were driven forward from the rear by drovers with long sticks. The rear was brought up by the very fat porkers who had to have special attendants, and a wagon followed for those who became too tired to walk."

The *Rockford Herald*, which recorded the goings-on of the town's largest pork-packing house (along with everything else that happened in the town), noted that the buildings burned three times. Yet the owner was not deterred. He kept rebuilding because the business was so profitable. Although it had not earned Rockford the name Porkopolis—a moniker applied to Cincinnati, Ohio—pork-packing surely built the town.

Hog butchering and pork-packing was seasonal work in Rockford, done in the winter months when carcasses could be kept cold. An entry in the *Rockford Herald* gives an idea of the size and scope of the industry: "HOGS—There have been some six to eight thousand hogs received at this place, a great number of which are still uncut and frozen stiff." It's easy to imagine frozen hog carcasses stacked like cordwood on the grounds of the pork-packing plant waiting to be cut into pieces. As the butchers worked, they packed pieces of pork into oak barrels made by local coopers. Before the barrels were sealed, coarse salt, saltpeter, and brine were poured over the meat to prevent spoiling. It would be early spring before the brined meat could be moved to market.

At winter's height, the East Fork of the White River was frozen. But as the days grew longer and warmer, and the snows stopped and the sun warmed the earth, the streams began to flow and the White River slowly began to thaw. Flatboats, built of tulip poplar—felled, stripped, cut, then fashioned into the functional boats during the off-season—were loaded with pork barrels and launched into the river. Young men poled and maneuvered the boats ever west and south, the waters carrying them as the White River spilled into the Ohio, then the Wabash, and finally into the mighty Mississippi.

Eventually, flotillas of up to a thousand boats a day reached their destination, New Orleans. Once there, the cargo was unloaded and the boats broken up for scrap wood. The young adventurers who steered the boats south made their way back home by steamboat, if they were lucky, or a combination of uncomfortable stagecoach and wagon rides and walking.

There was no doubt that the slaughterhouses clustered on the banks of the East Fork of the White River were the source of Rockford's prosperity. However, they were not the town's sole attraction. Before fires devastated the community, the bustling settlement boasted a Methodist church, a school, a Masonic hall, gristmills, shops, hotels, whiskey houses, and by 1852, a train depot. It was a stop on the north-south Jeffersonville, Madison & Indianapolis Railroad line.

Readers of the *Rockford Herald* perused advertisements from local businesses like W. H. Mason, dentist ("He has the newly invented instruments for extracting teeth and old fangs"), the Rockford Mill Company ("has just received a fresh supply of Bank Notes, of the best quality which they will give in exchange for Wheat, at the best market price. Those wishing to sell would do well to call before selling elsewhere"), and J. P. Fentress & Co., Merchants ("carries Dry Goods, Ready Made Clothing, coffee, sugar, salt, molasses, flour, vinegar, spices, indigo, lead, nails, axes, and various other articles too numerous to mention").

Community announcements also attest to the town's active cultural offerings: "Two balls came off here on the night of the 14th—a regular ball at the Odd Fellows rooms, and an independent, opposition ball at Postel's. Fast town, this" and "An association called the 'Rockford Literary Association' has just been organized at this place. It meets Tuesday evenings."

Prior to its destruction, the town's premier accommodation received an excellent review from the *Rockford Herald*: "ROCKFORD HOUSE— We are pleased to see that this house is rapidly gaining a most excellent custom—Dr. Woodward [proprietor] is one of the clever fellows, and make no mistake. Let all who desire to stop at a good House, where there is no card playing nor fighting nor cutting nor shooting nor threatening nor whisky-drinking, be sure to go to the Rockford House."

A robust business sector; a competitive, expanding pork industry; personal and professional services; stabilizing religious institutions; active civic and social clubs; as well as links to a blossoming nationwide transportation system were all available in the prosperous little town of Rockford in 1856. Yet none of those advantages could save it. Neither would the *Rockford Herald*'s crusading owner, publisher, editor, and star journalist, Dr. Jasper R. Monroe. He would, however, play a starring role in chronicling the demise of the community in general, and one family in particular.

When Jasper Monroe settled in Rockford, he'd already had an adventurous life. Born in New Jersey, Jesse or James (names he also used before settling on Jasper) moved with his parents and older brother first to Louisville, Kentucky, then to Vallonia, Indiana. His father died in 1839, within a year of the family's arrival in Indiana. His mother died a few years later.

This left the two boys alone. A young teen, Monroe enlisted with his older brother on a flatboat running out of Louisville for the South. And lucky for Jasper, Mr. Folsbury, the owner of the boat, "had a splendid line of books, including Byron, Moore and other poetical works, and the duties gave ample time for study."

The boat and cargo—flour, hay, and produce—were sold in Natchez, and when Jasper Monroe came back to Louisville he variously worked in a mill, purchased and ran a "furniture car," and drove a hack. And he worked on his writing. *Will Cobett's Vision, or the Devil and Tom Paine* was his earliest literary effort in addition to a lot of poetry, which Monroe would write for the rest of his life.

In the mid-1840s he studied medicine and apprenticed under several doctors in Clarke County, Indiana, a common way to get a medical education in those days. He then purchased a small farm in 1848 in Newry, Jackson County, where he set up a country practice. Two years later Monroe moved his young family—for by this time Jasper had a wife, Adeline, and two small children—to the town of Rockford, where he immediately stepped into a lucrative medical practice.

Yet, as he set broken bones and treated patients for the ague and malaria, his thoughts were never far from poetry and the politics of the day. Monroe had a lot to say about the state of the world, and he didn't hold back. His style was sarcastic yet witty. He lived and breathed politics and railed against anything he didn't believe in. His patients knew that being treated by Dr. Monroe also meant getting an earful about the evil southern Democrats and the expansion of slavery (Monroe was a devotee of the Whig party at that time).

His 1876 biographer wrote: "[Through the winter of] 1855 he found time to write many stories and poems, and to furnish correspondence for our county paper, and those of New Albany and Madison. In 1850 and

1851 he published essays against the grand jury system which are pertinent and if republished now would find twenty endorsers where they had hardly one at that time. He was hot against the isms and follies of that day, and published much in a burlesque style which he is no doubt heartily ashamed of now. Several of his poems and stories attracted marked attention at that time. Dr. Monroe was a zealous Whig and his opposition to the Democratic party partook of the bitterness of gall and wormwood; and so in February 1855 he started his weekly paper *The Rockford Herald* with a view of finally squelching that party in this county if not in the whole country."

Not only the brains behind the newspaper, Monroe was also the brawn, doing all of the typesetting and printing work himself on a press he owned. Never one to shy away from a challenge in pursuit of his goals, he hounded his patients and the businesses in Rockford for subscriptions and advertisements. To ensure there was no mistake as to the paper's origins and credibility, he always took pains to identify himself in its pages as Dr. J. R. Monroe, publisher and editor.

By the time Monroe started the *Rockford Herald,* he was firmly entrenched in the Know-Nothing party. The paper is laced with screeds against Catholics and foreigners, the former because he believed the Pope and the Catholic Church were attempting to rule the world, and the latter because recent immigrants were allowed to vote and it was these non-natives, he believed, who put Democrats in power. The fire and brimstone (or gall and wormwood as his biographer later called it) poured from the pages along with national and even international news lifted from other newspapers.

Monroe's politics and moral rectitude also extended to the popular evil of the day—alcohol. He started a Temperance Union in Rockford that held weekly meetings, and he ran the names of the men, women, and children who signed the Temperance pledge in his weekly paper. Cautionary tales about the evils of drink that always ended with ". . . and then he died," ran in every issue. Additional proof of his commitment can be seen in his policy of not letting establishments that served liquor advertise in his paper. A complete image of Rockford, including the saloons and whorehouses and gambling dens, doesn't emerge from the pages of the *Rockford Herald*. It's as if Monroe believed that if he didn't write about the seedy side of town, it didn't exist.

Despite the popularity of the paper, Monroe had trouble making ends meet as a newspaper man. He was forced to take some of his creditors to county court in Brownstown to get some of the seven hundred dollars owed him. He also continued to see patients. An ad in his own paper makes clear the maladies he preferred to treat, and isolates one ailment that required prompt payment: "Dr. J. R. Monroe may still be consulted at the Herald Office—Persons laboring under chronic or acute Rheumatisms, or Gonorrhea, or Syphilis, in any of their stages, may be cured by applying to Dr. Monroe, taking his prescriptions, following his directions, and paying him for his services. He pays particular attention to the ailments of females, and his assistance may still be had in the hour of their greatest peril. Persons with Ague applying to him will be cured promptly and permanently, but they must follow directions, and pay the bill at once."

Poor Rockford. By 1856, Monroe noted troubling signs of decline. The town had withstood numerous springtime floods of the White River and the vagaries of hog and corn prices on which its fortunes depended. But Monroe was following the development of another community, Seymour, merely two miles away.

"Few people," Monroe wrote, "come to this place [Rockford] but to buy goods, or trade in pork. While they continually go to Seymour if they want any mechanical job executed; and while there for this purpose, they very often do their little trading at the stores—making purchases, which, but for the mechanics, would have been made here . . . A country town must look to the country for its support—railroads will do nothing for it, except to give it a sort of mushroom growth. To thrive, it must be able to supply the wants of farmer, and without mechanics this cannot be done. A wagon, or plow, or rake, or hoe or harrow manufactory is worth more to a village than any number of bales of cotton and calico—not but what these latter are essential also."

The doctor had a particular admiration for the man behind Seymour's success, Captain Meedy Shields. Monroe lauded Shields's foresight in the pages of his newspaper, believing the man was doing everything right. He'd developed a town on paper, setting aside lots and money for churches and schools to be built in this new community. He aggressively supported businesses wishing to relocate.

Monroe wrote: "Seymour had been built up to the dignity of a considerable and thriving village by the foresight, determination and untiring industry of a single individual. To his unconquerable spirit, it is indebted not only for its present prosperity, but even for its existence. Unlike the proprietors of this place [referring to Rockford], Capt. Shields does not think two or three retail stores and half a dozen groceries are all that is necessary to constitute a town; but by liberal overtures, has supplied his village with a varied and good supply of mechanics. These are essential to the prosperity of any village town or city; and the idea of building up a town without them is preposterous in the extreme."

What Monroe seemed intuitively to understand is that mechanics would become the middle class. They would keep Seymour grounded. First, they built their factories, then they built houses in town, and soon they supported the schools and the churches. Their efforts would keep crime in check. Desperately wanting to be part of that social strata himself, Monroe finally succumbed to Captain Shields's enticements. During 1857, he moved his family, printing press, and opinions to Seymour, where he set up his next journalistic endeavor, the *Seymour Times*.

Dr. J. R. Monroe, the newspaper man, ruffled a lot of feathers with the opinions he wrote for the *Rockford Herald*. Based solely on his own political and personal beliefs, they had a strident tone, a moral rectitude, and a radical bent that rankled many of his readers and kept him out of the front parlors and social gatherings of the community's elite—he very tables where he longed to be seated.

In the decade following his move to Seymour, however, Monroe managed to hit on an editorial subject to rail against that put him completely in line with the people and groups he sought to impress. A Rockford family, the Renos, and the gang of outlaws they spawned would prove to be Monroe's ticket into the inner sanctums of influence and power in the region.

That the Reno Gang was a criminal scourge and worthy of any crusading journalist's attention is without question. But the intensity and viciousness of Monroe's campaign against the outlaws seems to have emanated from a darker place in his soul, a place likely shaped and hardened by his crushing experiences in an event that would forever change the nation—America's Civil War.

CHAPTER TWO

Meet the Players: John Reno and Allan Pinkerton

MEET JOHN RENO. HE'S A THIEF, AN ENTRY MAN, A CON MAN, A SAFE-blower, a bank robber, a train robber, a shover of fake currency, and a counterfeiter. He plays cards, but he's not very good at it. He's restless and leaves the forests and the fields of corn and the pork-packing houses of his birthplace, but he's not very good at leaving either. He keeps coming back. He seems drawn to the landscape of home—the pigs, the horses, the White River, the dense forests, the thickets—and the complicated family he grew up with.

By 1851, Wilkinson and Julia Ann Reno had six children—Frank (b. 1837), John (b. 1838), Simeon (b. 1843), Clinton (b. 1846), William (b. 1848), and Laura Amanda (b. 1851)—and by 1858 Julia Ann had had enough. No one knows what pushed her over the edge, but that year she filed for divorce from Wilkinson Reno. Although the paperwork was never finalized, after 1860 and for the rest of their lives she and Wilkinson lived apart. However, it was impossible for them to completely sever the relationship, to pick up and be done with one another. They would remain permanently entwined and entangled through numerous real estate transactions and their sons' future financial and legal problems.

John Reno, Wilkinson and Julia Ann's second-born son, claimed in his 1879 autobiography—the wonderfully colorful *The Life of John Reno:*

The World's First Train Robber, Written by Himself, a forty-six-page pamphlet he sold locally for fifty cents—that his father was an "uneducated man, and could scarcely count his own money correctly." John believed that he himself was his father's favorite and as such was often taken on trips to the market to sell wheat, corn, or hogs. His role was to act as money-counter. John, even as a kid against his father, knew how to run the scam. He knew he could count the money out "correctly" so that Wilkinson "would be as rich as ever in his mind, but short in pocket."

Although hard to believe, given what comes to be known about the elder Renos, John writes that his mother and father were strict Methodists. The Reno boys' religious training consisted of regular visits to the Sunday School of the Rockford Methodist Church, which they were compelled to attend from an early age. When John was about eight, he and his older brother Frank were permitted to go to Sunday School unaccompanied. After returning home, they had to stay indoors for the rest of the day to read their Sunday School papers. They were forbidden to play outside or engage in any sort of Sunday diversion. From age seven to about sixteen John attended the schoolhouse adjacent to the Reno farm during the school months (which, according to him, would have been a Christmas term running from January to Easter). "Although very attentive while at school," he wrote, "I was not apt at learning."

"Our parents being so strict . . . made us rebellious," wrote John. "And we did not hesitate to deceive them whenever we were out of sight . . . Our home seemed like a prison to us, and when away from its restraints we felt so light-hearted and free that we scarcely knew how to act."

When not in school the Reno brothers worked on the Rockford farm and were allowed only a half-day off on Saturday afternoons to hunt, fish, or swim. If caught skipping work or Sunday School, they were subjected to severe punishments, including beatings with sumac switches wrenched from the bushes in the front yard. Once, when John was told to dig up all the sumac bushes that surrounded the front walk, he instead cut them flush with the ground with a knife. He didn't fool his mother, though. A couple of hours later she called John into the kitchen and then locked the door behind him. "She then drew from under the table two of the bushes I had cut down and going to work upon me with all her might, beat and whipped me with them until they were both worn out. I carried marks made by this flogging for weeks afterward."

Wilkinson Reno employed what John called a "bad lot" of hired hands on the farm who spent their free time drinking and gambling. Hired-hand Hiram Mitchell was the first person to show John a deck of cards. Decades later John wrote that they were "the prettiest things I had ever seen," and he was anxious to learn to play them. Soon the Reno brothers were playing cards for stakes with the farmhands, which John claimed led to his first theft.

When John was fourteen, Wilkinson asked the boy to deliver a pig to Mr. Engleking, a dry-goods merchant in Rockford, who paid John $3.50 for the porker. On his way home to return the money to his father, John met a neighbor boy for a round of hearts. John lost the game and the money to the boy. Fearful of a flogging, he told his father that Mr. Engleking would pay him later. Then he set out to steal the money before his father discovered the lie.

Wilkinson always carried around large sums of money—he never knew when he might want to buy a pig or a horse or have a drink in the hotel. One night, not long after losing his father's pig money, John crawled into his father's bedroom to remove a banknote from his trousers. Unable to tell the denomination in the dark, the following morning he discovered he had taken a fifty-dollar note. He was frightened and wanted to return it, but by then Wilkinson was up and it was impossible to slip the note back into his pocket. Julia Ann, as was her habit, made Wilkinson empty his pockets at the breakfast table. Seeing he was short, she screamed at Wilkinson for losing the money—both these things (losing money and Julia Ann yelling) happened too frequently in the Reno home.

John told his older brother Frank about his problem, and they decided to divide the money between the two of them. They managed to get the bill into smaller denominations and then spent it all on poker, except for $3.50, which John kept to pay his pig-money debt. "I handed my father the money for the hog," John wrote, "telling him that Mr. Engleking had sent it by me. That ended the pig trouble."

When John was sixteen, tired of the beatings he received at the hands of his mother, he ran away from home, stealing a fine roan mare that belonged to Frank. It was 1855. As he rode away from the homestead he turned in the saddle and called out, "Goodbye forever!" But he got no satisfaction from his dramatic proclamation as his "voice was rather husky, and no one was in sight. I think they did not hear me." Two days later he reached Jeffersonville, about sixty miles to the south, where he attempted to sell the mare. Everyone was wary of buying such a fine horse from a boy. His cousin, sent by Wilkinson to trail John, caught up with the boy in Jeffersonville and gave him one hundred dollars in return for the horse.

John took the money, promptly lost it playing cards, and then spent months working odd jobs as he wandered through the South. He worked as a hand on flatboats running cargo along the big river. He worked for steamers hauling freight. When he got tired of the river he worked as a farmhand on plantations scattered throughout Alabama and Mississippi. He gambled, was stolen from, and beaten up. His adventures rivaled any of those from the dime novels that would appear later in the nineteenth century.

Early in his journey, he made his way to New Orleans, but was frightened by the large and raucous city. He wanted to return home, so he approached a man on a steamer that did the regular New Orleans to Louisville trade on the Mississippi River. John asked if he could work for passage upstream and was hired as a deckhand. About an hour's ride upriver from New Orleans, the steamboat was hailed by someone on shore near a plantation. Reno wrote:

"She rounded to and landed. Out went the stage plank. I fell in line with the 'rousters' and went to work rolling in molasses. There were fourteen stevedores or 'roust-abouts,' as they are called, on board, whose duty it was to bring on board wood and freight. Then the deck hands take charge and distribute it where it belongs. We took on board two hundred and fifty barrels of molasses and resumed our journey, to be again hailed within an hour."

This happened several times over the next thirty-six hours, and each time the boat was hailed, it seemed to Reno that the number of molasses barrels had multiplied. "We rounded to and found five hundred barrels of molasses this time. These must be loaded by our small force. It was now raining, and the mud on the banks was soft and sticky. When rolled on board the barrels looked like lumps of mud, they were so completely covered. Having no change of clothing, you can imagine how I looked when that job was done."

It was now night and "the mate is cursing, damning, kicking, and knocking down some of the men, just for a pastime. The whole crew is green, like myself, and were taking an initiatory degree in steamboating."

The next time they stopped John went ashore to see what had to be done, and "without exaggeration there were four acres of ground covered over with molasses barrels. I glanced at them, and my thoughts wandered back to the time when I chopped down the sumac bushes because grubbing them seemed too big a contract. How gladly I would give up the job I now had to have that back again: my hands were blistered and bleeding, and some of my fingernails were torn off, but there was not time for complaining."

After rolling barrels onboard for hours, Reno saw the light of a fire downriver and gave the boat "the shake." The sixteen-year-old boy hid in the woods and later wrote: "I will not attempt to describe my feelings when the steamer rounded from land and left me alone, without money, on that lonely bank of the Mississippi."

Reno was helped and abused by both blacks and whites as he made his way back north. He stole passage on several steamers but was always found out and put ashore. After spending a dismal night in a canebrake he woke to the "most dreary, dismal prospect that it has ever been my lot to witness . . . The tall, white trunks of the leafless trees stood thickly on every side, except where the river ran, their branches broken and interlocked with each other. Great, rugged branches were covered with rough Spanish moss hanging down, and their appearance can be described in no way so well as by saying that they looked like army blankets hung up by one of their corners."

John witnessed the cruelty of slavery while in the Deep South and was the recipient of blows and kicks doled out by bullies. He saw a black man being beaten for looking at a white man, and a white man beaten for speaking to a black man. He was swindled, cheated, and lied to. He staked hard-earned money on a card game—money earned by working as a raftsman (poling a raft upriver)—and lost every penny. So five months after saying "Goodbye, forever!" to his family home, he ended up back at the homestead in Rockford, Indiana, in his shirtsleeves and wearing a pair of borrowed pants that were so short they only reached about two inches below the tops of his boots.

"My journey," he wrote, "thus ended in this unspectacular manner."

The year John Reno ran away from home at age sixteen, Allan Pinkerton was setting up his first detective agency, the North West Police Agency, in Chicago, Illinois. Two decades older than Reno, Pinkerton had already lived a full life by 1855.

Born in 1819 in a working-class neighborhood of Glasgow, Scotland, Pinkerton had a few years of public schooling before his father died. He apprenticed to a cooper to learn a trade and to bring in some money for the family. A thickset, muscular, and intense young man, Pinkerton excelled at making barrels and was pleased to be learning a skill he could take with him wherever he went.

The 1830s and 1840s in England, Scotland, and Wales were a heady time for workingmen, as workers attempted to organize for what they saw as basic political rights. The Chartist movement, as it was called, supported the People's Charter written in 1838 and presented to Parliament that same year with over a million signatures.

The Charter demanded a number of things, including votes for all men, abolition of the requirement that members of Parliament be property owners, and removal of the secret ballot. Parliament voted it down and years of protest followed. Many leaders of the movement—having threatened to call a general strike—were arrested and thrown in prison. When Chartist demonstrators marched on Newport prison, Monmouthsire, in 1839, demanding the release of their leaders, troops opened fire, killing twenty-four and wounding forty others. Hundreds were arrested and dozens of men were transported on convict ships to Australia for their involvement. A second petition was submitted to Parliament in 1842—this time with three million signatures—and then a third in 1848. They were also rejected.

Although a very young man, Pinkerton threw himself into the middle of the Chartist movement, attending rallies and protests and entering into street brawls when necessary. Pinkerton was at the Newport Rising (as it came to be called) and witnessed the terrible treatment of the Chartists at the hands of English troops. He returned to Glasgow determined to break with the English Chartists, who he felt had bungled the whole march on the prison. He formed the Northern Democratic Association and attempted to unite others who were impatient with the mainstream English Chartists. As was typical of organizations of the time, the Northern Democratic Association held a concert in the parlor of a public house as a fund-raising event in the summer of 1841. There, Pinkerton first saw Joan Carfrae, an apprentice bookbinder who sang in the choir that performed. On March 13, 1842, they married. Joan was fifteen and Allan twenty-three.

The Pinkertons boarded a ship for Montreal less than a month later. In later years, Pinkerton would write to his son that he was a hunted man with a price on his head for his organizing activities, which pushed him and Joan to get married and leave the country. In typical Pinkerton fashion, his story may or may not be true. Pinkerton proved not to be the most reliable narrator when it came to himself.

The young couple took the 440-ton barque named *Kent* leaving Glasgow for Montreal. The journey was plagued with terrible weather, including a hurricane that buffeted the ship and blew it at least 250 miles off course. The *Kent* struck and foundered on the reefs off Sable Island, a desolate place some two hundred miles southeast of Halifax, Nova Scotia. The crew managed to get everyone ashore in lifeboats, where they were promptly set upon by natives and robbed of what few possessions they had managed to carry with them.

Over the next couple of days, crew members rowed out to the crippled ship and retrieved what they could. Fortunately for the shipwrecked passengers and crew, Sable Island lay on a sea-lane between Halifax and Liverpool, and within a week they were picked up by a ship headed to Halifax. From there, the Pinkertons made their way to Montreal with what Pinkerton later referred to as "our health and a few pennies."

In Montreal Pinkerton set to work for a cooper making barrels for packing beef but soon decided he wanted to relocate to the United States and to Chicago, where Robbie Fergus, one of his Scottish Chartist friends, had settled. So once again the Pinkertons gathered their belongings and headed off, this time by steamer down the St. Lawrence River and then into the mighty Great Lakes.

Upon reaching Chicago—at that time a filthy, stinking town with cattle and pigs roaming the streets and only twelve hundred human inhabitants—Pinkerton decided this was no place to settle. The young couple landed in Warsaw, a small town on the western edge of the state, just ten miles downstream on the Mississippi from Nauvoo, Illinois, the city founded two years earlier by Joseph Smith for his Mormon followers. Nauvoo was a flourishing city of twenty thousand, with many British immigrants enticed to the States by missionaries for the Church of the Latter Day Saints.

In Warsaw, the Pinkertons were robbed, once again, of everything except for one gold coin wrapped in a handkerchief. This was enough to get Allan and Joan back to Chicago. Robbie Fergus, who had set up a printing business in the young city, was able to house the young couple until they could get established. During the time the Pinkertons stayed with Fergus, Joan and Robbie collaborated on a book of Scottish country songs and ballads, which was the first book printed in Chicago.

Just a year later, Allan Pinkerton told Joan to pack her things once again because they were moving to Dundee, a tiny Scottish community thirty-eight miles northwest of Chicago. It was here that Pinkerton finally established his own cooperage. He built a single-story log cabin for the two of them and a small shack at the back for a workshop. Pinkerton placed his home on a grassy knoll within sight of the wooden bridge spanning the Fox River. From the bridge, farmers who needed barrels and churns would see his sign, Only and Original Cooper of Dundee.

Pinkerton worked fourteen-hour days, seven days a week, and by 1846 had eight employees. Joan Pinkerton cultivated vegetable and flower gardens and raised poultry. In later years, she considered her time in Dundee to be the happiest of her life. Fergus occasionally came to visit from Chicago, where he told the young couple of the tremendous growth of the city, which now had sixteen thousand inhabitants. The city was spreading out in a haphazard way with houses and buildings slapped together as fast as they could be built. It was a chaotic, yet exciting place to be, said Fergus. Plus, it was full of promise for an enterprising man. He couldn't entice the young couple to move at that point, but he certainly planted the seeds of opportunity in Allan's mind.

In June of that year, Pinkerton decided to cut young trees for his barrels from an island that lay in the middle of the Fox River. He poled his raft upriver, spent the morning cutting trees, then moved to another spot on the island. There he discovered a burned patch that looked like the remnants of a recent campfire. This struck Pinkerton as odd, so he returned that night, hiding his raft in the reeds. He crept up on the spot and then settled in behind some trees to see if anyone would show up. About an hour later a rowboat came ashore. Several men walked toward the campsite, built a fire, and settled in. Pinkerton could hear them talking about counterfeiting. The next day he contacted the sheriff of Kent County, who raised a posse that included Pinkerton. One night under the light of a quarter moon they all descended on the island. They surprised the band of counterfeiters and took them into custody along with a "bag of bogus dimes and tools used in their manufacture." The place is called Bogus Island to this day.

Pinkerton became an overnight celebrity in Dundee. Every farmer and tradesman who visited his shop wanted to hear him tell the story. Within a month, Henry Hunt, a local shopkeeper, asked Pinkerton to do a little job "in the detective line." Hunt suspected there was a counterfeiter working the town, and he and the other shopkeepers were losing money.

Before the Civil War and the creation of a national currency, banking was extremely local—each bank printed and issued its own banknotes. The Dundee shopkeepers would accept only those banknotes issued by Wisconsin Marine and Fire Insurance Company of Chicago. George Smith, a Scotsman from Aberdeen, owned the Wisconsin Marine and Fire Insurance Company. Hunt told Pinkerton that at least two bogus ten-dollar bills had been passed in Dundee. Pinkerton had never even seen a ten-dollar bill, much less a forged one, so Hunt pulled out one of the forgeries along with an authentic bill so Pinkerton could examine them both. Pinkerton could see that the Wisconsin Marine notes had a simple design, one that would be easy to imitate.

In what would later prove a trademark of Pinkerton's detecting style, he got right on the job. Hunt told Pinkerton that at that moment a stranger was at the stable getting his saddle repaired. Pinkerton—still in his work clothes—walked over and patted the stranger's horse while taking careful note of the man's appearance, which he later recorded as "a grey-haired swarthy man with keen grey eyes, about 65-years old, with a plain gold ring on his left hand." The stranger asked Pinkerton for directions to Old Man Crane's place. Hunt had suspected Crane of passing the counterfeit bills. Pinkerton gave detailed instructions and agreed to meet the stranger a bit later in a gully outside of town.

Pinkerton, excited about the prospect of cracking the case, walked to the gully. The stranger introduced himself as John Craig, a farmer from Fairfield, Vermont, who said he and Crane had done quite a bit of business together. Craig queried Pinkerton, who said he worked in a cooperage outside of town but was looking for a way to earn some extra money. Craig agreed to let Pinkerton have fifty bogus ten-dollar bills for 25 percent, or $125 in silver. The two agreed on a meeting spot for the transaction. Pinkerton walked back to Dundee, where he convinced Hunt and the other shopkeepers to scrape together the cash to pay for the bogus notes. Craig and Pinkerton made the exchange.

Pinkerton then asked Craig if they could do a bigger deal, say four thousand dollars in counterfeit money, in Chicago. Craig agreed to meet the Scotsman in the lobby of the Sauganash Hotel in the city. When the Vermont farmer handed over the fake money to Pinkerton, who was dressed in his finest suit for the occasion, Pinkerton gave the signal and a deputy sheriff of Cook County arrested Craig on the spot. Craig was handed over to Kane County—where Dundee was located— where he sat in jail as Pinkerton gave a deposition to the grand jury. Although indicted, Craig would never sit for a trial in Kane County because soon after the indictment he disappeared, "Leaving behind a certain law officer much richer than he had been," noted a disgruntled Pinkerton.

The setup and arrest of Craig took time—time Pinkerton could have used making money in the cooperage—so he asked Hunt and the other shopkeepers to reimburse him for his expenses. They told Pinkerton to ask for money from George Smith, the banker of Wisconsin Marine and Fire Insurance Company of Chicago, whose notes had been forged. So that's what Pinkerton did. He once again put on his best suit and shined his shoes and made the forty-mile trip to visit the Scottish banker. Smith, after listening to the story, told Pinkerton that he would pay him just this once, but that if Pinkerton did any more detective work on his behalf without his authorization, he wouldn't get a cent out of him. This was a valuable lesson for the young Scotsman, who learned never to work without a written contract in place.

Over the next year, Pinkerton split his time between the cooperage and regional law enforcement, rising swiftly through the ranks, first serving as deputy sheriff for Kane County before being asked by the sheriff of Cook County to be his deputy. In 1847 he sold his business for a handsome profit and told Joan to pack up once again. They left Dundee with their infant son, William, and headed for the city of Chicago, where Pinkerton would soon hold the title of Chicago's first detective. Within a few short years, he would strike out on his own and make deals with several railroad companies for detective services to the tune of ten thousand dollars a year in retainers.

As railroads connected more and more of the dots on the map in the Northeast and pushed farther and farther west in the 1850s, they encountered little resistance to their rapid growth. Yet as trains moved people and freight with increased regularity, the trains themselves and the towns in which they stopped became subject to an increase in crime. Confidence men, petty thieves, tramps, pickpockets, drunks, counterfeiters, and gamblers all frequented railroad stations and the trains. As passengers made their way through the jostle of people on a train platform, they could find their luggage missing or their purses stolen. It was the perfect setup for pickpockets and thieves. Baggage and freight cars, often left unattended at a station, were also targeted.

The train-riding public had a litany of complaints against the railroads, including unreliable schedules, unsafe equipment, lack of stations along the route, capricious ticket pricing, and thievery. Then there were the myriad problems on board the trains, not the least of which was poor ventilation, not enough seats, no toilets, no water, and no food service. Passengers had little recourse, particularly in railroad towns, as the laws often had yet to catch up to the speed in which the tracks were laid. The traveling public was not the problem of local marshals and sheriffs, and railroad companies, who had their hands full with the seemingly endless opportunities for expansion, paid little attention to the nattering of unhappy passengers.

But when the railroads themselves, particularly as the trains sat in the sidings or in rail yards, fell victim to thievery of freight, money, and livestock amounting to millions of dollars' worth of goods, the railroad owners began to pay attention. Self-protection, and not passenger complaints, prompted railroad companies to hire private police to work the trains. Contractors like Allan Pinkerton and his detectives were hired to investigate the losses.

Pinkerton knew there would always be a need for good detectives. Theft, graft, counterfeiting—these were just a few of the activities that would keep him in business. Even at this early date—when John Reno was still a boy running back home to Rockford, Indiana—plans were being made that would lead to the collision of the famous detective from Chicago with the young runaway from Rockford.

Chapter Three

The Birth of Seymour

THE RISE OF ANY POWERFUL CRIMINAL FORCE IS A PRODUCT OF CIRCUM-stances coming together at just the right time to produce an environment ripe for exploitation—personalities, social circumstances, politics, and even geography determine whether an outlaw enterprise gains a foothold.

If Rockford had the dubious honor as the birthplace and home ground for the outlaw Renos, Seymour was their fiefdom. Perhaps it's not surprising given that the very origin of the town carried with it an ambiguous morality from day one.

No one thought much of it when local landowner Meedy Shields, a clever and ambitious man, began buying up more and more land south of Rockford. Although he had inherited over a thousand acres from his father—given to the senior Shields by the government in the early part of the nineteenth century when he signed on to be a land agent—Meedy was always on the lookout for more. But there was a particular element of deceit in the man's acquisition of this land near Rockford, a land grab that beautifully illustrates that in the mid-nineteenth century, as today, politics was not only a moneymaking career but also a means to amass personal power.

What Meedy knew, and others did not, was that the newly formed Ohio & Mississippi (O&M) Railroad was going to lay tracks in the region. This east-west line would connect Cincinnati, Ohio, to St. Louis,

Missouri, and was going to cross the north-south railroad line (Jeffersonville, Madison & Indianapolis) somewhere in Jackson County. Shields was no fool. He knew the great potential for land that lay at the intersection of two railroad lines.

Shields was the product of an industrious family who had arrived in southern Indiana in 1816 when Meedy was eleven. At the time, the Shieldses were one of only five white families in all of Jackson County. They may have migrated to the area thanks to Meedy's uncle John Shields. He was recruited by Lewis and Clark to join their cross-country expedition in 1804. On that expedition, John Shields served as gunsmith, blacksmith, and general fixer. He was later recognized by the United States government for having performed "exceedingly well."

Meedy, who grew to be a small, barrel-chested young man with dark, wide-set eyes, started running flatboats at age fifteen on the White River, hauling barrels of pork to New Orleans. Once there, the flatboats were busted up for lumber and Meedy would make his way back to Rockford by land. He evidently liked the work—whether it was the excitement of seeing the exotic world of New Orleans with its mix of cultures and languages, or just that it was lucrative—because he remained in the freight business for about twelve years.

In 1832, a seasoned veteran of adventure as a flatboat runner, Meedy enlisted in the Indiana Militia. He wanted to fight in the Black Hawk War against the Native American splinter group of Sauks, Kickapoos, Meskwakis, and Potawatomis led by Black Hawk and known as the British Band because they sometimes flew a British flag just to infuriate the Americans.

The British Band did not subscribe to the 1804 Treaty of St. Louis negotiated by William Henry Harrison, then governor of the Indiana Territory and future president of the United States. The 1804 treaty opened lands of the Old Northwest—as the region was called—for white settlement. Consequently, more and more people poured into the territory, settling on Indian land that Black Hawk's confederation believed they still owned.

By the 1830s the British Band was ready to make one last stand for control of their land. It was a depressing and lopsided war lasting only a few months. Forty-four whites died compared with hundreds of Indians. It was the springboard for what would become known as the national policy of Indian Removal. All Native Americans would be persuaded to sell their lands in the region and move west of the Mississippi. For his participation in this military campaign, Shields made rank of captain and was known as Captain Shields for the rest of his life, a title he embraced.

When Meedy Shields returned from his stint in the Black Hawk War, he married Eliza P. Ewing, daughter of a wealthy farmer in Brownstown, the county seat of Jackson County. He then took up farming on the Shields' old homestead in Rockford. It was his political career, however, and not farming, that would fix him firmly as a powerful, influential man. Though he had no more than three months of formal schooling, Meedy Shields would eventually serve in both the state legislature and the state senate of Indiana.

Meedy got his political start in 1846 when his older brother William, elected the year before to the fledgling Indiana State Legislature, died unexpectedly while in office. Meedy took William's place as the representative from Jackson County, and in that role was privy to proposed improvements to the state's infrastructure. He knew what bridges would be built and where. He knew about proposed turnpikes. And he knew about plans for new railroad lines.

He also knew that railroads trumped travel by road, so he began buying shares of a newly proposed east-west rail line and got himself appointed to the Board of Directors of the Eastern Division of the Ohio & Mississippi Railroad Company. When the midwestern section of the east-west line was finished, it would connect New York to St. Louis, a distance of over one thousand miles.

Shields began courting the surveyor from New York State, Hezekial C. Seymour, who was to be the general contractor for the east-west project. He brought Seymour to his land outside of Rockford. His swampy, forest-covered land. The land with the mule pasture. Yet, Shields wasn't daunted by the property's current condition. Instead, he presented his vision to the railroad man—a vision that included draining water from the wetlands and creating a three-mile-long gravel berm through the swampiest section, upon which the tracks would be laid.

Hezekial Seymour was taken in by the smooth-talking Shields. With a stroke of a pen, he inked in the proposed Ohio & Mississippi rail line on the survey map. It ran directly through Shields's swamp. Maybe the suggestion by Meedy that his dream community be called Seymour was enough inducement for the surveyor, though other enticements probably made the offer even sweeter.

The development of railroads in America had a most profound effect on all aspects of the settlement of the country, from emigration, land policies, the rise and fall of towns and cities, and industrialization, to, ultimately, the concentration of wealth in a true upper class. From its nascent beginnings as short tramroads or railways where horse-pulled passenger wagons moved along rails over short distances, and rail-guided cars filled with coal or ore from mines were propelled by gravity, the railroad of the early nineteenth century had to wait for clever people to bring steam power to the locomotive.

By fits and starts rail lines began connecting towns and ports, primarily in the Northeast. The Baltimore & Ohio was America's first common carrier railroad, meaning it was expected to haul anything, within reason, offered to it by the general public when the city of Baltimore chartered it on April 24, 1827. Railroad companies were individually chartered, each applying for its own charter from the state of origin, until the 1840s when the federal government created a system whereby companies could apply for articles of incorporation. This streamlined and fast-tracked the development of new railroad companies. If it was determined that the company would benefit the common good, the company was then eligible for federal subsidies. This not only meant money from the government to lay the lines, but also meant, over time, huge land grants that the railroads could then sell to individuals. This fiercely competitive business was flooded with would-be entrepreneurs. Alliances were made and broken and, prior to the Civil War, it was often difficult to sort out who would emerge as the big players in any transnational railroad scheme.

Both federal and state governments encouraged railroad development. During the 1830s, when states chartered railroads, they granted monopolies much as they had for canal construction. The U.S. Supreme Court had ruled in 1837 that state charters did not have the power to grant railroad monopolies. By the 1840s, many states permitted the formation of railroad companies by the simple act of public incorporation, which also opened up the possibility of competition. The Supreme Court ruling also helped the railroads by supporting their use of eminent domain. In other words, the courts backed the railroad company's right to take land legitimately owned by someone (in theory, landowners were offered fair market value for the land), reasoning that the railroads could put land to better public use. There was little a landowner could do to prevent a railroad company from taking his land. In the area of civil litigation known as torts, the courts routinely ruled in favor of the railroads. Plaintiffs had to demonstrate negligence on the part of the railroads to win a settlement. These were just more judicial and legislative acts favoring the financing and growth of the railroad industry. So, from the late 1830s to the Civil War, a number of fledgling railroad companies soon expanded into a vast network linking the major northern cities east of the Mississippi River.

The northern railroad companies in control of the east-west lines were driven farther and farther west. Railroad development in the South took a very different path. The southern states—the states profiting from the institution of slavery—concentrated on building local lines that would connect tobacco and cotton plantations to port cities. And these local railroads were forbidden to cross state lines, because each state maintained firm control over what they saw as their railroads. The southern railroad lines were laid primarily by slaves, making the railroad labor costs well below those of their northern neighbors.

Calls for a transcontinental railroad arose in Congress as early as 1838. However, legislators from the South always blocked railroad bills, because they saw, among other things, these bills as a violation of their states' rights. They also believed a transcontinental system would inevitably push northern industrialization westward, something that would hurt their interests, so southern legislators voted as a block to prevent transcontinental railroad plans from moving forward. When most of the southern states seceded from the Union in 1861, and all the southern legislators left Washington, the Railroad Act, a bill aimed at linking the Pacific to the Atlantic, was easily pushed through Congress with the blessing of President Abraham Lincoln. This railroads' constant push westward meant that those who owned land on a proposed rail line stood to benefit greatly from the flow of people, commercial goods, and even ideas that came by way of the "iron horse."

It was a raw day in November of 1852, and the men who had shown up to bid on lots were stamping their feet against the cold, as were their horses. Meedy Shields likely hauled a wooden table out of the back of the wagon he'd driven to the edge of his pasture, then spread and smoothed his plats marked with the proposed lots of the proposed town. Although he recognized a few faces, Shields didn't know everyone, and he was glad, for that meant the word-of-mouth advertising had worked.

As they stood in a clearing where Shields pastured his work mules, it's not unlikely Shields had just a moment of doubt as he scanned the dense forest, swamp, and occasional meadowland that was to be transformed into his dream town, Seymour. The doubt, if it existed at all, was quickly brushed aside. Meedy knew he had a winner, as did the men in front of him. The town on the railroad crossing would be a town of the future. "Mr. Shields, the founder of the town, who had nothing to show as an inducement to investment but the prospect of railroads (on paper) that were soon to come, was most happily surprised at the eagerness of bidders," wrote one historian.

In a few short years, hotels and train depots would replace the swamp adjacent to where the buyers now stood. The future first ward of the town was now just a dense forest. Bidders squinted their eyes and, in their minds, dug the trenches that drained the water and wielded the axes that cleared the trees. They imagined, through the seductive enthusiasm of the seller, their homes and businesses, and then marveled at their good fortune at being able to buy a lot in a future railroad-crossing town.

For his part, Shields, always the shrewd businessman and leaving nothing to chance, would build a sawmill on the edge of his planned town. For the next three years he would clear the land and furnish all of the lumber used to build the new houses in Seymour. But his genius for development didn't stop there. Meedy Shields thought on a larger scale. He knew that the railroads would revolutionize the way goods were distributed to markets.

In 1850s southern Indiana building or creating things outside the home hadn't changed much since early pioneer days. Manufacturing establishments were small and individually owned, averaging only four employees per business. They were simple in organization and equipment, composed primarily of craftsmen working with hand tools, perhaps aided by horse or waterpower. Most manufacturing was closely tied to nearby agriculture and natural resources—processing grain in flour and grist mills, packing pork in barrels made by local coopers, distilling liquor, and clearing the vast hardwood forests for timber.

The arrangement and structure for this kind of commercial enterprise in Meedy's region was based on technologies rooted in the past. When planning a town, why not try to entice manufacturing on a larger scale? Why not encourage mechanics to set up shops? Why not give land to the railroads to build depots and rail yards and sheds for repairing locomotives? It was a bold vision for Seymour, but it turned out that there was one big problem Meedy Shields needed to solve.

Even after the Ohio & Mississippi Railroad line was completed, and a passenger depot was built in Seymour where the trains would stop, the north-south Jeffersonville, Madison & Indianapolis trains did not and would not stop in Seymour. They continued on to Rockford, two miles north, before stopping. If someone needed to transfer from the east-west line to the north-south line, they had to make the two-mile trek to Seymour on foot or by wagon.

Always the crafty politician with a willingness to use his position for personal gain (although in this instance it could be argued it was for the good of the community), Shields introduced a bill in the state legislature that required a train come to a complete stop when it crossed another line. Trains ignoring this rule would face a stiff fine. Though it was a naked maneuver that would provide enormous personal benefit to Shields, he stiffly defended his proposal as necessary for "safety reasons."

Enacted in 1857, Shields's bill rang the death knell for Seymour's older neighbor, Rockford.

Early train travel was grueling. Depending upon destination, you might take multiple railroad lines, a canal boat, an omnibus, a stagecoach, and a steamboat. Railroad tracks were often shared by several railroad companies who ran their trains at uncoordinated times. Little attention was paid to establishing connections for through travel. Early passengers were even left on the side of the tracks to wait for the next train to come through. Sometimes passengers would have to walk across town to get on another train run by another company to continue their journey. Or in the case of Seymour, make the two-mile trek to Rockford. Until the latter part of the nineteenth century there was no guarantee that a passenger would even be left off at a station or depot, because there was no requirement that railroad companies provide them.

In the early days of railroad travel there were no reliable timetables and no ticket agents to assist in arranging a journey (conductors sold tickets on the trains), and it was difficult to plan a journey of any length because there were hundreds of local times in the United States (time zones didn't yet exist). If there was a schedule or timetable, there was no way of knowing what the time listed really meant. Although local newspapers printed a train schedule somewhere on their pages, the time zone problem wasn't finally resolved until 1883 with the creation of four time zones across the country.

Yet these problems did not deter people from using the railroads. Trains and railroads held a deep fascination for Americans. Trains held out the promise of a better life. Railroads represented progress and opportunity. They were the embodiment of the very idea that the world was bigger than a farm or a village. Trains began to connect parts of the country that had hitherto coexisted in a national geographic vacuum—a world filled with mountains and rivers and forests and prairies. Railroad tracks became to rural towns like the wire to the poles for the newly invented telegraph—something electrifying was being transmitted. Robert Louis Stevenson knew this when he wrote *Across the Plains*, an account of his train journey from New York to San Francisco in the 1880s. "If, in truth, it were only for the sake of wages that men emigrate, how many thousands would regret the bargain! But wages, indeed, are only one consideration out of many; for we are a race of gipsies, [sic] and love change and travel for themselves."

People, ideas, farming implements, hardware, barbed wire, wagon wheels, barrels, food, books, newspapers, letters, parcels, ready-made clothing, orphans, fabric, cattle, lumber, corn, hogs, and wheat were transported by train. Trains held the promise of a new start and reinvention. They also held the promise of anonymity for those who wished to disappear. It was not uncommon for a family member to get on a train and never be heard from again. And railroads could also portend deep disappointment for those who lived in towns and villages bypassed by the train. Much like Eisenhower's interstate highway system of the 1950s, many towns that were bypassed were doomed to endure a slow but sure death.

The rail route selected by the surveyors meant everything to existing towns. The future lay in the lines drawn upon the map. Historian John Mack Faraghar wrote about some small, mid-nineteenth-century communities strung along Sugar Creek in Illinois, just to the east of Springfield. In 1851 the residents of Auburn—a village settled about forty years earlier by pioneers from Auburn, Maine—held their collective breath as they waited for news of the proposed route of the Chicago and Alton Railroad. Auburn lost. The line would run one mile east of town. It soon became clear that the railroad had cut a deal with the landowner Phillip Wineman, who offered the company donations of land in the midst of a "new paper village he platted there and named after himself."

"It seemed a pity," Moses Wadsworth of Auburn later wrote, "that so pretty a site as that of the old town should be abandoned for so unpromising a one as the north-east quarter of section 10 then appeared—much of it a mere swamp—but railroad corporations possess no bowels of compassion, the practical more than the beautiful being their object."

The village of Auburn lost its purpose. Within a year the stage line closed its operations in the town and the post office was relocated to the new town of Wineman. Many residents moved to the new village as well, dragging the buildings they had built on ox-drawn sledges and then setting them up on lots purchased from Wineman. A farmer bought up all the lots in the old town of Auburn and he plowed up blocks, even the public square, and planted corn in their place, obliterating signs of the village within a couple of growing seasons.

In 1857, the same year the Indiana railroad bill passed requiring trains to stop where rail lines crossed, Shields persuaded Dr. J. R. Monroe to shut down the *Rockford Herald* and move his family and newspaper business to Seymour. It was a brilliant public relations move. Meedy understood that a newspaper filled with notices of civic and enterprising activities would be a tangible reminder that Seymour was a growing and thriving community, a town that was more than just a railroad crossing. It was a place to be lived and worked in.

Encouraged by the prospect of more paying customers, Monroe set up shop in the heart of bustling Seymour and began writing and publishing his weekly, the *Seymour Times*, patterned on the now defunct *Rockford Herald*. His relocation was pivotal for himself, for the town, and for Shields. Within a few short years of Monroe's arrival in Seymour, the place would confront a dilemma that threatened its existence. The roots of the struggle Monroe, Shields, and the citizens of Seymour encountered were woven into the Federalist states' rights arguments that erupted even before America's thirteen colonies were figuring out how to coexist after winning the Revolution.

In the late 1850s, when Seymour was becoming a town, Julia Ann Reno filed divorce proceedings against Wilkinson. She sought the care and guardianship of Laura Amanda and William, the two youngest children. In an effort to keep the family together, the older boys convinced their parents to sell part of the farmland in Rockford, take the proceeds, and move together to Missouri. The elder Renos stayed in Missouri for only a matter of months because Wilkinson could not find land he wanted to buy. They packed up once again and moved back to Indiana.

John's parents continued to quarrel and went back to Jackson County as discontented as before. As the boys saw it, the family had squandered four thousand dollars of the money their land sale had brought. The elder Renos rented a house in Seymour and moved in together, but, according to John, "it was plain there would soon be a separation." Julia Ann, Laura Amanda, and William moved back into the farmhouse near Rockford. Wilkinson then bought a house along Indianapolis Avenue adjacent to the railroad tracks in Seymour. The three older boys—Frank, John, and Simeon—bounced between the houses. Clinton, the Reno brother folks didn't hear much about, lived in Rockford's new tavern, Postel's, with a local madam, Adie Reed.

Some think that maybe the Renos didn't leave Rockford for Missouri because of marital discord. Some think it was because of the fires. Shortly before they left the farmhouse, presumably for good, Postel's tavern in old Rockford was set ablaze. This was just six months after the burning of the Rockford House and many other buildings in the center of town. The destruction of Postel's tavern was deemed a blessing by most of Rockford's citizens, for it was evidently a saloon and whorehouse. The paper reported that it was purposefully set on fire and destroyed. Adaline Reed conducted business out of the old tavern and "the house was much frequented and under very bad repute." The well-meaning citizens believed she was "poisoning the morals of the youths of the vicinity," and the businessmen believed she was injuring their businesses. Very little was saved, as the building was allowed to burn to the ground. Postel's tavern and Adie Reed's business migrated to another building and was soon back in operation.

By 1860, following two more episodes of arson, most of the people of Rockford had deserted their old homes, salvaging what they could, and moved into the adjacent town of Seymour. Reading the advertisements on page three of the *Seymour Times* is reminiscent of reading page three of the *Rockford Herald*. Rockford businesses moved lock, stock, and barrel two miles down the road and set up shop. Yet, through all the fires that raged through old Rockford, the Reno farmhouse never burned. And the remnants of the town—the land under the charred buildings—was sold lot by lot to Julia and Wilkinson Reno, at rock-bottom prices. An actual fire sale.

Accusations swirled about the Reno family's involvement in the fires, but nothing was ever proved. There was even a rumor circulating through town that Meedy Shields, the founder of Seymour, and Wilkinson Reno were in cahoots. Shields would be selling the lots in the new town to Rockford people and Reno would be buying their burned-out lots in Rockford. Both men stood to gain by the fires. Within a few short years, Julia and Wilkinson Reno owned most of the ghostly, burned-out town, where blackened shells of houses stood between those few buildings that had somehow escaped the numerous conflagrations.

Post-fire Rockford was not for the faint of heart. A peek into the rough-and-tumble life shows up in the January 10, 1861, edition of the *Seymour Times*. Editor J. R. Monroe writes, "George Barnes was shot in a fracas in Hibner's grocery at Rockford on Monday by Richard Winscott. The ball struck a rib three inches below and an inch inside the left nipple, ranging downward and backward, and going where, nobody knows. Winscott was before Esqr. Whitson on Tuesday and was discharged. Barnes' condition is critical."

As nature sought to reclaim the town, and trees and underbrush grew through and around the burned buildings, Rockford—Wilkinson Reno's Rockford—would become the perfect hiding place for a gang of thieves, robbers, and counterfeiters.

Soon after Wilkinson Reno moved to Seymour, and Julia Ann and the two youngest Reno children returned to the farm near Rockford, John asked his mother for a clean shirt. She sent him upstairs in the old farmhouse to get it. While searching in a clothespress he came upon a bag of gold. He didn't count the money, although later his father said it contained $1,100. John took the sack of coins across the pasture and down the lane to what was left of the town of Rockford. He found his cousin (perhaps Trick Reno) and asked him to hold onto the money for a while until he figured out what to do next. The cousin stole three hundred dollars from the sack before returning the rest to John. What could John do? He couldn't make a big deal about his cousin stealing part of his stolen money.

Wilkinson soon found his gold was missing and figured out who likely took it. He had his son arrested for the theft. John was brought before Seymour's Justice of the Peace, Travis Carter. Just as court was called to order, Wilkinson must have had a change of heart, for he signaled John to run. The younger Reno bolted. He fled the county in company with "a young woman of Rockford" identified only as Mollie. The young couple landed in Clay County, Indiana, renting a farm two miles west of Brazil. Buying both stock and farming implements, John went to work. But being in one place for any length of time was not in John's nature—he grew discontented before the crops matured. He sold out, sent Mollie home, and took the train to Indianapolis.

When John Reno arrived at the magnificent Union Station in Indianapolis, where six railroad lines came together like the center of a spider, web, he found the people of the city "wild with excitement." It was April 14, 1861, the day after Fort Sumter was fired on.

Reno was about to embark on an odyssey that read like the stuff of pulp fiction.

The United States was only a half-century old when Seymour was founded. The great midsection of the country where Indiana lies was geographically carved up and bisected by rivers and canals in the early part of the nineteenth century. Within two generations, it was further divided by railroads and roads. The region—known then as the Northwest—was rapidly and continually in the process of becoming settled.

The Second Continental Congress anticipated this population surge when they passed the Northwest Ordinance of 1787, signed into law by George Washington and the U.S. Congress in 1789. This ordinance prescribed basic law for the huge area of forests and plains north of the Ohio River and east of the Mississippi—land that later became the states of Ohio, Indiana, Illinois, Michigan, and Wisconsin.

"The Ordinance of 1787 is one of the most important documents in American legal history," writes legal historian Laurence Friedman. Everyone expected the frontier spaces to fill with settlers. When the population reached a certain threshold, the various territories would enter the union as free, sovereign states. The ordinance laid out the roadmap to statehood. Until there were five thousand free male inhabitants, "of full age," living in the territory, a territorial governor and three judges had the power to make laws.

The first governor divided the Northwest Territory into huge counties. The judges had to live in the district, or county, they were to represent, and any two of them could "form a court." They were to exercise "common law jurisdiction," a reference to the British traditions that underpinned American jurisprudence. The judges were to be "substantial people" who owned a "freehold estate" of at least five hundred acres. The governor and a majority of the judges had the power to "adopt and publish in the district such laws of the original States, criminal and civil, as may be necessary, and best suited to circumstances of the district."

Congress held on to the power to disallow these laws. This last prescription brilliantly prevented the local lawmakers from pondering exactly how to re-create the wheel. Territorial lawmakers were forced to borrow from a set of laws that had already been proven—they had to look back toward the eastern states. This also assured some regularity in legal codes across the land.

Many territories ended up with a cut-and-paste version of statutes from the states from which the lawmakers had come. For example, because the original governor of the Northwest Territories was from Pennsylvania, nine-tenths of the laws adopted were from his home state.

When a territory had five thousand male inhabitants of full age, it entered into a second stage. Now the governor and judges had to share power with elected representatives—one for every five hundred men, up to a total of twenty-five legislators. After that, the legislature could decide how many representatives it wanted. Each legislature would nominate ten people (who lived in the district and owned at least five hundred acres of land), and then Congress would choose five out of the ten to serve on a Governor's Council. The governor, the Governor's Council, and the legislature had authority to make laws as long as they were "not repugnant" to the ordinance.

When 65,000 free male inhabitants lived in a territory, it was eligible for statehood. In 1803, Ohio was the first portion of the Old Northwest Territory to be granted statehood. The remaining counties were grouped together as the Indiana Territory. Indiana applied for statehood in 1816 and held its constitutional convention the same year. The convention drafted Indiana's first constitution, which among other things, provided for a state-supported system of education (unfunded for many decades) and forbade slavery (though this provision was not enforced or was circumvented by calling slaves indentured servants). In December of that year, Indiana became the nineteenth state to enter the union.

Once a territory became a state, it had complete power to make and unmake its own laws. However, most lawmakers in new states hadn't the time, skill, or inclination to make up new laws. Many legislatures simply adopted the laws they had originally cribbed from other states when they were still territories. In the first half of the nineteenth century, states were responsible for regulation and intervention within their own states, not the federal government. At this point in America's history the federal government was tiny and actually controlled very little money, so it gladly ceded these powers to the states.

States built turnpikes, roads, canals, and even railroads. States chartered banks and enacted their own regulations on banking. There was no federal banking system in place or even a national currency, so banks printed and issued their own notes. As one can imagine, counterfeiting was rampant. Consequently, banking tended to be very local as many merchants were leery about accepting a banknote from a bank they didn't know. An unsound bank—where there were more printed notes than gold or silver to back it up—could sink a community, as happened in the Panic of 1837.

States also relied on a fee system rather than taxation as a way to shift the financial burden to users. Litigants paid judges for their lawsuits, newlyweds paid the justice of the peace for their weddings, and local users paid assessments for roads in their regions (although many regions offered the option to work for four days out of the year on maintenance and repair of roads if someone couldn't pay the assessment). In many cases, a sheriff was paid according to how many people he put in jail. Even the state penitentiary in Jeffersonville, Indiana, was a private, for-profit institution, which, when toured by Dorothea Dix midcentury, was declared unfit for humans.

"People like to tell entertaining stories about the early years of territories and the frontier states," writes legal historian Friedman. "But there was also trained legal talent on the frontier, along with the fraud and animal cunning." Still, the level of legal sophistication in each town depended upon its size, economic base, and leadership. And sometimes, more importantly, the town's leadership had to be able and willing to uphold and enforce the laws that were on the books. For Seymour, it was this last concern that would push many in the community, including Monroe and Shields, down a morally bankrupt path.

Allan Pinkerton believed himself a very moral man. He didn't drink—except when necessary as an undercover agent. He knew right from wrong. He was an abolitionist whose houses, first in Dundee and later in Chicago, served as stops on the Underground Railroad. But Pinkerton was also an opportunist. Sometimes these two sides to his nature didn't quite line up.

In 1860 when Seymour was a young town, John Reno was about to be on the lam for stealing his father's money, and Dr. Monroe was calling for merchants to band together to fund a woolen mill, Pinkerton headed a midwestern private regional police force of growing repute. It was then that he renamed the company Pinkerton's National Detective Agency. His motto—the eye that never sleeps—was illustrated on his sign and his stationery by one open eye.

The Pinkerton Code created by Allan Pinkerton dictated company behavior. His employees—called operatives, agents, or detectives—could never accept bribes or compromise with criminals. They were to partner with local law enforcement agencies, refuse divorce cases or cases that initiated scandals, turn down reward money (agents were well paid), and never raise fees without the client's prior knowledge. And they were required to keep clients apprised on an ongoing basis. The Pinkertons, as they collectively came to be known, had the power to arrest criminals anywhere in the country in conjunction with local law officials.

Allan Pinkerton shrewdly saw the need and then created the first national police agency.

A curious change came over Pinkerton during the formative years of his private detective work. This man, once a radical proponent of the working man while in Scotland, began to work on behalf of big business. His clients were railroad companies and express companies. His job was to protect their property, which often meant casting a suspicious eye toward the growing number of railroad employees.

Conductors were often the subject of Pinkerton's scrutiny because conductors had the most power and freedom on a train. They collected tickets, and money for tickets that hadn't been bought at stations. They could give free seats to their friends. They could pocket money from ticket sales. They could sleep or socialize while on the job. In a big business being run like a modern corporation, railroad owners believed that theft of time was almost as bad as theft of property.

Throughout the mid-nineteenth century, a substantial portion of Pinkerton's business was devoted to spying on railroad conductors to "test" their honesty. Were conductors pocketing money? Were they doing their jobs? Pinkerton operatives rode trains as paying passengers and observed. They sent detailed notes back to Pinkerton about the conductors' activities. Railroad employees hated the undercover detectives and started referring to them as vipers, spies, scoundrels, jailbirds, and "thieves set to catch a thief," for the rest of the nineteenth century.

Throughout Allan Pinkerton's life his agency would provide private police services to the well-to-do. The Pinkerton National Detective Agency acquired enormous power in their work on behalf of the wealthy as they crossed legal jurisdictions including state borders, and in a couple of cases, international boundaries. And, for all intents and purposes, if they could not get the cooperation of local officials, they personally kidnapped criminals to bring them to justice.

There was no state police. There was no FBI. There were only the Pinkertons.

In his work on behalf of the railroads, Allan Pinkerton had dealings with a young lawyer from Illinois representing a Chicago-based railroad. When this lawyer, Abraham Lincoln, was elected president of the United States in 1860, Pinkerton saw his chance to bust out of the Midwest and head to Washington, D.C., the seat of political power. He could imagine himself working for Lincoln. He imagined himself establishing a Secret Service detail to provide protection for the president.

His first act on behalf of Lincoln would come sooner than he anticipated.

As rhetoric between the North and the South escalated with Lincoln's election, one of Pinkerton's operatives discovered an assassination plot being hatched in Baltimore, Maryland. The plan was to murder president-elect Lincoln when he changed trains in that city while on his way to his inauguration.

Pinkerton had to warn the president.

CHAPTER FOUR

The Reno Boys and the Civil War

WHEN JOHN RENO ARRIVED IN INDIANAPOLIS ON APRIL 14, 1861, THE day after Fort Sumter was fired on, and found the people of the city "wild with excitement," the prospect of going to war thrilled the twenty-one-year-old. The Renos were staunch Republicans, so it's possible that fighting for the Federals was appealing. Then again, John Reno was an adventure seeker, and what greater adventure than war?

After news of Fort Sumter, Hoosiers rallied behind their political leaders, resolving, in the language of an Indianapolis meeting, "to repel all treasonable assaults . . . peaceably, if we can, forcibly, if we must."

During this chaotic time, Reno signed up for Johnathan W. Gordon's light artillery. The recruits went to the Indianapolis fairgrounds to drill but found out within a few days—when they were handed muskets—that they were not going to be artillerymen after all. "The majority of the company were dissatisfied with this," wrote Reno. "And refused to become infantrymen, and to end this controversy Governor Morton himself had to come out and disband the company." Reno ended up enlisting and mustering into the Indianapolis City Grays under Captain Dobbs for a three-year stint. They drilled "constantly" and were sent out to the battlefield on the Fourth of July.

There were about 300,000 men of military age in Indiana, and over the course of the war two out of every three eligible men went off to fight. Every family was touched by the war. Brothers, fathers, and sons became soldiers. Hoosier soldiers were slaughtered at Bull Run, stood fast on the first day of Gettysburg, and were even scalped by Cherokee warriors in the mountains of North Carolina. Four of the five Reno brothers saw action in the war that devastated families and towns and entire regions. It was a terrible watershed moment in a country less than a hundred years old.

"On the thirteenth of July, we fought in the battle of Rich Mountain," wrote Reno. "Our company was 'A'. We were armed with Enfield rifles, and did the skirmishing in the Rich Mountain fight. I was one of twenty-five who climbed over the breastworks under fire with Colonel Jerry Sullivan. After getting over, we received at once a telling volley from the enemy. I wheeled to go back and turned right into the Colonel's arms. Taking hold of me by the shoulders, he turned me 'right about face,' and cried out, 'they are running, man; follow them up!' True enough, they were retreating, and the volley they had fired was their parting salute. This was the closing scene of the six or eight hours of fierce fighting."

The war death toll for the whole state totaled over 25,000 men, or almost 13 percent of those who served. Deaths from battle numbered more than 7,000, while over twice that number died of diseases like malaria, dysentery, and typhoid. Disease decimated entire regiments. Many thousands more returned home injured and maimed, with debilitated bodies or minds, and memories that would never allow them or their families to forget the horrors they witnessed as part of the nation's bloodiest war.

In 1861 the 50th regiment of the Indiana Volunteers was recruited in Seymour, and forty-two-year-old Dr. Monroe volunteered and was mustered in on October 22, 1861. He was commissioned a surgeon. At home were a wife, Adaline, and four children. A dozen years later he recalled: "Everybody was willing to go and skin out South Carolina, or to make some sacrifice for the cause . . . Everybody wanted to go and nobody had the slightest idea of getting hurt, or that the rebels would ever do anything in the world but to run away on sight of the terrible 75 thousand, or any squad thereof. Everything was rosy, but it wasn't quite so sunny-like later along, and it got quite forbidding and squally in 1862 and '63 . . ."

By that winter, Monroe sought reassignment because of the way Colonel Cyrus Dunham and Lieutenant Colonel Horace Heffren treated the enlisted men. Monroe, never one to hold his tongue, complained about the officers' "insolent tyrannizing" and "enslavement" of the men. Monroe was reassigned to the 49th Indiana Volunteers and joined the unit at Cumberland Gap, Kentucky.

The ill and injured soldiers from the 49th Indiana Volunteers were spread out in small camps between Lexington and Cumberland Gap—a distance of over a hundred miles. Measles, pneumonia, and chronic diarrhea were rampant, and in spite of Monroe's best efforts, many of the men died. Monroe sent word to Governor Morton to send food, medical supplies, and more surgeons. Years later, Dr. Jas. G. McPheters remembers that when he first encountered Monroe that spring, Monroe was "an active healthy man, busily employed night and day, attending the sick. He was small and slender, but sinewy, apparently in excellent condition."

Another officer of the 49th recalled that Monroe did not appear to have much physical endurance, although he was a physician and surgeon of considerable talent. He also reported that Dr. Monroe, the rabid temperance advocate, "used liquors to some extent and was in the habit of going on 'sprees.'" He added that he knew of two sprees while Monroe was in the service, one about the time of the capture of Cumberland Gap, when he saw him sitting in a tent "beastly drunk."

Finally, Monroe's own health broke down. He was attacked with a partial paralysis, affecting and rendering his left arm almost useless. "It was that curious kind of spinal trouble that gives the victim an irresistible inclination to turn round in attempting locomotion," according to a profile of the doctor in the *Seymour Weekly Times*. "This affected the mind, and most of the month of July and a part of August of that year were almost a blank to the Doctor. But in spite of his indisposition, he continued his labors among the sick in camp until about the first of July. In this condition a resignation was reluctantly sent in."

Dr. McPheters, who saw Monroe in July, said he was in bad condition with rheumatism and gastric trouble. He also said he knew Monroe "drank very hard and, after quitting drink, resorted to opium which caused mental 'hebetude'" or dullness. He added that he always supposed the severe service Monroe saw as a surgeon "caused him to resort to stimulants."

Monroe was discharged and spent a month in a hospital in Lexington before traveling back to Seymour in August 1862.

The *Seymour Times* continued publication during the doctor's absence, covering the war and the goings-on about town. The week after Monroe's return to Seymour, he wrote about his own health in the third person.

"By the army surgeon, Dr. Monroe's disease was pronounced to be located in the brain and nervous system. His left arm had been partially paralyzed for a long time, and the senses of hearing and taste have been entirely destroyed on the left side. He has but partial control over the voluntary muscles of the left side of the body. The memory and mental faculties generally have suffered, and a distressing sensation of falling forward and to the right has been continually present. To this almost total loss of appetite and exhausting night sweats have been accompaniments since the middle of May."

With so many men and boys dying on the battlefields far from home as Union generals bounced from one disastrous defeat to another during the first years of war, it was no wonder that Republican Hoosiers began to show dissatisfaction with the way the war was being conducted. Some of this questioning may have been influenced by the traditional ties of family, culture, and trade, which many Hoosiers, especially those in southern Indiana, had with the South and its people. Southern Indiana, after all, shared a long boundary with Kentucky—a border state—and Missouri, another border state, lay just a train ride away.

To make matters worse, the Federal government ordered a draft conscription in the fall of 1862. For loyal Indianans, being forced to fight against slavery was an outrageous contradiction. Several other conscription calls were made in the following three years.

The war came home to the people of Jackson County and Seymour through letters and the newspaper. A small piece in the October 8, 1863, issue of the *Seymour Times* read: "Letter from Capt. C. A. Gordan; Chattanooga, Tenn., Sept. 27th, 1863. Dear Sir: To relieve the anxiety of the

friends and families of the boys from Jackson and Bartholomew counties, I here give you a list of the casualties in our regiment. Wounded—
Company F. Capt. Joseph C. Potts, privates B. R. Prather, Chas. Parker,
William Elbing. William Nolt, missing; William Banto, killed. Company E. Sarg't Nathaniel Jenkins, Corp'l Alfred Clifton, private, Smith
Whitaker, and Barton Myer. The above are all the casualties in our two
companies. The loss in the regiment was forty. All the Seymour boys are
all right." It's likely the community breathed a collective sigh of relief at
that last line.

A small notice appeared in a January 1863 issue of the *Seymour
Times*. "Dr. Monroe, at the request of the governor (accompanied by Drs.
Hagins and Price) left here last Saturday for the battlefield near Murfreesboro, to assist in caring for the wounded, which will account for the
lack of editorial in this issue."

The Battle of Stones River (better known as the Battle of Murfreesboro), fought near Murfreesboro, Tennessee, between the Union
Army of the Cumberland and the Confederate Army of Tennessee, left
enough dead on the battlefield to populate a small city. The night before
the battle began, the two armies bivouacked just seven hundred yards
from each other, and their bands started a musical battle that became a
non-lethal preview of the next day's events. Northern musicians played
"Yankee Doodle" and "Hail, Columbia." They were answered by "Dixie"
and "The Bonnie Blue Flag." Finally, one band started playing "Home
Sweet Home," and the others joined in. Thousands of Northern and
Southern soldiers sang the sentimental song together across the lines. The
battle raged between December 31 and January 2, 1863, and there were
23,515 casualties—one-third of the soldiers were killed, wounded, or
captured—making it the bloodiest battle of the war based on percentage
of casualties. At the request of the Indiana governor, Monroe went to
Murfreesboro with battlefield experience but also dread at what he would
find. He had previously mustered out of the army because of "fatigue,"
which was most likely shorthand for having a nervous breakdown or suffering from severe post-traumatic stress disorder. Going to Murfreesboro
would prove to be a severe test.

Sam Watkins of the First Tennessee Infantry, CS was amazed at
the bloodshed. He wrote: "I cannot remember now of ever seeing more

dead men and horses and captured cannon all jumbled together, than that scene of blood and carnage . . . the ground was literally covered with blue coats dead." The scene became known as the Slaughter Pen because Union soldiers recalled it looking like the slaughter pen in the stockyards of Chicago.

This is what Dr. Monroe walked into.

After Murfreesboro, the doctor had another and worse paralytic attack, which confined him to his bed for many weeks. He sold the *Seymour Times* to Braxton Love and John R. Jennings, but after several months, upon recovering, he bought the paper back.

The Reno brothers of Rockford used the Civil War as a way to supplement their income—they were Republicans, and proud of it, but they never let their political affiliation get in the way of making money. They would not be called upon by Indiana's Republican Governor Morton to tend to the wounded, like Dr. Monroe was. For the Reno brothers, the war was all about money and, perhaps, the element of danger.

Some of the Reno brothers became bounty jumpers and bounty brokers. As a way to drum up recruits, the federal and often state and local governments offered a bounty to men who enlisted or enrolled in a regiment. Bounties ranged from one hundred to three hundred dollars depending upon when they enlisted. This payment was in addition to the monthly private's pay of eleven dollars. A bounty jumper took advantage of the bounty system by enlisting, receiving the bounty, and then deserting before seeing action. There are cases of some men bounty jumping multiple times by enlisting under different names or using their own names in different states. Later in the war, bounty brokers emerged—men who would find substitutes to serve in place of someone who didn't want to enlist. The person looking for a substitute paid a fee to the broker, and the broker would also collect a portion of the enlistment bounty.

A bounty jumper could easily make one thousand dollars on top of his monthly pay, which was a small fortune. It was equivalent to nearly three-years' wages. If a man was a bounty jumper more than once, he could become rich. It's impossible to know how many enlistments and re-enlistments the Reno brothers made during the Civil War under false names, but we do know from the official records that both Simeon and John deserted and re-enlisted.

Simeon Reno enlisted at least twice during the period of one week in 1865. He's listed as a deserter from the second enlistment three months later. It's possible he may have enlisted in other states as well as Indiana, or that he may have enlisted under assumed names.

William Reno enrolled as a private in 1864 for a term of three years, and there's no record that he deserted. The oldest Reno boy, Frank, enlisted for three months. He enrolled at the very beginning of the war on April 22, 1861, and mustered out in Indianapolis on November 24, 1861. Except for his age of twenty-four, there is no description of him on the enrollment card.

There is no record or mention of Clint Reno ever serving in the Civil War, although there is a mention of him in the *Seymour Times* on July 2, 1863: "Clint Reno is well prepared to furnish everybody with groceries for the Fourth of July. He stands ready to also buy all the produce that farmers can haul to town."

John Reno's autobiography provides detail and color about his time during the war. After the battle of Rich Mountain, his unit moved to Beverly, West Virginia. John was detailed to General J. J. Reynolds's staff as assistant wagon master. While in company with Lieutenant George Wallace, that officer lost his pocket book, containing four hundred dollars. There must have been something about John Reno's look or behavior that caused people to assume he was up to no good. John was arrested on suspicion of taking the pocket book, and was placed in the guardhouse at Reynolds's headquarters. Found not guilty, he returned to duty.

Around two years after enlisting, John Reno decided to go to Norfolk to have some fun. On payday he got roaring drunk and was arrested and severely beaten with musket butts while resisting the arresting officers. When he recovered consciousness, he found himself covered from head to foot with deep cuts, scratches, and bruises. Reno was placed in a cell "ten or twelve feet below the surface of the ground." He was apparently in a cellar under a large brick jail. The floor of the cell was made of stone and cement. A small stream of water ran down the wall in one corner, and having no outlet except to seep through the floor, there was no more than three feet of dry floor to sit on. Green moss had grown all over the ceiling and partly down the walls, and the place was so damp and foul that a match or lamp would not burn. "About two o'clock in the morning I was attacked by rats . . ." he wrote about his first night in the cell. "They would run all over me, and when I would knock one off I could hear him chuck in the water . . . I never passed such a night of torture." Reno awaited trial by court-martial for fourteen days. During his spree he had badly injured two of the provost guards.

For some reason, Reno was released without court-martial and told to follow his regiment, which had left for Bermuda Hundred, North Carolina. John Reno didn't head south toward his regiment but instead wandered around Norfolk. He eventually made his way back to Rockford, where he spent time with his girlfriend Mollie, and hid from the U.S. Marshal, aware that he could be picked up at any time for desertion. He wrote: "My mother seemed glad to see me too—apparently she had forgotten the eleven hundred dollars I had stolen from the clothespress before I left. She was not in very good health . . . My father and her constantly quarreled."

During his time in Rockford the following notice ran in the *Seymour Times*: "The Post Office at this place was entered on Monday night and robbed of all the letters it contained. No clue has yet been obtained to the perpetrators of the act. We hope our citizens hereafter will be on the alert and thereby put a stop to the occasional petty thieving that has been carried on in this place for some time." Banknotes were often sent through the mail, which made the post office a tempting target for a thief.

After a Seymour counterfeiting ring was busted up, Reno left town. He was sure he'd be taken in for desertion, so he remained on the road until Atlanta was captured by the Federals.

Reno writes that after the draft of 1864 he became a bounty broker ". . . running men, mostly negroes, from Tennessee to Kentucky and Indiana, [and] selling them as substitutes."

On one occasion he took on a black man at Marietta, Georgia, "who was good for four hundred dollars as soon as I could get him to Chattanooga . . . Near Calhoun, the guerrillas, or bushwhackers, fired on us.

When at Ringgold I went to look at my man, whom I had left asleep in my berth in the caboose, and found him dead. A ball had come through the side of the car and entered his heart. I rolled him up in a government blanket and buried him the best I could."

Reno found himself in Nashville waiting for something to turn up. Hearing that large bounties were being paid at Bowling Green, Kentucky, he went to the jail in Nashville and found three bounty jumpers who had been jailed for drunkenness and put to work on the chain gang. Reno paid their fines and set out with them for Bowling Green, reaching an agreement with them that he was to receive half of their bounty money. He thought this would be twelve or fourteen hundred dollars—substitutes at that time bringing nine hundred dollars and a quick sale.

In Bowling Green, John located a "rich old rebel" who had been in town three or four days looking for a substitute, nearly wild with despair at the thought of having to fight for the Federals. He agreed to pay John $950. When John returned to the hotel, he found his three jailbird friends had left and joined with another man. Reno agreed to enlist on behalf of the old planter himself; he changed into ragged clothing, let the old man lead him to the provost marshal's office, and was examined. He reports that the examination consisted of merely stripping naked and walking across the floor, whereupon the examining doctor said: "He will do," to the immense relief of the planter. It was now noon and the marshal's office was closed. John was to return at two to be mustered in. When he and the planter returned, a messenger entered the office with them and handed a dispatch to the provost marshal ordering him not to accept any more drafted men or substitutes since the war was fast drawing to a close. The planter paid John $50 instead of the $950 promised.

Within a month, the Confederate Army surrendered.

All the Reno boys found their way back to the old farm near Rockford. The war had hardened them. Although some of the Renos had figured out how to make money by cheating the system, they had also witnessed horrible deaths, heard the pitiful cries of the wounded and dying, and walked on the blood-soaked ground of battlefields. It might not have taken them long to figure out what to do next when they found that their father owned most of the property in Rockford, including what was left of the burned houses and businesses. It probably seemed like an ideal place to set up their new enterprise with friends made during the war—a group of counterfeiters, thieves, safecrackers, gamblers, pickpockets, and confidence men. Two miles south, in the little city of Seymour, lay the junction of two great railroads. The Reno brothers figured they'd never have to leave home, for those railroads would bring business to them.

A thousand miles to the south, Allan Pinkerton stood on a wharf in New Orleans harbor, counting cotton bales on a dock for the Federal government when he heard that the war ended. The war had not gone as planned for the Scotsman, who had longed to be within Lincoln's private orbit. Instead, he was making sure the government wasn't being cheated of its supplies. When he heard the news later, by telegram, that Lincoln had been assassinated, all he could think was that it would have never happened if he had been at the president's side.

Chapter Five

Allan Pinkerton Goes to Washington

In early 1861, two men made their way from the great midwestern section of the country to the East Coast. One, Abraham Lincoln, was on his way to be sworn into the office of president. The other, Allan Pinkerton, was on a mission to make sure Lincoln reached the capital city alive. On February 11, President-elect Lincoln, his family, and some close family friends boarded a train in their hometown of Springfield, Illinois. Their journey would take them on a meandering route through numerous cities, including Indianapolis, Cleveland, Buffalo, Trenton, Philadelphia, Harrisburg, and Baltimore, before reaching Washington, D.C., on February 23. Two weeks earlier, Samuel Morse Felton, president of the Pennsylvania Central Railroad, contacted Allan Pinkerton in Chicago, asking him to come to New York City as soon as possible on a matter of greatest importance.

What Pinkerton learned from Felton was very serious but not surprising, given the mood of the country. Felton revealed there was a plot to assassinate Lincoln. It would happen as he switched railroad lines in Baltimore, where he had to travel across the city from one train station to another. Pinkerton begged Felton to maintain the utmost secrecy about what he knew to give the detective time to come up with a plan.

To get to Washington by rail from the North or West, it was necessary to travel through the city of Baltimore. Maryland would be known as a border state during the upcoming war, sending troops to both Confederate and Union regiments. Baltimore identified closely with the South.

So did most of Maryland's eastern shore—a low area confined between the Chesapeake Bay and the Atlantic Ocean—which raised tobacco.

Baltimore's police chief, Marshal George P. Kane, was a notorious secessionist. He'd later be placed in jail at Fort McHenry along with Baltimore's mayor, both charged with inciting riots. Pinkerton operative Timothy Webster, who was sent to Baltimore to assess the situation waiting for Lincoln, reported that the city was filled with Southern agitators and spies.

Webster, a naturally gregarious man with dashing good looks, was sent undercover by Pinkerton, posing as a rebel sympathizer. The operative was so convincing he was brought into the very group organizing the plot to assassinate Lincoln. Webster reported the mechanics of the plot: the group would create a distraction on the train platform; then one of the cohorts, chosen by drawing straws, would pull out a knife and stab the president-elect.

Norman Judd, a friend of both Pinkerton and Lincoln, was in charge of the presidential entourage from Illinois to Washington. Pinkerton sent Judd a sealed envelope via operative Kate Warne in which he outlined the plot as relayed by Webster.

Judd arranged for Pinkerton to meet the president-elect in his room at the Continental Hotel in Philadelphia at 6:00 p.m. on the evening of February 21. During the meeting, Pinkerton suggested Lincoln leave that evening on the 11:00 p.m. train from Philadelphia to Washington—much earlier than Lincoln had planned. Lincoln refused. He had promised to address the Pennsylvania legislature in Harrisburg, correctly believing them to be crucial allies in the work to come. Also, Lincoln was not entirely convinced by Pinkerton that there was a deliberate plot to murder him.

Pinkerton and Judd spent the rest of the night discussing alternate plans to ensure the president-elect's safety.

The following morning, Secretary of State William Seward's son, Fred, called on Lincoln at the Continental Hotel to report that Lieutenant-General Winfield Scott, head of the United States Army, had received information about an assassination plot. Fred had to wait several hours to deliver his message. "After a few words of friendly greeting with inquiries about my father and matters in Washington,' Fred remembered, 'he sat down by the table under the gas-light to peruse the letter I had brought.' After a few moments, Lincoln said to Fred: 'If different persons, not knowing of each other's work, have been pursuing separate clews that led to the same result, why then it shows there may be something in it. But if this is only the same story, filtered through two channels, and reaching me in two ways, then that don't make it any stronger. Don't you see?'"

Then, Fred related, "noticing that I looked disappointed at his reluctance to regard the warning, he said kindly: 'You need not think I will not consider it well. I shall think it over carefully, and try to decide it right; and I will let you know in the morning.'"

Lincoln and his party traveled on to Harrisburg, where he addressed the state legislature and raised the flag over the state house. Pinkerton made plans to spirit Lincoln out of the Pennsylvania city in the early evening, at least twelve hours before he was scheduled to leave. The rest of the entourage, including the Lincoln family, would stick to the original schedule.

At 5:45 p.m., Judd went to the hotel to collect the president-elect, who had changed into a traveling suit. Over the years, much has been made about what Lincoln wore during that clandestine journey—was it a women's shawl thrown around his shoulders and did he have a "Scotch plaid cap" upon his head? Was he wearing a long, threadbare military coat with a soft wool cap? Pinkerton was adamant that it was the latter and was furious when several newspapers printed the first description—a description Pinkerton believed made both him and the president look foolish. That depiction of Lincoln's traveling garb strangely haunted Pinkerton for the rest of his life.

Lincoln and his former law partner, Ward Lamon (later Lincoln's biographer), traveled alone on a special train from Harrisburg to Philadelphia. As soon as the train left the station, Pinkerton arranged for a linesman of the American Telegraph Company to climb the poles at the depot and cut all the wires in and out of Harrisburg, to prevent word getting out that Lincoln was traveling. Before the wires were cut, though, Judd telegraphed Pinkerton in Philadelphia to let "Plums" (Pinkerton's code name) know that "Nuts" (Lincoln) had departed safely.

Pinkerton operative Kate Warne had already secured the rear sleeping car of the Washington train, saying she needed the entire compartment for her invalid brother. Samuel Felton led Pinkerton and Lincoln to the last car, where Warne had drawn all the curtains and was waiting to escort the president. At 3:30 a.m. the train pulled into the Baltimore station, where it had to wait for the connecting train on to Washington.

Pinkerton later wrote: "An officer of the road entered the car and whispered in my ear the welcome words, 'All's well' . . . An hour and more the train waited . . . a drunken traveler on the train platform sang 'Dixie,' singing over and again how he would live and die in dear old Dixie. Lincoln murmured sleepily, 'No doubt there will be a great time in Dixie by and by.'"

Pinkerton operatives stood at strategic positions along the route between Baltimore and Washington, flashing lanterns to Pinkerton, who stood on the train's rear platform, signaling back that all was well. At 6:00 a.m. the train pulled into Washington, and Lincoln was hustled into a carriage and whisked off to the Willard Hotel on Pennsylvania Avenue, across the street from the White House. There he was met by William Seward for breakfast. At that time, Pinkerton telegraphed Judd in Harrisburg, where the telegraph wires had since been fixed: "Plums arrived with Nuts this morning."

The newspapers had a field day with Lincoln's arrival in Washington at that ungodly hour of the morning and about twelve hours earlier than the official itinerary. They wanted to know why he was *sneaking* into the capital city. When the rest of the presidential party—including an unhappy Mary Todd Lincoln and the children—arrived in Baltimore, more than ten thousand people crowded the Calvert station in Baltimore. As the train halted, the people—believing that Lincoln was aboard— gave three terrific cheers for the Confederacy, three more for Jeff Davis, and three loud and prolonged groans for Lincoln. Plot or no plot, this would have been a potentially dangerous moment for the president-elect.

At the Willard Hotel Lincoln thanked Pinkerton. The detective traveled back to Chicago, probably thinking he had clinched a job in the Lincoln government. A niche had opened up, and Pinkerton was pleased that Felton had thought to contact him when the plot emerged.

The detective had assessed the situation and delivered Lincoln safely to Washington. With the inevitability of war on the horizon, Pinkerton stood to gain enormously from what could be viewed as a test run of his abilities. Surely his quick thinking and well-crafted plan to save Lincoln's life meant that he—and only he—could provide this kind of special service to the Union. He was a detective and a spy, and had charge of a couple dozen competent operatives, both men and women.

Above all, however, Pinkerton was an opportunist, and here was an opportunity.

Much has been made over the years of whether the Baltimore plot was real or not. When Lincoln and Lamon parted company in Philadelphia, Pinkerton said or did something that irked Lamon, for later he would write in Lincoln's biography that there had never been a plot, and that the whole conspiracy was a "mare's nest gotten up by the vainglorious detective [Pinkerton]." Although knowledge of the plot came from two sources—Samuel Felton via Pinkerton, and General Scott via Fred Seward—there was still speculation about its existence, as no one was ever arrested for the treasonous act. George Templeton Strong wrote in his diary, "It's to be hoped that the conspiracy can be proved beyond a cavil. If it cannot be made manifest and indisputable, this surreptitious nocturnal dodging or sneaking of the President-elect into his capital city, under cloud of night, will be used to damage his moral position and throw ridicule on his Administration."

Eight days after the fall of Fort Sumter, President Lincoln received two letters. The first was from Norman Judd, the second from Allan Pinkerton. Judd's letter, addressed to "Dear Lincoln," read as a reference letter for the Pinkerton Agency. "I believe that no force can be used to so good advantage in obtaining information," wrote Judd. "His men can live in Richmond and elsewhere with perfect safety. Of course profound secrecy is the key to success. If you approve, Pinkerton can come to Washington and arrange the details."

Pinkerton's letter, addressed to "His Excellency A. Lincoln, Prest. of the U.S.," was hand-delivered by the dashing English-born operative Timothy Webster, who had been with the detective agency since 1853. The letter read, in part, "When I saw you last I said that if the time should ever come that I could be of service to you I was ready. If that time has come I am on hand." Pinkerton wrote that he had a "Force from Sixteen to Eighteen persons on whose Courage, Skill and Devotion to their country I can rely. If they with myself at the head can be of service in the way of obtaining information of the movements of Traitors, or Safely conveying your letters or dispatches, on that class of Secret Service which is the most dangerous, I am at your command."

Pinkerton instructed the president to trust Webster, who could get either a written or verbal message to him safely. Webster also provided Lincoln with a copy of a "Telegraph Cipher" that Lincoln could use if he preferred to contact Pinkerton that way. The letter ended, "My Force comprises both Sexes—all of good character and well skilled in their business."

President Lincoln wrote a brief reply to Pinkerton summoning him to Washington for a meeting with him and the Cabinet on May 3rd. Webster rolled Lincoln's message into a tiny ball and concealed it in the head of his walking stick before strolling out of Lincoln's office.

At that point, there was no easy way to get to the nation's capital, as the Baltimore & Ohio (B&O) Railroad had ceased operation and would remain shut down for several weeks following a riot in the city. When Federal volunteers of the 6th Massachusetts Infantry were being transported from the North through Baltimore on April 19, Southern sympathizers had attacked the troops outside the main Baltimore terminal. Shots were fired, and in the end nine civilians and four soldiers were dead. Dozens more were wounded. B&O president John Garrett and Baltimore mayor George W. Brown decided to suspend rail service until things cooled down. Both the South and the North claimed the B&O Railroad for their own use to transport troops and supplies. The railroad would be a source of contention throughout the war as Federal and Confederate troops fought for control over segments of the line.

It was just when Pinkerton was traveling east to meet with the president that the B&O railroad ceased its operation in and out of Baltimore. Washington was now effectively cut off from the North and West. New York papers had to be delivered to the nation's capital by Pony Express. Pinkerton traveled from Chicago to Perryville, Maryland, then boarded a boat to sail the length of the Chesapeake Bay to Annapolis, where he then caught a train.

Once in Washington, Pinkerton made his way to the White House, later writing, "Around the executive mansion everything was in a state of activity and bustle. Messengers were running frantically hither and thither; officers in uniform were gathered in clusters, engaged in animated discussions of contemplated military operations; department clerks were bustling about, and added to these was a crowd of visitors, all anxious, like myself, to obtain an interview with the Chief Executive."

He was ushered into the long room that served as Lincoln's office and cabinet meeting room. Several members of the Cabinet were there with the president. Pinkerton was asked to be seated. President Lincoln told him that they were entertaining the idea of organizing a secret service department to ascertain the social, political, and patriotic status of numerous suspected persons in and around the city. Pinkerton lobbied hard for the job, yet by the end of the interview no decisions had been made. The detective was told he would hear from someone shortly and was sent away.

Pinkerton waited in Washington for a message from the White House. He later wrote about the city, "I found a condition of affairs at once peculiar and embarrassing, and the city contained a strange admixture of humanity, both patriotic and dangerous. Here were gathered the rulers of the nation and those who were seeking its destruction. The streets were filled with soldiers, armed and eager for the fray; officer and orderlies were seen galloping from place to place; the tramp of armed men was heard on every side, and strains of martial music filled the air."

After several days with no word from Lincoln (he later wrote that he believed the idea was lost amid the "confusion of the moment"), Pinkerton left for Philadelphia to attend to some railroad business. When he checked into his hotel, he found a telegram waiting for him. It was from George B. McClellan, recently appointed Major General of the Ohio Volunteers (consisting of combined forces from Ohio, Indiana, and Illinois). McClellan wrote: "I wish to see you with the least possible delay, to make arrangements with you of an important nature." He was in Cincinnati and requested Pinkerton come at once. Pinkerton, who had worked for McClellan when the latter was president of the Ohio & Mississippi Railroad, immediately boarded a train and headed to Ohio, ready to take whatever job McClellan proposed.

McClellan told Pinkerton he wanted the detective to establish a secret service department under his command, with the objective of obtaining information from behind enemy lines. Pinkerton and his operatives were to observe troop strength, equipment, military movements, and, when possible, the intentions of the enemy. The detective jumped at the chance. It would be a delicate business, though, and Pinkerton thought about how to proceed. He chose his best operatives, men and women, who could work alone or in pairs, and then sent them on different routes throughout the South. They were all to adopt new personas. One pair traveled as husband and wife, while another toured as a rich Englishman accompanied by his manservant. Timothy Webster, Pinkerton's most experienced operative, who had passed as a secessionist in Baltimore and allegedly helped expose the plot to assassinate Lincoln earlier that year, infiltrated rebel spy rings throughout the South. Pinkerton himself adopted the *nom de guerre* Major E. J. Allen, which he used during the war, as he believed his own name was too high profile and had grown to be a synonym for "detective."

Allan Pinkerton was a driven man who could get by on two or three hours of sleep. He seemed possessed of boundless energy. A tireless worker with reckless courage and a formidable grasp of detail, he expected nothing less from his operatives. The war would test and ultimately change all of them.

In the mid-nineteenth century, the science of criminology did not exist. Detection work was at its most basic, relying almost entirely on betrayal by informers. Parisian detective Eugene Francois Vidocq had established his Bureau des Renseignements in 1832, paving the way for the modern detective agency. Vidocq used ex-criminals as detectives because he believed they best understood the workings of the criminal mind.

Pinkerton differed from Vidocq in two fundamental ways: he didn't want to hire criminals because they were too difficult to control, and he liked to rely upon deduction—or following clues—to solve cases, a method later popularized by Sir Arthur Conan Doyle's character Sherlock Holmes. At that time, few knew that the ridges and whorls on fingerprints could be a unique way of identifying people, and criminal identification by fingerprints did not become widespread until the twentieth century. Crime scenes were not protected. Once gawkers or passersby had walked around bodies or disturbed robbery scenes it became almost impossible for police or detectives to establish what had happened and in what order.

Pinkerton's National Detective Agency operatives were chosen carefully by Pinkerton, who looked, first and foremost, for people who were loyal and clever. Operatives assumed different identities and disguises to fit the particular case. A large room in the agency's headquarters in Chicago could rival that of the costume department of any large theater. It was filled with changes of clothing, wigs, accessories, and makeup. Pinkerton taught his operatives to use the art of disguise. Men might dress as old women. Women might dress as men. An operative could be made up to look younger or older, richer or poorer. The objective was always to infiltrate, observe, and engender the trust of whoever was the target or the target's closest allies. Operatives learned to develop their memories and powers of observation so they could later file extensive reports with Pinkerton.

The detective agency was always quick to adapt to new technologies—particularly telegraphy and photography—and because the agency worked for a number of big railroads, the operatives always had access to free railway passes.

Pinkerton developed his own system of keeping track of criminals. A card was filled out for each lawbreaker, noting physical description, name, aliases, dress, habits, mental characteristics, criminal specialties, and mode of operation. It sounds so simple compared with more sophisticated twenty-first-century techniques, but this information had not been systematically collected before. Pinkerton also attached photos to his cards—mug shots—and then circulated copies of photographs of wanted criminals to lawmen all over the country. Pinkerton's "Rogues Gallery" system was later adopted by other law agencies, including the FBI.

Pinkerton's stint as McClellan's secret service operative was a disaster. For whatever reason—and there is much speculation about why this happened—Pinkerton and his operatives consistently overstated the strength of the Confederacy forces that lay in McClellan's path. Early in the war, General McClellan had been promoted to lead the Army of the Potomac. The battle theater lay primarily in Virginia. Due to either bad advice, natural reticence, or a combination of both, McClellan hesitated attacking the enemy on several occasions, opting to wait for reinforcements, when in fact, he had the superior army strength at the time. The Army of the Potomac lost battle after battle, and McClellan was soon demoted. Pinkerton, as McClellan's right-hand man, lost his post as head of the secret service. However, the great detective stayed in Washington, determined to help the Federal cause and to be compensated for his expertise. Various government departments contracted with Pinkerton for his spy services during the remainder of the war.

Pinkerton operatives continued to gather data from around the South, while Allan Pinkerton decided to tackle espionage rings in the capital. "Here, too, lurked the secret enemy, who was conveying beyond the lines the coveted information of every movement made or contemplated," wrote Pinkerton. "Men who formerly occupied places of dignity, power and trust were now regarded as objects of suspicion, whose loyalty was impeached and whose actions it was necessary to watch. Aristocratic ladies, who had previously opened the doors of their luxurious residences to those high in office and who had hospitably entertained the dignitaries of the land, were now believed to be in sympathy with the attempt to overthrow the country, and engaged in clandestine correspondence with Southern leaders."

Somehow, sensitive Union military information—including maps and proposed lines of attack—was being leaked to the Confederates. The name of one Washington society doyenne, Rose O'Neal Greenhow, surfaced time and again because she made no secret of the fact that she was in complete sympathy with the South.

The widow Rose O'Neal Greenhow and her eight-year-old daughter, Little Rose, lived in a large brick house in a fashionable section of Washington, D.C., a house that her friend Confederate General P. T. G.

Beauregard said was "within easy rifle range to the White House." In her late forties, she was considered a great beauty, and powerful men were drawn to her house like flies to honey, where they hoped to partake of more than her excellent port and brandy. She had torrid love affairs with a number of men, including Captain Thomas Jordan, a West Pointer, distinguished veteran of the Mexican-American War, and quartermaster in the U.S. Army. Jordan decided to spy for his native Virginia. He enlisted Greenhow's help in establishing an espionage ring. She was happy to assist.

At the start of the Civil War, Washington was a city with a decidedly southern feel—at least a third of its residents were born in either Maryland or Virginia. Abraham Lincoln received less than 3 percent of the vote in Maryland, and a paltry 1 percent in Virginia. Most of the men of the secessionist Confederate government and its military hierarchy had held posts in the Federal government in Washington and had left behind friends and family when they moved across the Potomac River and into Virginia.

Washington was thrown into a state of barely organized chaos. Union troops poured into the city to be drilled before going into battle, with many regiments housed near one of the three dozen fortifications being built to encircle the city. Soon soldiers were housed everywhere— even in the Capitol building, whose dome was still being constructed, and the east wing of the White House. Naïve farm boys and young city slickers from Maine to Indiana moved along the muddy streets, wide-eyed at the availability of every sort of sinful activity, including card games, prostitutes, and taverns selling "likker" that would burn your insides.

The population of the fledgling city, the seat of the Federal government, consisted of bakers and blacksmiths, fishermen and farmers, carpenters and government clerks. There were several monumental public buildings—the Treasury Department, the Capitol whose dome would be completed while war raged on the perimeter of the city, and the Smithsonian Institution, also known as the Castle.

The Capitol, the Castle, and the Washington Monument (only one-third finished) were corners of a massive triangle whose interior was empty of buildings. Cattle grazed around the base of the unfinished Washington Monument. There were 3 veterinarians, 6 undertakers, 17 milkmen, 67 innkeepers, 148 doctors, 180 lawyers, and 242 tailors in the city. Smith's on Seventh Street sold the season's latest hats and caps.

Charles Shafer worked in his watch shop, not far from the Washington Carriage Factory, which was on D Street between 9th and 10th. Benter's Restaurant on C Street advertised its fish and oysters, as well as its wine, liquor, and cigars. The studio in which Mathew Brady would photograph the most famous faces of the Civil War was already up and running in a building on Pennsylvania Avenue, halfway between the White House and the Capitol.

Mary Henry, daughter of Joseph Henry, the Secretary of the Smithsonian Institution, lived with her family in the Castle. In her early twenties, Mary kept a diary throughout the Civil War noting everything from lectures held at the Smithsonian, to battles witnessed from the tower of the Castle. She also wrote about visits to the regiments encamped around the city. In May 8, 1861, as young recruits filled the city she wrote: "Gov. Sprague's men are decided to be the finest here not excepting the proud N.Y. Seventh. He has clothed most of them himself. They are stationed in the Capitol. The streets are filled with soldiers & the sound of the drum is heard unceasingly from morning until night. A squad of men in very pretty grey suits with red trimming have just left the Institution. The N.Y. Zouaves have a very undesirable reputation. They have been quite disorderly since their arrival."

As spring melted into summer, the muddy streets of the city that could formerly bury a carriage wheel up to the hub became dry and dusty, although they were never without a generous layer of manure from the many horses that pulled carriages and wagons. The fetid smells mixed with the humidity of a city built on a swamp.

In 1861, many of the 75,000 residents of the District of Columbia who were able moved out of the low-lying city during the summer months because of the rampant and seasonal spread of malaria, typhoid, dysentery, and diarrhea. Tens of thousands of additional people using the Potomac River for drinking and washing, with army encampments built on the banks of the river without adequate latrines, made the capital city almost unbearable.

Rose Greenhow decided to stay in town during the humid summer of 1861. With the help of the traitorous Captain Jordan, she devised a scheme to extract information about Yankee troop strength and strategies from her many knowledgeable suitors. Among her conquests was Union Colonel Erasmus D. Keyes, who called her "one of the most persuasive women that was ever known in Washington."

Senator Joseph Lane, Democrat from Oregon, visited Greenhow as often as his ill health would allow. He wrote to her, "Believe me, my dear, I am not able to move as a young man should. Please answer."

But her most strategic conquest was Republican Senator and abolitionist Henry Wilson from Massachusetts. He also happened to be Lincoln's chairman of the Committee on Military Affairs and a future vice president under President Grant. Wilson sent Greenhow love letters, some written on congressional stationary, all signed only "H." In one he wrote: "You know that I do love you. I am suffering this morning. In fact, I am sick physically and mentally and know nothing that would soothe me so much as an hour with you. And tonight, at whatever cost, I will see you." Wilson had a wife and children at home, to whom, he said, he was very devoted.

Captain Jordan taught Greenhow a cipher in which symbols stood in for different letters, numbers, or words. Jordan also taught Greenhow how to use Morse code, by which she could send messages to the other side of the Potomac by manipulating her window shades on the upper story of one side of her house. She also became adept at using Morse code on the street, letting words rain forth by the flutterings of her fan.

An accomplished seamstress, Greenhow spent hours at her sewing machine affixing pockets to the undersides of dresses and creating ingenious little bags that would hang from the hoops under a skirt. No one would dare search a refined lady who wished to cross into Southern territory—which Greenhow counted on as she pressed a small circle of socialites dedicated to the cause into service. She also fashioned small silk purses—the size of a silver dollar—that she'd sew around ciphered notes and then tuck into the folds of an informant's hair.

Greenhow's notes were all intended for General Beauregard. It soon became obvious to Federal troops that there had to be a leak of military intelligence, because Beauregard and his Confederate Army seemed to know exactly what the Grand Army was going to do and when they were going to do it. The information she passed to Beauregard may have led to the rout of the Union Army by the Confederates at the First Battle of Bull Run.

What Greenhow didn't know in 1861 was that Allan Pinkerton was on to her.

After Pinkerton's involvement in the Baltimore assassination plot of Abraham Lincoln, and in spite of his disastrous turn with McClellan, the detective was on both the president's and his administration's radar. And Pinkerton made sure of that by offering his assistance at every opportunity. Soon-to-be Secretary of War Edwin Stanton hired Pinkerton to keep a strict watch on Greenhow's house. Pinkerton's operatives were to note every person entering or leaving. They should try to ascertain who the visitors were and whether they attempted to communicate with any "suspicious persons." Pinkerton was to report to Stanton daily and to continue surveillance until instructed not to.

With the same dogged determination Pinkerton would later show in his dealings with the Reno Gang, he performed his duties with gusto. Allan Pinkerton made it a priority to bust up the Greenhow espionage ring. His operatives continued their surveillance of Mrs. Greenhow and her premises, taking note of all her visitors, including senators, congressmen, society women, and military men. One afternoon, after Mrs. Greenhow and her daughter left for the day, Pinkerton and three of his operatives broke into her house and searched it thoroughly, finding nothing. Mrs. Greenhow later bragged that Pinkerton missed a note on her desk written by Jefferson Davis.

Within a month, Mrs. Greenhow was placed under house arrest. A legal search turned up maps, Beauregard's codebook, and some notes in cipher.

On January 1, 1862, Rose O'Neal Greenhow was sent to Old Capitol prison. Her young daughter, Little Rose, accompanied her. There they occupied the same cell. Rose, with the use of Little Rose as a decoy, continued to pass coded messages to the enemy. After refusing to take the Oath of Allegiance to the Union several times, mother and daughter were sent to the South. The Confederate government then sent Greenhow to Europe as an ambassador from the South, where it was hoped she would charm European nations to support the Southern cause.

While in England, Greenhow wrote a scathing, scandalous, and supercilious book, *My Imprisonment and the First Year of Abolition Rule in Washington* (1863), in which she is the heroine of her tale of woe.

Of the search of her house by Pinkerton and his detectives she writes: "An indiscriminate search now commenced throughout my house. Men rushed with frantic haste into my chamber, into every sanctuary. My beds, drawers, and wardrobes were all upturned; soiled clothes were pounced upon with avidity, and mercilessly exposed; papers that had not seen the light for years were dragged forth. My library was taken possession of, and every scrap of paper, every idle line was seized; even the torn fragments in the grates or other receptacles were carefully gathered together by these latter-day Lincoln resurrectionists . . . I was a keen observer of their clumsy activity, and resolved to test the truth of the old saying that 'the devil is no match for a clever woman!' I was fully advised that this extraordinary proceeding might take place, and was not to be caught at a disadvantage."

While Allan Pinkerton, "the eye that never sleeps," and his Washington operatives worked to crush the Greenhow spy ring, operatives Timothy Webster, Pryce Lewis, John Scully, Kate Warne, and Hattie Lawson roamed through the South in search of information to pass on to the Union command.

This quest would have disastrous results. In addition to contributing to General McClellan's earlier misfortunes, within a year, Timothy Webster would be executed by the Confederacy as a spy and two other operatives imprisoned. The death of Webster hit Allan Pinkerton hard. Webster was Pinkerton's best operative; he'd become like a son to the older man. After the war, Pinkerton had Webster's body moved from its pauper's grave in Richmond, Virginia, to Illinois. His name was carved on a monument in the Pinkerton family plot in Graceland Cemetery, Chicago. His body was buried elsewhere.

CHAPTER SIX

Seymour Takes a Stand

IN 1864 JOHN RENO, A DESERTER FROM THE UNION ARMY, RETURNED to his family's farm outside of Rockford, Indiana. He was joined by his brother Frank, who had served his five months and then mustered out of the army, and their younger brother Simeon. Soon the three brothers moved from the family farm and into the deserted buildings of nearby Rockford. A number of "questionable looking tenants . . . some of the best known thieves, gamblers, cutthroats, and counterfeiters in the country" drifted into Rockford. This collection of characters, men befriended by the Renos during the Civil War, would now be known as the Reno Gang in the literature of the day.

It's difficult for a modern reader to imagine the upheaval, chaos, and dislocation the Civil War created. The war raged throughout the South and spilled into the West and up into the North as far as Vermont. Southeastern Indiana experienced organized raids by Confederate troops under the leadership of General John Hunt Morgan. While most of the local men were engaged in fighting elsewhere, in the summer of 1863 Morgan led 2,500 troops through the small towns of North Vernon, Vienna, Salem, and Corydon terrorizing townspeople, burning buildings, and raiding livestock, horses, mills, and stores for money and supplies. Indiana Governor Morton frantically organized home troops to pursue the raiders. They were soon joined by Federal troops under the command of Major General Ambrose Burnside, who chased Morgan's men from town to town. In Dupont, Indiana, the Confederates burned the town's storehouse and stole two thousand smoked hams before leaving. The soldiers eventually discarded the rapidly spoiling hams along the trail as they began to attract flies.

Men like Dr. Monroe returned home from the war physically and emotionally battered from what they had experienced. It's not difficult to imagine boys like the Renos, whose sense of morality was already challenged, entering the war in search of adventure and then coming home hardened and unconcerned about what was right and what was wrong. Their moral compasses—weak and wavering before the war—were completely out of whack by the end of the conflict. Men of similar ilk found each other. When not fighting, they spent their free time devising ways to amass great fortunes by robbing, stealing, and cheating. The Renos and their newfound associates—unlike Monroe or Meedy Shields or Travis Carter—were not returning to a place where they felt any sense of civic obligation. They had not built the town. They had not cleared the land and drained the swamps and laid foundations for their houses. The only way the Renos would ever be viewed as leaders was through notoriety.

When in town, the Reno brothers and their associates made themselves at home in their *de facto* headquarters, Seymour's Rader House, where they played cards, drank, and planned their next jobs. This hotel, built near the train platform, had a saloon on the first floor and rented rooms above. In 1864, soldiers and travelers who had to stay the night in Seymour while waiting for connecting trains reluctantly stayed in the loud, noisy, and less than respectable Rader House. The gang had a perpetual card game going at a table in the corner of the hotel's saloon. When they could, they cheated travelers out of their money. If that didn't work, they resorted to robbing rooms.

Occasionally, those just passing through Seymour ended up dead or missing.

That same year the Reno gang began robbing local businesses and wealthy farmers in the area. In December, Frank Reno, Sam Dixon, and Grant Wilson rode to the next county and robbed Gilbert's Store and the United States Post Office in Jonesville. The three men were caught by Federal marshals but were soon released after posting bond—a pattern to be repeated time and again over the next several years.

By 1865, Seymour had a population of close to two thousand and was by far the largest town in Jackson County. All sorts of traffic came through Seymour—people on their way to other places, soldiers on their way home—in addition to the grifters, confidence men, and gamblers who frequented railroad towns. In many ways, Seymour didn't seem to be a destination. Rather, it was a way station, a layover, and often an annoyance, on the way to someplace else.

A letter to the *Seymour Times*, signed RAILROAD, gives a glimpse into the swirl of activity at the train station: "We are very frequently annoyed by small boys standing around the railroad station, especially during train time—they annoy not only the employees, but also the passengers getting off and on the trains. Boys, we wish to treat you kindly, therefore we ask you to keep away. We also ask parents to keep their children away from the station. Their being here results in no good to them, but may result greatly to their injury. One boy has lost an arm here and who knows but your boy may be the next one, not only to lose his arm, but his very life. Parents, we warn you in time, will you heed our warning? But there is a class of larger boys with whom we have no patience—boys old enough to know what is required and expected of them—boys whose mustaches are beginning to sprout, and who begin to 'ape the airs of men,' these young gentlemen (?) both annoy and disgust us and all decent people, by hanging around the sitting room of the Depot, and insulting every female passenger that gets off the train. Young men, if you don't wish to have your names exposed to become reproach to all respectable people this must be stopped."

The Reno Gang and other confidence men used this transient and always moving population near the railroad stations to make a quick buck. In 1865, five men set up a tent on a vacant lot near the railroad crossing. The purpose? A snake show. The tent was divided in two, the front section for the show, the back for gambling. The snake men hired agents to hang around the depot when the trains were pulling in. *Snake show, snake show! Come see the snake show!* The agents were particularly interested in enticing soldiers returning from war into the tent. Once there, the con artists would invite them into the back section and attempt to swindle them out of their paychecks. Soldiers who looked like they might rat on the operation were threatened. Some of the men connected with the snake show branched out into a band of roving thugs that knocked down and robbed people in the streets of Seymour after dark. City officials were overwhelmed. Fortunately for them, the snake-show men had a feud among themselves. One was shot, "unfortunately not fatally," Monroe comments, but this rid the town of the show. Several of the men stayed in the area, moving to the Reno properties in Rockford.

On February 18, 1865—a Saturday night—three members of the Reno Gang crossed a line. They blackened their faces and pulled on half masks and rode out to the house of Mrs. Joel Richards. Her husband was still away in the army. Their two children were asleep upstairs in the remote farmhouse. When Mrs. Richards came to the door, she must have been terrified at the sight of the masked men who greeted her. The men demanded all of her money, and when she gave them two dollars they dragged poor Mrs. Richards from her house. They took the rope from the windlass of the well, threw it up over a piece of wood projecting from the top of the smokehouse, and made a noose on the other end of the rope. This they put around the woman's neck. Poor Mrs. Richards was hauled up off the ground and left to hang in the air for a few minutes as the men held onto the other end of the rope. They let her down, again demanding more money. Gasping for breath, Mrs. Richards told them, again, that the two dollars were all she had. They hoisted her up off the ground once more, this time letting her hang until she was nearly dead. They finally dropped her to the ground, where she landed in a heap. The robbers mounted their horses and rode off, taking her two dollars with them.

Several days later an editorial in the *Indianapolis Daily Sentinel* condemned the "outlawry and thievery." The unnamed author, likely Monroe (the column is written in his style), wrote: "This is one of the most inhuman outrages we ever recorded, and the people of Jackson county should organize a vigilance committee that will hunt down and hang the scoundrels. So many crimes have lately been committed in that county that the people should make common cause to bring the perpetrators to speedy and condign punishment."

It was the first call for a vigilance committee in Jackson County.

By mid-July the lawlessness was so rampant in Seymour that after a soldier was robbed of $400—"all he had"—Dr. Monroe wrote: "We would advise soldiers and others who are compelled to stop here not to drink, nor to go to sleep, nor to move about unless in sufficient numbers to over awe the gangs of thieves and assassins that infest this place."

In the following week's *Seymour Times* Monroe did not hold back in his call for vigilante justice, believing the law was so inadequate that "it is nonsense to depend upon it." He proposed that a vigilance committee "composed of sober and respectable men" be organized in Seymour, and that "Lynch law should be sternly administered." Monroe wrote that because the law was doing nothing about the rampant lawlessness, it was starting to look like all the townspeople were themselves members of the band of robbers. "Nothing but Lynch law will save the reputation of the place and its citizens."

The bitterness Monroe felt after the Civil War gushed from his editorial pen as well. In the August 3 issue of the *Seymour Times*, Monroe's editorial took on "Andy" Johnson and all of Washington over the pardoning of former rebels. "The work of pardoning rebels whose hands are red with the nation's best blood goes bravely on," he wrote. "In fact, the pardoning of the bloody scoundrels who murdered and starved to death our brave soldiers, seems about all the business going on at Washington." Monroe's fury at the Johnson administration's policies toward the rebel South spilled forth from many of the *Seymour Times* editorials. The editor seemed to view these actions on the part of the Federal government as a personal affront and betrayal of all he had sacrificed by administering to the sick and dying men at the front.

Perhaps Monroe's call for vigilante action in Jackson County was one way the doctor could grab some control in a country where the men in charge seemed so unwilling to prosecute those he believed had wreaked havoc upon the land. If Washington wouldn't blame and punish the former rebels for atrocities perpetrated at places like Andersonville Prison, at least the people of his county could make quick work of those who chose to live outside the law in their midst.

Newspaper editor Monroe was really dedicated to two things—the annihilation of the Reno Gang and the promotion of the town of Seymour. The one would further the other. Monroe badgered and hounded the people of the town to continually make civic and economic improvements as a way to ensure Seymour's prosperity. He used his paper as a bully pulpit and wrote, equally vigorously, for lynch law and a new woolen mill.

Seymour was home to people who attended the large brick Methodist Church in town, and to children who went to one of the several public schoolhouses. It was home to George Green the mayor, and to Travis Carter, John Love, and Mr. Butler, the men who scraped together the financing for the new woolen mill. The rolling hills just south of Seymour were too steep for farming but perfect for sheep herding, and from these flocks would come the wool for the mill. An Agricultural Society was being formed and new fairgrounds were planned for the fields at the edge of town. The first ordinance the Seymour Council passed in the year 1866 was to establish the first fire department in Jackson County. Hooks and fire ladders would be placed at specific places in each ward and "in case of removal by cause of fire that the same be returned to the places designated for their keeping."

Most of the people of Seymour went about their business and lived their lives. The men operated planing mills, woolen mills, and flour mills. They ran groceries, dry-goods stores, hotels, livery stables, and pharmacies. They were tinsmiths, blacksmiths, and photographers. They worked on the railroad maintaining track, fixing locomotives, and loading cars with freight. Doctors and lawyers filled downtown offices. Women raised families, cooked, cleaned, and kept gardens. The farmers on the edge of town raised sheep, pigs, and field crops like winter wheat and corn. The town council and municipal officials were drawn from the town leaders like Travis Carter and John Groub—men who felt deep pride in their community and planned to guide Seymour toward an ever prosperous future.

Seymour, like most towns, was home to an assortment of characters ranging from gamblers and prostitutes to mill owners and schoolteachers. The gambling houses, saloons, and hotels along Indianapolis Street, which ran parallel to the railroad, were, for at least four years, the part of Seymour that received the most attention. The county history written in 1886 claims that the Reno brothers themselves didn't engage in the petty robberies and burglaries that took place near the railroad stations. This may or may not be true. What is true is that the little scams—playing cards, stealing purses, and passing counterfeit bills—brought in chump change. But the very presence of the gang and their ability to somehow paralyze local law enforcement from taking action against them made the petty crimes possible. The gang created an atmosphere where the towns-people became somehow convinced that they deserved to be mistreated.

Chapter Seven

Koniakers and Boodle

John Reno, definitely the brains and sometimes the brawn of the Reno Gang (until he was sent to prison), had a special affinity for counterfeit money. Reno knew it was easy to make a killing with the bogus notes, especially with a master engraver in the gang.

Imagine a time when the states had responsibility for chartering banks, a time when neither a federal banking system nor federal regulations covered banking. In the mid-nineteenth century, between 1837 and 1862, thousands of local, state, and national banks popped up all over the country, some of them conducting business out of post offices, even stores. Economic historians may call this the "free banking era," but for counterfeiters and forgers, it was a free-for-all era. Each bank issued its own note with its own design, and currency varied in shape, size, and color. With so many different banknotes in circulation, shops, individuals, banks, and other commercial enterprises often had no way to know if a note was real or a forgery.

By 1860, there were 1,562 state banks in operation, which caused massive confusion in the marketplace. In addition to attracting counterfeiters, the state system of chartering banks created other problems. First, banks issuing their own notes as currency made it difficult to determine the relative value of each different note. In the first half of the nineteenth century, banknotes were like promissory notes and could be redeemed for specie—gold or silver coin—which gave the notes value. But, with no federal oversight, the money supply and the price for goods were highly unstable. These two problems led to a third—frequent runs on banks, resulting in substantial losses for anyone crazy enough to be a depositor. Consequently, travelers often carried bulky gold or silver coins because their banknotes might not be recognized or accepted anywhere outside of their hometown.

In 1861, the U.S. government stepped in. Congress passed a law allowing for the printing and distribution of Demand Notes backed by $250,000,000 of U.S. credit. This act was drawn up, in part, to finance the Union side of the Civil War. Demand Notes were also known as "greenbacks" for the distinctive green ink used on the reverse side of the bills. The reverse side of most banknotes (including Confederate money, called "graynotes") was usually left blank. Demand Notes were viewed with suspicion until Secretary of Treasury Salmon P. Chase explained to the banks and the public that the five-, ten-, and twenty-dollar notes were redeemable in coin on demand at the offices of the assistant treasurer in Boston, New York, Philadelphia, St. Louis, and at the Depository of Cincinnati.

"They must be always equivalent to gold," wrote Secretary Salmon P. Chase. "A sufficient amount of coin to redeem these notes promptly on demand will be kept with the depositaries, by whom they are respectively made payable." In spite of the convoluted language, this statement calmed the public and the state banks, which began accepting the federally issued Demand Notes as currency.

In 1862, Congress passed the First Legal Tender Act, granting legal tender status to new U.S. Notes. The five-, ten-, and twenty-dollar bills looked very similar to the Demand Notes, but the phrase requiring payment in specie "on demand" was eliminated, and the U.S. Treasury seal was added. The U.S. Note, also known as a Legal Tender Note, became the paper money issued for almost a hundred years, 1862 to 1971, in the United States.

Within two years, the country had moved from thousands of state-issued notes of all different sizes and colors, along with a reliance on gold and silver coins, to a uniform dollar backed by the promise that the federal government could convert those dollars to gold at any time.

The National Banking Acts of 1863 and 1864 established some federal control over the banking system. Creating national banks wrested control of the money from state charter banks. The country could now rely on a uniform national currency. An active secondary market in treasury securities was established to finance the Civil War. For the first time there were notes issued by the nation, for the nation, based on the future credit of the nation.

An unintended consequence of the issuance of greenbacks (like Demand Notes, Legal Tender was also called greenbacks) was the skyrocketing of counterfeiting on a national scale. Now rather than working on numerous designs, plate engravers could concentrate on creating and perfecting a single design for each note, which could then be passed all over the country.

In Indiana, the Reno Gang took advantage of this golden opportunity and brought several of the best counterfeiters in the country into their fold. The plan was simple. The Renos would supply the counterfeiters with real currency that could be washed and reused for making bogus money of higher denominations.

Counterfeiting had its own language. Counterfeit currency was called coney or queer. A coney man or a koniacker was the person who made or controlled the bogus money. Counterfeit bills were often tied into bundles called boodle, which was sold by coneys or dealers for ten dollars of real money per hundred dollars of coney. Boodle carriers then distributed the fake bills to shovers, who paid between twenty-five and forty dollars per hundred depending on the quality of the notes. The better the quality, the more real money a shover had to pay. To shove meant to pass counterfeit bills in public as real money. If a shover didn't have the down payment for the bills, he or she could approach a middleman, who would advance the bogus dollars in return for 50 percent of the take. These layers within layers meant that even a person with drive but no means could get in the game.

Often shovers worked in teams—particularly if they had taken the coney on credit—and one person would stand outside a shop and hand the shover one counterfeit bill and some change. The shover would enter the shop and try to buy some small item with the bogus bill. If the shopkeeper balked, the shover could take back the bill and reach into his or her pocket and pay for the item with change. Successful shovers or passers had to be well dressed and clean, and to appear above suspicion in any shop where they tried to pass bills. They'd go from shop to shop and town to town working their con.

In the 1850s and 1860s, enterprising publishers began producing counterfeit detectors or pamphlets that merchants kept next to the register. In the days of the state banking system, when a shop owner received a bill, he could look up the name of the bank on the banknote in the counterfeit detector and see if any bogus bills had been circulated under the name of that bank. If they were lucky, they'd find a description of the counterfeit note.

John Thompson published the most successful weekly counterfeit detector in the 1850s and 1860s, called *Thompson's Bank Note Reporter*, which was available by subscription weekly and semimonthly. The descriptions in *Thompson's Bank Note Reporter* were often indecipherable and cryptic, and without an example of a "good" note to compare the bogus note to, it was near impossible to figure out what was in front of you. Yet many merchants subscribed to a counterfeit detector like *Thompson's Bank Note Reporter* because just displaying it on the counter might scare off a shover.

Some clever confidence men began creating their own counterfeit detectors, which they would pass out to merchants. Then the con men's associates would trail behind, passing counterfeit notes that weren't listed in the pamphlet. With the proliferation of state banks issuing a blizzard of banknotes, and so many ways to be conned, merchants in cities and towns were wise not to take any notes from banks they didn't recognize as local.

There was always an engraver at the center of a counterfeit ring. Before the issuance of greenbacks there were several ways an engraver could create a realistic bill—he could raise the denomination by washing the bill with an acid bath where the numbers were, and then, using a die, switch a lower number for a higher one. He could change the words on a bill using the same method—washing, then substituting letters. Banknotes from banks that had gone under could be bought in bulk on the black market, then completely washed and reprinted with a made-up bank that sounded real. Sometimes coney men got their hands on a dead bank's printing plates, which they'd hand over to the engraver, who would create more money using the plates. Engravers, although skilled, were not well paid under the state banking system. It wasn't surprising to find former bank engravers working in what they hoped would be a more lucrative enterprise.

The issuance of greenbacks raised the stakes. Now an engraver had to be adept at creating dies of both lines and portraits (usually they had skill at one or the other). The master engravers who had real skill at both were in high demand. And the payout for accurate-looking greenbacks was tremendous because the bills were accepted everywhere.

A perennial problem in creating realistic coney was the paper. The government began to use a very particular rag paper created from cotton and linen fibers, which they controlled access to. This meant engravers either had to be creative and imitate the weave of the paper using a very fine hatching design on the plate, or use greenbacks that had been washed or bleached to remove the ink: the original laundered money. Sometimes it was just easier to raise the numbers on bills, changing a one to a ten, or a ten to a one hundred dollar bill.

As the public gained confidence in the new national currency, the counterfeiters saw their opportunity. Engravers were being put out of work. As state banks folded, the production of greenbacks became concentrated in just a few cities and engraving shops before the Bureau of Engraving was established. Good engravers were looking for work and were able to find it within counterfeiting rings. A story in the *New York Times* from 1862 claimed that six thousand varieties of counterfeit banknotes were contaminating the money supply. The piece concluded that counterfeiting was "a national evil demanding a national remedy."

In the South, Confederate notes were losing value by the day and southerners were keen to get their hands on Yankee dollars. Shovers had no problem passing false dollars in the Confederate States, where few had actually seen the new national currency.

It soon became apparent that counterfeit bills were also flooding the North. By 1864, it was estimated that about half of the money in circulation was bogus. Secretary of Treasury Chase understood the seriousness of the problem. He asked Secretary of War Edwin Stanton to release William P. Wood, superintendent of the Old Capitol Prison in Washington, D.C, so Treasury could employ him to help track down the coney men.

Wood, by many accounts of the day, seemed an odd choice. A hero of the Mexican-American War, Wood's tenure at Old Capitol Prison had fueled the rumor mill in Washington for years. It was whispered he was a spy for the South. That he did things his own way and often exceeded his authority. That he passed counterfeit Yankee dollars to Union prisoners in the South so they could purchase food, clothing, and other items from their Confederate guards.

Secretary Chase didn't go through the formalities of seeking approval from Congress or the president when he created his ad hoc agency of Treasury with the hiring of Wood. Giving Wood the directive to crack down on counterfeiters, Chase let his man do as he pleased.

The first thing Wood did was to hire three coney men as operatives, one of whom was plucked from a Chicago jail. These men were allowed to set up scams to entrap counterfeiters. In the end, the operatives often profited from their own stings. The operatives might turn in the bogus currency and pocket the real dollars they found at the scene. Or maybe they'd keep part of the counterfeit money and sell it to shovers. Some operatives made money by offering suspects immunity or protection for a fee. The men who worked for Wood were aggressive and played fast and loose with the law, but they got the job done.

When Hugh McCulloch replaced Chase as Secretary of the Treasury in 1865, he was determined to make this ad hoc agency legitimate and permanent. In what is an oft-repeated yet unsubstantiated apocryphal story, McCulloch met with Abraham Lincoln on April 14, 1865, just hours before President Lincoln and his wife went to Ford's Theatre. At their meeting McCulloch told Lincoln that the fake currency was undermining the trust in the national currency and that local law enforcement was incapable of putting a stop to the problem. McCulloch told Lincoln he recommended the creation of a permanent, aggressive organization of government operatives trained to target counterfeiters. Lincoln said, "Work it out your own way, Hugh. I believe you have the right idea."

On July 5, 1865, William P. Wood was officially sworn in as the first chief of the U.S. Secret Service. By year's end, Wood had thirty Secret Service operatives in the field. One of these operatives, Samuel Felker, crossed Allan Pinkerton's path more than once, and the two men squared off in court on several occasions. The public disliked Wood's unorthodox and unethical methods, but he didn't care. Wood had a knack for getting counterfeiters to turn on each other, which created chaos in the big counterfeiting rings in the East.

Wood was also mapping who was who in the world of counterfeiting in the greater United States. In the upper Midwest Mississippi region, where the Renos held sway, Frederick Biebusch, a German immigrant, was a prominent middleman and financier for counterfeiting gangs operating in Missouri, Indiana, and other states along the Mississippi River. Biebusch maintained close ties with master engraver, dealer, and Reno associate (John) Peter McCartney, who was known as the "King of the Koniackers." Ben Boyd, a skilled engraver who made beautiful counterfeit greenbacks, was also in the Biebusch orbit, as was financier Nelson Diggs. John Frisby and Louis Sleight, who lived in Nauvoo, Illinois, controlled that state's counterfeiting business. All of these men were known associates of the Reno Gang, but especially close to the gang were McCartney and Boyd, who laundered the gang's money along with counterfeit boodle.

Chapter Eight

Incident at Pana, Illinois

In September of 1866, John Reno made a trip to Illinois with his buddy George Mace. Mace had just been released from the penitentiary south of Seymour in Jeffersonville, Indiana. Reno and Mace rode the trains, stopping at Indianapolis for a few days, and ended up in Pana, where Mace registered at the hotel as "George Nace" and Reno as "Sam McBeth." Nace was George's real last name, only in Seymour was he known as Mace. Reno used Sam McBeth because he'd gotten a railroad pass from railroad engineer Sam McBeth, which allowed him to ride the trains for free.

About the time the two men left Seymour, a fine horse belonging to Giles Goss disappeared. When in Pana, Reno, short on cash, wired his mother Julia for money under his assumed name. Apparently the Seymour telegrapher noted the name Sam McBeth and found it suspicious. Why was this man wiring Julia Reno for money? He told the sheriff, who told Goss. Thinking there must be a connection to his missing horse, Giles Goss and two detectives headed to Pana.

Reno (as McBeth) got a notice from the Pana express agent that there was a package waiting for him in the office. When he went to collect it, the express agent happened to be an old schoolmate from the little Rockford school. Recognizing Reno, he refused to give him the package addressed to McBeth. Reno went round to the depot to telegraph his mother again when he saw George Mace being arrested by two men and taken to a waiting room. Reno followed and was then himself arrested. It was about 9:00 at night, and they were taken out to the "commons" and

80

placed in a little blockhouse the men called the "calaboose." Neither Reno nor Mace had an inkling what was going on.

After midnight a man came to the door and ordered George out. John assumed they'd take him out of earshot, question him, then bring him right back. Sometime later the door opened again and John was ordered to come out. Reno got up off the straw tick mattress he'd been lying on. For some reason he left his coat, with a loaded revolver in the pocket, inside the calaboose.

"I was quickly jerked off the doorstep and a rope was thrown around my neck, and I was led in this way a distance of about a mile down the railroad tracks," Reno wrote in his autobiography. "The man who had hold of the rope was drunk so that he would constantly fall down, jerking me to my knees, since my hands were tied helplessly. I managed, with difficulty, on account of the pressure of the rope on my throat, to ask them what they were going to do.

"'We have hung that long-legged son of a b----,' they cursed, 'and we're going to serve you the same way.'"

Back in Seymour, plans were being made to hold a fair in October. The newly formed Agricultural Society purchased land at the edge of town and was now erecting a building on the new fairgrounds.

There was already a race track just off the road between Seymour and Rockford that attracted people from around the county. The Renos loved the races, and when they were flush, wagered great sums on the horses. From the Renos' perspective, an autumn fair at the new fairgrounds meant even greater numbers of people would come to the races. This would put money not only into their pockets, but also into the coffers of the gambling houses and saloons that lined Indianapolis Avenue. They could imagine the cash flowing as they played hearts and poker. They could almost hear the men yelling and frantically betting as two roosters rose together in a flurry of feathers and feet and attacked each other with their man-made spurs attached to their heels.

Earlier in the year, town-founder Meedy Shields died at home of inflammation of the stomach. His estate was valued at $375,000. Monroe writes: "Capt. Shields was in many respects a remarkable man ... of great ability and force of character. All that prevented him from becoming one of the foremost men of his party (for he was a politician by nature) was the want of an early education. His ability was of the practical kind. He had no theories. Any problem he couldn't work out satisfactorily, he dropped ... His business transactions reached almost every man in the community ... Mr. Shields was respected by all and honored and loved in his own family."

Dr. Jasper R. Monroe and his wife, Adaline, filed for divorce. She received $4,500. Not long after this, Dr. Monroe, age forty-five, married Mary R. Clark, age twenty-one.

In May of 1866, the city of Seymour elected George Green mayor and George Slagle marshal. A. A. Davison and J. W. Hollinsworth tied 29–29 for a seat on the city council. In August, Slagle resigned as city marshal and Dick Winscott was elected to fill the vacancy.

Monroe wrote, "No town in the state is in a worse sanitary condition, and even while inspired with a lively fear of the cholera the officials took no step to improve it." A small stream ran through the lot of the *Times* building and acted as a natural drain for much of the town. Monroe advocated drying it out, stating that "half of the miasma of the town would be swept away." He also recommended that the practice of setting privies over the stream should be stopped.

Back in Pana, John Reno was dragged to a barn, where he was led up into the loft. "I could see by the flashes of lightning outside, that there were about fifty men sitting around," wrote Reno. "They now began to talk 'horses' to me, asking a great many questions and, being unable to get a satisfactory answer to them, they kicked me off and let me hang by my neck, where I was in great agony. This they repeated at intervals of about five minutes each, until I had been hung by the neck until nearly senseless for five different times. The last time I was hung up I did not come to for a long time, and when I did come to I 'played possum' on them."

Reno seems not to have realized he was being asked about stealing a horse—literally. When he came to that final time, and was led back to the calaboose, he found George flopped down on the tick mattress. After talking they discovered they had received the same treatment. They compared their experiences and found they both lied under questioning but about different things. George denied having ever been in prison, whereas John said George had. John said the names on the hotel register were true, and George said they weren't.

"Had I been guilty of any offense, I would have been looking for them, and I would not have left my Navy revolver behind me," wrote John. "I often wished that I had had it in my hands when they came [to get me from the calaboose]. The people of Pana would have known at least three of the party—because they would have been found there the next morning."

The marshal brought the two men breakfast and appeared very surprised and "astonished" to hear about them being mobbed the night before. John recognized the marshal as the man who had opened the door for the mob to drag him out. John asked for an attorney, who secured his release, and then Reno went to the courthouse to swear out a warrant for the mob. He had seen several faces clearly in the flashes of lightning. When he entered the mayor's office to get the warrant signed, he recognized at once that the man sitting behind the desk was one of the three men who dragged him into the barn with the rope around his neck.

John changed his mind about the warrant.

Before leaving town, Reno met Giles Goss on the street. By now he knew Goss was searching for a stolen horse. Somehow John had learned that Goss was present at the mobbing and was sure he was to blame for this "cruel lynching."

Reno wanted revenge.

John wrote: "I later came home in the company of Mr. Goss, and had abundant opportunities for getting even, but as time elapsed since his brutal treatment of me, my thirst for vengeance subsided. He is living today [1879], I believe, and if his eye should fall upon these pages he will know that the man he caused to be hung like a dog, in so cowardly a manner, for no better reason than mere suspicion, had too much honor and manhood in him to shoot or stab him in the dark as he so rightly deserved."

Dr. Monroe ran a story in the September 13, 1866, issue of the *Seymour Times* under the title THE RENO TWIST: "John Reno of this county, and George Mace met with rather rough treatment at the hands of the Mayor, Marshall, deputy Marshall and home citizens of Pana, Illinois, a few days ago. Mr. Goss of this place had a valuable horse stolen some weeks ago. He was in Pana in search of his horse. Reno and Mace being there were arrested on suspicion and locked up. In the night the officials above named, with some unknown men, all in disguise, took them out of the jail and deliberately hung them till they were nearly dead. The hanging was done to extort a confession, but both men persisted in their innocence. Reno was strung up five times till consciousness was gone. Fifteen minutes elapsed the last time before he came to. The men constituting the mob were drunk . . ."

In December of 1865 the Indiana State Legislature renewed an 1852 statute legalizing vigilantism. This act authorized the formation of companies for the "detection and apprehension of horse thieves and other felons and for mutual protection." This was sometimes referred to as the Reno Law in late nineteenth-century southern Indiana newspapers.

There had to be at least ten men to form a company, and each company had to draw up articles of association. They had to state a reason why the association was being formed. Each year the articles of association had to be filed and recorded in the office of the County Recorder, and a certified copy of this record would be received as "*prima facie* evidence in any court of this State." Affixed to the articles were the names and addresses of each member. The association had to draw up a constitution and bylaws. Members of the association "who in the pursuit and arrest of horse thieves and other criminal offenders against the criminal laws of their State," had all the powers of constables. Constables did not have the right to act as judge and jury to those they arrested. They did not have the authority to lynch. And yet . . .

Vigilante movements were called various things in nineteenth-century America, including horse thief detection societies or anti-horse thief associations, vigilance committees, regulators, mutual protection associations, detecting and pursuing societies, aid and detective societies, and detective clubs. They most often arose in response to a typical nineteenth-century American problem: the absence of effective law and order in a frontier region. Vigilante movements sprang up hundreds of times over the course of the century as settlers pushed west beyond the relative safety and familiarity of the Atlantic seaboard.

In many towns in southern Indiana, particularly after the Civil War, the regular system of law enforcement—the town or county sheriff or the town marshal—often proved woefully inadequate to keep the peace. Usually, lawmen were elected officials who didn't need to have any qualifications to get the job. Many people in southern Indiana were sympathetic to the South during the war, including citizens of Seymour, who felt they had much more in common with people in Kentucky than those in New York. Dr. Monroe could easily whip up little dust storms with his frequent commentaries on Copperheads and Democrats in his decidedly Republican-leaning newspaper. When he began to rail against the Reno Gang, it marked the beginning of what would be an intense war of us versus them. The lawmen and courts and juries in Jackson County were overwhelmed and overworked with Reno business in the mid-1860s. Like some of their neighbors to the west, the elected lawmen began to rely on the Seymour Vigilance Committee, aka Jackson County Regulators, aka Jackson County Vigilance Committee, to help them do their jobs.

A vigilance committee roundup of criminals and outlaws followed by their flogging, expulsion, or killing not only solved the problem of disorder but had an important symbolic value as well. Vigilante action was a clear warning to disorderly inhabitants that the newness of a settlement wouldn't be an opportunity for the erosion of the established values of civilization. "Vigilantism was a violent sanctification of the deeply cherished values of life and property," wrote Richard Maxwell Brown in his critical study of American violence and vigilantism.

Looking at the first fifty or sixty years of court records in Jackson County reveals how difficult it was to convict someone of a crime in the late 1860s. It appears that judges, lawyers, and members of juries were all susceptible to bribery, as were sheriffs, marshals, and jail guards.

Jurors were also afraid, and rightly so, of retaliation. The name Reno appears frequently in the court records: James Reno—grandfather of the Reno brothers—was indicted for mayhem and arson; Wilkinson Reno for inciting a riot, assault, and numerous tussles over real estate; Frank, John, William, and Simeon Reno for robberies both large and small, and counterfeiting; and Clint Reno for running a gaming house. But the state had little or no control over juries who through fear, friendliness, or corruption often failed to convict. Additionally, the lack of jails or their often flimsy construction made it nearly impossible to prevent those in custody from escaping. Several members of the Reno Gang busted out of jails more than once, confounding and humiliating those who tried to hold them.

Although all the elements of a system of law and order were firmly in place, John and his brothers spent years making a mockery of the justice system in Jackson County. They obtained false witnesses on their behalf. They made witnesses "disappear." They packed juries and bribed officials. The Reno brothers seemed to have the whole system in their pocket. Through a combination of bribery, intimidation, and their ability to post large bail bonds (sometimes as much as $15,000), they operated the gang on the fringes of town with impunity for several years.

Did the Seymour Vigilance Committee register their association with the county? It doesn't appear so, but in every other way they behaved like the many other horse thief detection companies found around the country. They were highly organized, had a strong leadership, and believed they had the right to step in and protect their community. Maybe, because there was a law on the books authorizing this kind of group, they believed they could act first and then, if need be, apologize for not jumping through the correct legal hoops.

CHAPTER NINE

The First Train Robbery

ON A RAINY, AUTUMNAL NIGHT—A NIGHT WHEN THE WIND BLEW THE rain sideways and soaked anyone stepping out for even a moment—the eastbound Ohio & Mississippi train from St. Louis thundered toward Cincinnati with over $50,000 locked in two safes in the express car.

The O&M's tracks between Cincinnati and St. Louis had been laid just a decade earlier, and the railroad had transformed the region. Cars filled with everything from dry goods, crops, cattle, hogs, hardware, and lumber rolled through once virgin landscape and connected East with West. Pulled by enormous twenty-two-ton steam locomotives with prominent cowcatchers attached to their fronts and towering stacks that belched acrid, blue wood smoke, these trains also carried all kinds of passengers, including soldiers returning home from the war, young men searching for a fresh start in the seemingly endless frontier, families visiting relatives, and people headed to town for supplies.

In his 1878 book, *A History of the Growth of the Steam Engine,* author Robert Thurston wrote gushingly that it would be "superfluous to attempt to enumerate the benefits which it has conferred upon the human race, for such an enumeration would include an addition to every comfort and the creation of almost every luxury that we now enjoy."

On this particular dreary evening in early October of 1866, the O&M train stopped in Seymour just long enough to pick up freight and some passengers, many of whom had likely spent at least part of the day in the train depot or in one of the hotels or gambling houses crowding the streets near the tracks, waiting for a connection that might or might not be on time. Passengers waited as long as possible before leaving the relative dryness of the overhanging eave of the station before dashing to the open doors of the train.

The O&M picked up its passengers in Seymour and continued its journey east. Less than a mile from the depot, the O&M engineer saw someone on the tracks ahead signaling to the train with a red lantern. The red lantern was used when something was wrong. He shouted to the brakemen on top of the cars to *put on the brakes!* They turned the big metal wheels on top of each railcar that manually applied the brakes, sending up a cascade of sparks off the metal rails and a high-pitched squeal of metal-on-metal as the train shuddered and skidded several hundred feet.

The train's deceleration was the signal for two men sitting on one of the wooden seats in the last car. They began moving forward through the trains. These were rough-looking young men, of average size or maybe a little on the small side, with dripping hats pulled low and the shapes of huge revolvers visible through the large pockets of their wet jackets. When the men walked past, the other passengers moved a little closer to each other, as if for protection.

By the time the train stopped, whoever had been swinging the signal lantern had extinguished the light and disappeared down the side of the steep embankment and into the tangle of bushes, vines, and low trees bordering the track.

Realizing there was no emergency, the engineer, likely swearing loudly, brought the boiler back up to a head of steam. The train slowly began moving forward again, jerking each car into motion.

As the locomotive picked up speed, the men making their way forward through the cars reached the railcar hooked behind the tender box of the engine. They stopped to pull on two cardboard (then called pasteboard) masks—one painted white and the other black—that completely covered their faces. There were round holes cut where the eyes and mouths might be. With hats jammed onto their heads and coat collars turned up, the two masked men looked like ghouls or apparitions. The robbers then stepped into the express car through the unlocked rear door.

In the mid-nineteenth century, important documents, money, payrolls, and valuables like jewels were transported for clients in special railcars owned by express companies. These companies—such as American Express, Wells Fargo, and the Adams Express Company—promised point-to-point delivery of the goods entrusted to their care. Within the express railcars, the money and valuables were locked in iron safes. A company employee called a messenger rode in the car and was responsible for transferring the contents of the safe to another express company employee at each station. This system had been in place since before the Civil War and to date had not run into any trouble.

But that was about to change.

That night, Adams Express messenger Elam Miller was sitting at a small wooden table in the middle of the car, entering into the ledger the names of items just picked up in Seymour. He looked up in shock as the robbers burst into the express car and moved toward him. They both put heavy Colt Navy revolvers to Miller's head and demanded—in voices muffled by the masks—the keys to the two safes.

Miller, a small, trim man wearing the Adams Express uniform of a navy blue coat and waistcoat over a white shirt, broke into a sweat although it was a cool night. He told the men he only had the key to the little—or the local—safe. The local safe held valuables that were delivered to the smaller destinations along the train line.

As Miller drew the key slowly from his waistcoat pocket, the robber in the white mask grabbed it from his hand and opened the small safe. Inside, he found $18,000 in cash, some jewelry, and several small packages.

The black-masked robber found a couple of canvas satchels in the corner of the railcar, which he then filled with the contents of the small safe. There was another, larger safe in the car holding money bound for points east. But Miller didn't have keys for the large one, known as the through safe. It had been filled and locked by another Adams Express agent, not Miller, and could only be opened and emptied by an express agent with a key in another city.

But the robbers were in luck. The through safe was on rollers. Since they couldn't get into the big safe, they put their shoulders to the iron box and pushed the heavy container across the railcar and out the open broad side door. They watched as it hit the weeds and tumbled down the side of the muddy embankment.

By that time, the train had picked up speed, so one of the robbers pulled the bell cord to signal the train to stop again. As metal skidded on metal, sending off another shower of sparks, the robbers hugged the money-filled canvas bags close to their bodies and jumped out the side door of the slowing car. They rolled down the slick embankment and disappeared into the cold, murky darkness.

Elam Miller watched in astonishment.

It was October 6, 1866, and he had just witnessed the world's first robbery of a moving train.

Later, Miller estimated that fifteen minutes elapsed from the time the robbers entered the express car to when they jumped from the train. As the train slowed that second time, and after the robbers jumped, Miller yelled to the engineer that the express car had been robbed. The engineer, swearing again, threw the train in reverse and slowly backed it to Seymour, much to the bewilderment of the passengers. Once there, Miller told his incredible story to the O&M route agent on duty.

Miller, the route agent, and several other railroad men commandeered a handcar from the rail yard adjacent to the train station and worked their way along the tracks to where Miller thought the safe had been pushed from the train. The wind was lessening and the rain had eased up to a slow drizzle, but the men were still soaked through and cold.

The railroad men held their lanterns high on the left side of the handcar looking for evidence of the large safe in the weeds lining the track. It was easy to spot the flattened grasses where the safe had first landed. It appeared to have rolled end-over-end several times before coming to rest. A trail of skid marks through the wet grass and mud led into a thicket where the safe had been pushed or dragged another hundred feet. The safe—a large iron box on wheels—was filled with $38,000 in gold coin, making it extremely heavy. The possibility of it being carried off by two robbers was very unlikely.

The men leapt from the handcar and scrambled down the embankment. They followed the slick trail made by the weight of the safe being pushed along the ground and found, by looking at the footprints left in the mud, that the two robbers had been joined by a third man. The railmen also saw that someone had tried to break into the iron box by hitting the thick metal of the safe door repeatedly with something heavy but was unsuccessful at getting the box open. The relieved railmen and Miller strained and sweated as they pushed the intact but dented safe up the muddy slope. They then loaded it onto the handcar and made their way back to the train station in Seymour.

At the station the shaken and exhausted Adams Express messenger telegraphed his supervisor in the Chicago home office to tell him about the robbery. The supervisor then telegraphed Allan Pinkerton of Pinkerton's National Detective Agency.

The robbery of the O&M out of Seymour, Indiana, caused a ripple of excitement across the country. It was common knowledge that trains now carried large amounts of cash—payrolls, banknotes, even gold—but no one had robbed a moving train of its lucrative payload. Although a train had been robbed in Kentucky, in that case the masked bandits had stopped the train and robbed the passengers. Railcars had been robbed of freight while parked in rail yards, a feat requiring only opportunity on behalf of the burglars. Robbing a moving train was something entirely different. The first problem was figuring out how to get on and off the train, which meant stopping the train. Less than a decade later the James Gang would pile logs and boulders on the tracks, forcing the engineer to stop the train or risk derailment. The Reno Gang had taken a simpler approach, merely waved a red lantern on a flat and desolate stretch of the tracks to cause the engineer to stop the train. The robbers had to know the layout of the train and where the express car was, how to get into it, and how best to intimidate the messenger into handing over the keys to the safes. Then they needed an escape plan.

Express companies had been moving valuables around the country for decades but hadn't used the railroads until just before the Civil War.

As railroads expanded their reach into the heart of America, connecting cities to the frontier, express companies realized that partnering with railroads would be a win-win. Gold from mining camps, payrolls, bank deposits, tax money, and jewels, which were moved by stagecoach and wagon prior to the partnership, were always vulnerable to attack by robbers.

Two days after the robbery, the *Indianapolis Daily Journal* splashed across their front page: "Daring Robbery Near Seymour—Adams Express Rifled—Fifteen Thousand Dollars Stolen." The reporter noted that "[The robbers] are represented to be about five feet eight or nine inches in height, and of about one hundred and fifty pounds in weight," and that "pasteboard masks covered the entire face." The piece concluded with a reward announcement: "The company offers $5,000 for the arrest and conviction of the robbers, or one-half that amount for either."

The *New York Times* also ran a small piece on the front page of the October 8, 1866, edition under the headline "Express Car Robbed." They reported the bare details of the crime and that "The Company offers a liberal reward for the arrest of the thieves."

Adams Express, whose clients were out thousands of dollars, had the Pinkerton National Detective Agency of Chicago on retainer. The detective agency held retainers with a number of railroads, and also with express companies (including Adams Express) that moved packages around the country. One of the Pinkerton Agency's railroad jobs was to investigate any problems that might arise with the transporting of valuables.

Just months earlier, Allan Pinkerton had made two recommendations: first, that the doors to the express cars be locked at all times, and second, that the rollers be taken off all the safes, making them much more difficult to move. Neither recommendation was put into place. The Seymour robbers were able to enter the Adams Express car easily through the unlocked door. And although they couldn't get into the big safe, they were able to roll it out the side door rather than wasting time pushing and shoving the heavy iron box across the wooden floor of the railcar. In hindsight, it seemed like the express company was begging to be robbed.

As soon as Allan Pinkerton was contacted by Adams Express after the October 6 robbery, he telegraphed two of his operatives, Larry Hazen in Cincinnati and John Egan in St. Louis, telling them to get to Seymour immediately. Within twenty-four hours, the detectives met in Seymour and visited the spot where the robbers had leapt from the train. Although by that time many sets of footprints surrounded the impression where the safe had briefly lain, the detectives managed to isolate three sets that interested them. These footprints created a muddy trail leading away from where the safe had been and into the cluster of buildings by the train station. Hazen and Egan noted the approximate size and unusual details of the prints—a worn-down heel, a distinctive hobnail pattern— then followed the prints directly to the small house of Wilkinson Reno. The father of the Reno brothers lived near the O&M rail station. At that point, the detectives didn't enter the house but were fairly certain they were looking at one or more of the Reno brothers for the train job.

The next day was Election Day in Seymour. Southern Indiana took elections very seriously. Residents discussed national politics in the saloons, on street corners, and in the papers for weeks before elections. Because there were many Southern sympathizers in the state, particularly in the southern part that bordered Kentucky, every single election in southern Indiana during the Civil War era was hotly contested. In 1866, right after the end of the war, the election became a referendum on President Johnson and Reconstruction.

President Andrew Johnson was a Southern Unionist Democrat whom Abraham Lincoln chose as vice president for his second term. As the horrendous war was coming to a close, Lincoln hoped that by putting a southerner on the ticket—Johnson was from Tennessee—he could bring the Confederate states back into the Union as quickly as possible. When Johnson became president after Lincoln's assassination, he betrayed Lincoln's faith in him by firing cabinet members, enacting his own Presidential Reconstruction plan, and opposing the Fourteenth Amendment.

Because Johnson was a Democrat, and the Democratic Party was the party of the South, the more outspoken Republicans in Seymour had their say in the local Republican paper, Monroe's *Seymour Times*. A week before election day, Dr. J. R. Monroe offered his opinion: "Next Tuesday is election day and every man who is entitled to vote is requested to bear in mind that the Wilkes Booth-copper-Johnson party, who are now asking the suffrage of free and enlightened citizens, used their whole influence during the war to disorganize and break up the Union. They were opposed to all means and measures which were calculated to assist the soldiers in their efforts to suppress the rebellion . . . When you go to cast your vote consider these facts and remember that the principles of the party have not changed and that when you vote for a Democrat you vote for a rebel."

A snide editorial comment about local Democratic candidate Jason B. Brown, a lawyer who would weave in and out of the Reno story over the years (and who was re-elected to the Indiana House of Representatives that Tuesday), had run a week earlier in the same paper: "It is not our intention today to discuss the doctrine of innate wickedness. We affirm, however, that evil communications and poor whisky will demoralize any man without innate wickedness. The Democratic candidate in this District for Congress, when younger he was a better man; evil communications and poor whisky has made him what he is."

As the election neared, discussing politics could easily turn into drunken, bloody affairs. On that Election Day, liquor ran freely as candidates tried to entice potential voters to vote for them. For some people, like the Reno brothers, every election was another chance to make money by wagering for or against candidates. Although professed Republicans, the Reno brothers were not interested in politics, per se, but only in the men who held office and how easily they could be bought.

Great sums of money changed hands in the saloons over the outcome of the election. Detectives Hazen and Egan melted into the rowdy saloon crowd and watched as John Reno, his brother Simeon, and their friend Frank Sparks bet heavily on their candidate to the tune of almost $1,500—money Hazen and Egan were sure came from the Adams Express robbery.

Earlier, during their two-day investigation of the robbery, the detectives questioned the route agent and railroad men who were at the train station that Saturday night. Some of them had seen John and Sim Reno boarding the train in Seymour. On Election Day afternoon, as detectives Hazen and Egan hung back and tried to blend in with the boisterous crowd, they were able to compare their impressions of the footprints they had found on the trail leaving the abandoned safe with footprints left in the mud of the street by John and Sim Reno and Frank Sparks. The detectives were convinced they had a match.

The following day, October 10, the detectives obtained warrants for the arrest of the two Reno brothers and Frank Sparks. They had no problem getting the warrants, but they couldn't find anyone to serve them. No one in town wanted to confront the Renos. The detectives were not going to let the opportunity to nab the train robbers slip through their fingers, so they did what Pinkertons would come to be known for throughout the rest of the nineteenth century—they took matters into their own hands. They unilaterally declared themselves officers of the court.

They could do this because the Pinkertons were in a murky legal position and they capitalized on it. Although the detective agency always worked with and supported local law enforcement, more often than not, the locals already had their hands full. Locals considered laws broken on trains to be under the purview of the railroad companies and their hired security forces. So that morning the Pinkerton detectives came up with their own plan to take the Reno brothers and Frank Sparks into custody.

As the westbound train pulled into the station around midday, John Reno—as was his habit—came sauntering out of the Rader House hotel. He was like a kid when it came to trains; he watched them come into town and he watched them as they left town. This morning he stood on the platform watching who was getting off the train. The detectives waited until the platform filled with porters hauling baggage and packages, and with passengers leaving and entering the railcars. Then they came up on both sides of Reno and grabbed his arms, forcing him into the last car on the train.

They placed "nippers," or heavy iron cuffs, on John's wrists and threw him onto a wooden seat. Sim, who was drinking in the hotel, was looking out the front window and saw what had happened. He ran onto the platform, yelling to his brother, and then ran into the railcar he'd seen John forced into. He came face-to-face with a large man who slapped a pair of nippers on his wrists as well and threw him onto the wooden seat next to John.

While one detective stayed with the Renos, the other went into the Rader House and yelled for Frank Sparks to come outside. Sparks ran to the train platform to see what all the commotion was about. The detective told him the Renos were in the last railcar and wanted to see him. Once there, the detective pushed Sparks onto the wooden seat and slapped nippers on him as well, adding him to the cuffed Reno brothers just as the train was pulling out of the station.

When the detectives and their charges reached Brownstown, the county seat of Jackson County about eleven miles west of Seymour, the detectives hauled their prisoners off the train and pushed them toward the two-story brick county jail, where they were locked in a cell pending a bail hearing before a judge.

Detectives Hazen and Egan took the next train back to Seymour, then walked to Wilkinson Reno's house. Although Wilkinson wasn't home, that didn't stop them from entering the house. They were determined to get evidence that would tie the Reno brothers to the train robbery. Although they did have probable cause—footprints leading from the big safe to the house—Hazen and Egan knew they couldn't get the cooperation of local law enforcement. Earlier that day, the local marshal refused to serve the warrant on the Reno brothers out of fear of retaliation. So the two detectives, figuring it would be easier to apologize later than ask for the search warrant, began rummaging through each room.

In a back bedroom, where John Reno often slept, the detectives found a pair of pants, torn at the knees, and two coats, all of them muddied and damp. They also found two pasteboard masks, one black and the other white, and two large .38-caliber Navy revolvers. Strewn about the house were several piles of banknotes and some watches, odd items to be lying about in plain sight.

Hazen and Egan had heard about the Reno brothers' reputation and knew they had been accused of numerous robberies—both large and small—and for passing counterfeit money within a five-hundred-mile radius of Seymour. They also knew that two miles north of the little city was the abandoned town of Rockford, now home to scores of thieves, pickpockets, murderers, safe-blowers, and counterfeiters, who were drawn to the charred remains of the town like iron filings to a magnet. These men were in league with Wilkinson's sons John, Frank, Simeon, and William, and were members of the Reno Gang. So as the detectives tore apart Wilkinson Reno's house, they hoped to find either the money from the Adams Express robbery or evidence of past wrongdoings.

Even as the detectives scoured Wilkinson Reno's house for the money stolen from the express car, they knew they might already be too late—the Reno boys and Frank Sparks could have handed off most of the stolen money to their confederates in Rockford, who might have passed it on to Pete McCartney and Ben Boyd, two of the best counterfeiters and shovers in the region. The Adams Express money might already be laundered through the slipstream of counterfeit money spreading around the Midwest, landing in the tills of small banks and general stores. Or perhaps the money hadn't made it that far and was buried in a burned-out lot in Rockford to be dug up and circulated when all the fuss died down.

As the detectives systematically tore the house apart, they found molds for making counterfeit half- and quarter-dollars, several jimmies and other burglar's tools, and a set of skeleton keys in a cache between the ceiling and the garret.

Counterfeit coins were fairly common in the mid-nineteenth century, and people were aware of it, so anything that felt lighter than a genuine coin or didn't look right was suspect. In addition to not having the heft of a real coin, the color was wrong, the surface was often crude and pitted, and there was usually a seam where the two halves of the mold came together. Nineteenth-century molds for counterfeit coins were usually made of plaster of paris or clay. A genuine coin was carefully pressed into each half of the mold—the head on one side and the tail on the other—and the two pieces were then secured together and molten metal (brass, lead, pewter, or some other base metal) was poured into it and allowed to cool. The two pieces of the mold were pried apart, revealing the fake coin.

Interestingly, half a century later, counterfeit coins were still a problem. According to *Dickerman's United States Treasury Counterfeit Detector and Bankers* (1901), counterfeiting of half-dollars was rampant. *Dickerman's* noted that "Old issues [from the mid-nineteenth century] were extensively counterfeited; composition generally used was German silver and brass, they were heavily plated, and had fair appearance."

In addition to coins, members of the Reno Gang also made counterfeit banknotes of varying quality—Pete McCartney and Ben Boyd served as teachers to other gang members who were just learning the trade.

The burglary tools the detectives found were standard tools of the burglary trade for the time. Just a few years later, the monthly newspaper the *Manufacturer and the Builder* published a description of burglars' tools as a way to educate their readers: "It is indeed doubtful which displays the greatest amount of ingenuity, the honest mechanic who tries his best to make so-called burglar-proof locks, fastenings, shutters, doors, and safes, or that class of dishonest mechanics who provide the professional burglars with the most ingenious tools to pick locks, loosen fastenings, open doors and shutters, and rob safes . . . The burglars' tools in the language of the profession are called 'kits,' and are divided into several classes: they are jimmies, chisels, wedges, hammers, skeleton keys, nippers, drills, punches, jacks, clamps, etc."

The detectives confiscated the burglars' tools, the molds, and the piles of cash to be used as evidence against John and Sim Reno.

What the Pinkerton detectives discovered in Wilkinson Reno's house was a glimpse into the world of the Reno brothers. At age twenty-eight, John, and his younger brother Sim, age twenty-three, were already experienced criminals. At that moment, they stood at the head of a vast criminal network of thieves, counterfeiters, thugs, pickpockets, murderers, and confidence men that terrorized the upper Midwest. Brother Frank Reno, age twenty-five, was cooling his heels in an Illinois jail for the robbery of a county treasury office but would rejoin the gang in the spring after John bailed him out. And youngest brother William, age eighteen, would be sucked into the family business before the year was over.

The following day, five days after the train robbery, the weekly *Seymour Times* was published. The headline, in bold capital letters with words set off by stars, was *THE WORLD'S FIRST TRAIN ROBBERY** OCTOBER 6, 1866**SEYMOUR*. Monroe briefly described the robbery, then wrote: "On Wednesday detectives were here and arrested John and Simeon Reno and Frank Sparks, on what grounds we do not know. They were taken west, probably to St. Louis." Monroe learned days later that the robbers were actually taken eleven miles down the road to the jail in Brownstown, the county seat of Jackson County, where John and Sim Reno and Frank Sparks sat in jail cells for ten days awaiting their first court appearance. The brick county jail, built thirteen years earlier at a cost of $3,950, was "rectangular in form with a front forty-eight feet, running back in depth twenty-four feet, in height two stories," and sat on one side of the town square.

Simeon Reno and Frank Sparks were led from their jail cells across the Brownstown square to the Jackson County Courthouse. They appeared before Judge Bicknell of the Jackson County Circuit Court on October 19, 1866. John Reno was arraigned the following day, and all of them posted bonds—$2,500 apiece for Sparks and Sim Reno, and $8,000 for John Reno, who was considered the head of the gang. Sim's mother, Julia Reno, covered Sim's bond with her property. Wilkinson Reno and three other men (including Lycurgus Shields, son of Meedy Shields!) put up property to pay John Reno's bond. According to court documents, Frank Sparks's bond was covered by the property of Mr. James Filer.

The train robbers were told to appear in circuit court on the first day of the next term in February 1867, and were free on bond until then. The timing was perfect for the accused robbers. They arrived back in Seymour by train just as the Jackson County Agricultural Fair—the first fair held in the county since the beginning of the Civil War—was getting underway on October 23.

On the outskirts of Seymour, farmers would bring their best cattle, horses, sheep, chickens, and hogs and put them in temporary pens. Animals would be entered into the livestock competition and admired by their neighbors strolling the fairgrounds, getting a glimpse into what everyone had been up to during the past year. There would be exhibitions of baked goods and produce, farm grains and needlework, which would be judged and awarded prizes. Innovations in agricultural equipment and labor-saving devices would be showcased at the fair. Sponsored sporting events like horseracing would draw huge crowds.

According to the *Seymour Times*, the Reno brothers and Frank Sparks were seen at the Jackson County Agricultural Fair betting heavily on the horses, making their wagers with what was presumed to be Adams Express money.

Four months later on February 4, 1867, the Jackson County Grand Jury was called into session in Brownstown's courthouse. The courthouse (which would be destroyed by fire just three years later) was a large brick building with a white cupola that dominated one side of the town square. The county jail, where John, Sim, and Frank were remanded in October, anchored another side of the square. The Aetna House, a large brick hotel, stood directly across the square from the courthouse. Although Brownstown was the county seat—the town was established in 1817 and stood smack in the center of the county—by 1867 the rapidly growing town of Seymour was more than double Brownstown's population. Seymour's town fathers petitioned the state more than once to have Seymour declared the county seat, but Brownstown stubbornly managed to cling to its status.

Finally, on February 22, 1867, four and half months after the train robbery, the accused robbers were to appear before the judge to be indicted for committing the world's first train robbery. Judge Bicknell called each of their names. John Reno failed to appear. "The said defendant John Reno being three times solemnly called fails to appear," read the court record.

The three men were formally indicted for "forcibly and feloniously" taking from Elam Miller "by violence and putting him in fear," one safe key worth $30, three canvas bags worth $1 each, $10,000 in gold coin, $33,000 in banknotes "commonly called National Currency," and $33,000 of "said United States Treasury notes commonly called Greenbacks." (The same $33,000 was listed twice.)

Because John Reno didn't show, his bail was revoked and his new bail set at $7,000. The court ordered that Wilkinson Reno, who posted the original bail, bring his son into court and surrender him to the custody of the sheriff until the new bail was paid. Later that same day John Reno was brought to the courthouse. John was thrown into jail, where he shared a cell with John Brooks, who was indicted the same day for the murder of Marian Cutler. Reno got out of jail less than a week later, after his father posted another bond.

Because the Adams Express company lawyer, Jason B. Brown, was not ready to prosecute the case, a trial date was set for the August term of court, which gave Sim Reno and Frank Sparks (and soon John Reno) another six months of freedom as they sauntered out of the courtroom. When the president of the Adams Express Agency, E. S. Sanford, heard of this postponement, he became furious even though his own lawyer called for the delay.

According to Allan Pinkerton's account of the case of the Reno Gang, Sanford suspected these men were not going to stop robbing express cars as long as they were free. The Reno brothers had hit upon a new way of accumulating great sums of money. The brothers intended to keep the lucrative business of robbing express cars to themselves and their handpicked associates. This was now their territory.

Pinkerton agreed with Sanford that with this robbery the Renos had pulled the stopper out of a bottle. It was only a matter of time before the Renos or copycat robbers hit another train. For Pinkerton the stakes were high—neither his ego nor his business could withstand failure at this point in his career. In 1866, Pinkerton had arrangements with several railroad companies for detective services to the tune of ten thousand dollars a year per company in retainers. But he was also owed payment from the Federal government for his service during the Civil War. With a staff of over twenty operatives and several branch offices, Pinkerton was struggling to make ends meet. Taking on a greater role in protecting railroad shipments was a shrewd move.

Once a train left the station in a town or city—and moved beyond the authority of the municipality's police force—it entered that murky no-man's-land of law enforcement where the Pinkertons thrived. They assumed enormous power in their work on behalf of wealthy railroad owners as detectives crossed legal jurisdictions including state borders and, in a couple of cases, international boundaries. And if the Pinkertons couldn't get the cooperation of local officials, they often resorted to kidnapping criminals to bring them to justice. In Allan Pinkerton's mind, the end justified the means.

The Reno Gang couldn't have known what they were up against when the Pinkertons came into the picture in October 1866.

CHAPTER TEN

Talley and Brooks Meet the Vigilance Committee

THE FIRST TIME THE VIGILANCE COMMITTEE MADE AN APPEARANCE IN Jackson County was on March 30, 1867. John Talley and John Brooks, who were indicted and charged with murder in the first degree, were the targets. Several months earlier, on a snowy night in a far corner of Jackson County, the two men entered the remote log cabin of Marian Cutler, an old and likely mentally unstable woman who lived alone. They raped and strangled her, then ransacked the cabin in search of anything of value. Talley and Brooks then attempted to torch the place before leaving, though the fire snuffed out. The two men left with about ninety dollars in their pockets.

They were captured almost immediately, after bragging in a saloon about what they had done. Taken to the county jail in Brownstown, they sat in cold jail cells in shackles awaiting trial. John Reno shared a cell with John Brooks for a short time while waiting for his bail to be reduced for his participation in the first train robbery. While there, Brooks told Reno the whole story of participating in the crime. He also told of helping to murder a man near Vincennes, where he and Talley split four thousand dollars in gold. Brooks had been very "successful at covering up his crimes, but when accused of murdering this woman, his tongue simply refused to do its bidding." A strange feeling came over him, Brooks said, and he confessed the "whole matter before a justice of the peace." As

Reno would discover later, he was fortunate his bail was reduced by one-half, because that allowed him to leave the jail and his cellmate Brooks sometime in mid-March before the vigilance committee came knocking.

Late in the night on the 30th of March, horses with silent riders began appearing from all directions of the county, gathering in an open field about a mile from Brownstown. As one newspaper later reported, "After some 250–300 had gathered in the clearing, they assumed an almost military body with officers appointed and brief commands given. The riders formed a double column and rode slowly and silently toward Brownstown."

What Dr. Monroe had written as early as 1865 in the *Seymour Times* was coming to pass. The people were taking justice into their own hands, fearful, perhaps, that the legal action against Talley and Brooks would be continued from one term of court to the next and then finally dismissed. The courts in Jackson County, rife with legal manipulations and payoffs, had proved time and again that they had a tough time meting out justice.

The riders rode past the County Poor Asylum and the town's burial ground, then headed up the small incline to the middle of town where the courthouse loomed over the town square. The double column of riders formed a circle around the stone jail that stood across the street from the courthouse. The leader of the riders called out for the sheriff to deliver the persons of John Talley and John Brooks. Jackson County Sheriff John Scott didn't answer. Earlier that evening, catching wind of what was going to happen, Scott locked the jail door and barred it from the inside as heavily as possible, "padlocking and bolting it with extra equipment," wrote the *Seymour Times*. Scott then escaped through a rear window and made his way to another part of town so he couldn't be found by the mob and made to hand over the keys. He wanted no part of this. The vigilantes took a battering ram to the wooden door and sledgehammers to the brick jambs surrounding the door. The door was smashed to bits and "the throng poured into the dark jail, tore the cells of the screaming prisoners to pieces and dragged Brooks and Talley out to the lawn."

The mob half-dragged and half-carried the prisoners across the street to the yard beside the courthouse. They selected a tree. It was early spring in Indiana and the leaves had not yet made an appearance, so the branches of the trees in the town square spread like dark menacing arms in the night sky. Talley quieted down, but Brooks cried and begged for mercy. Talley said he wanted to see a minister. Reverend Wilbur Benton, who lived a few doors from the courthouse, was brought to the scene still in his bedclothes with a coat hastily thrown over his shoulders. Benton was given a few minutes to pray for the doomed men. Two of the vigilantes threw ropes over a limb. Talley suggested they might choose a larger tree so that the bodies would swing clear of the trunk. The men agreed, pulled the ropes down, and threw them over the branch of a bigger tree. The nooses, already tied, swung slowly on the end of the dangling ropes—a chilling reminder of what was to come. Barrels were rolled under the tree and turned upright beneath the swinging nooses.

Talley, helped by two of the vigilantes, climbed up on one of the barrels. He asked if he might put the noose around his own neck and tighten it. They let him. He then stepped off the barrel.

Brooks was hysterical as he was hoisted upon the other barrel and held in place. A man on a horse rode up and fitted the noose around Brooks's neck. The barrel was pushed from beneath him.

The bodies of Talley and Brooks were left hanging from the tree through the night as a grisly reminder to all who saw them that things were about to change in Jackson County. The following morning the bodies were cut down and carried into the courthouse, where they were laid out on the wooden floor. After the coroner proclaimed them dead, the two men were buried on the grounds of the County Poor Asylum.

In a creepy follow-up to the Talley and Brooks story, Edwin Boley discovered an article in the August 28, 1879, edition of the *Brownstown Banner* while researching the Reno Gang: "The usual inquest was held by Coroner David F. Wilson, and the bodies buried at the spot on the Fair Grounds indicated by the picket enclosure, which was then part of the county asylum farm. Subsequently the graves were invaded, the heads of both men cut from their bodies and buried in the spring branch on the east side of town. Later they were removed and thoroughly boiled and cleaned. Finally, the skulls were secured by Col. C. L. Dunham, who expressed them to New York, to whom or for what purpose we do not know . . ."

Col. C. L. Dunham had been Talley and Brooks's lawyer.

The lynching of Talley and Brooks grabbed headlines around the region. Most newspaper reports, while decrying the deplorable act, also admitted that if any people had a right to take action into their own hands, it was the people of Jackson County. Two days after the lynching, the *Indianapolis Daily Journal* published a long piece about what it called the "citizen action." It described Jackson County as a place infested for years by gangs of notorious desperados, who almost uniformly escaped conviction when brought to trial. "In and about Rockford and Seymour there are a number of men who are known to be villains of the deepest dye, house-breakers, safe-blowers, burglars, highwaymen, and strongly suspected of diverse murders," it said, "who seem proof against all efforts to bring them to justice through the regular channels."

The local outlaws managed to evade punishment in various ways, including amassing great fortunes so they could always make bail, buying off or killing witnesses, providing alibis for each other, and hiring shrewd lawyers. "If," the article continued, "under these circumstances, society protects itself by inflicting summary punishment upon outlaws who are able to place the courts at defiance, the criminal law of self-defense must be their justification."

In the *Seymour Times*, Dr. Monroe suggested that the vigilantes' work would not be finished until the county was rid of "thieves and cut-throats and till honest people can move about without being knocked down and robbed, or can go to sleep with some assurance that they won't be murdered before they wake." Monroe also used the mob action as a springboard to rail against the legal system, going after, in particular, lawyers. "Let it come to pass that no lawyer of influence can be brought to the defense, by foul and villainous means, of notorious criminals, and crimes will become less frequent," he wrote. "There is little difference between the lawyer who, by all rascally means attempts to defeat justice and to acquit the criminal whom he knows to be guilty—who pockets a part of the blood-money—there is little difference between his guilt and that of the murderer he defends, and both should meet the swift justice meted out to the hardened wretches by the noble men who met at Brownstown Saturday night . . . While the country is full of lawyers too lazy to work, and who must live by their wits, it will be full of thieves and murderers. Each class is necessary to the other . . ."

Monroe had to be present in Brownstown the night Brooks and Talley were lynched. The details in his piece about the lynching are too rich in detail—too believable—to be someone else's eyewitness account. "Brooks was terribly agitated," he wrote, "and begged for his life. He offered to confess everything, and to give the names to companies of men banded together for illegal purposes, reaching from the Ohio to Indianapolis. But his denial last court of his previous confession and his well-known character for lying, caused the crowd to put no faith in nor care anything for his confession . . . he died harder than Talley. The bodies hung about three fourths of an hour, when the men mounted their horses and rode off." Before leaving, Monroe says, the vigilance committee took a vote on whether or not they should hang some men accused of a robbery in the southern part of the county who were now free on bail. The vote was unanimous to hang them. Also "a citizen of Brownstown was visited and informed if he was caught in any more dirty tricks he would go the way of the others."

In that same paper, editor Monroe ran the following item of interest: "That accommodating and clever young gent. Sam Woodward run a special train to Brownstown last Sunday morning to accommodate the numerous crowd that was anxious to visit the scene of the fearful tragedy just transpired. Sam is the prince of good fellows, and we vote him a heap of thanks."

A pointed finger, or manicule [☞] drew attention to the note.

CHAPTER ELEVEN

The Second Train Robbery

AFTER HIS RELEASE FROM JAIL, JOHN RENO SPENT TIME AT THE ROCK-ford farm. He tended a corn crop, making seven hundred dollars when he sold it in the fall. He put the money in his pocket and set up a horse race at New Albany, matching the Butler horse against "Old Joe," the butternut horse from Jeffersonville. He expected to double "his pile by this horse betting" but instead lost every single dollar.

Saturday night, September 28, 1867, was not much different from any other Saturday night in Seymour. It was the town's busiest night of the week—work had ended and men with pay in their pockets came to town to spend it. The saloons, gambling houses, and hotels along the avenues that ran parallel with the two railroad lines regularly filled with men eager to spend whatever money they had on liquor, gambling, and women.

The streets would be lively with people moving between favorite watering holes. Laughter and the plink of piano music spilled through open doors and windows. There was some shouting from those who had already drunk their week's pay, and the occasional whinny of a horse tied up in the livery next to the depot. In all the Saturda-night commotion, it's likely that little notice was taken of the strange movements taking place on the Ohio & Mississippi train platform.

It had been almost a year since John and Simeon Reno and Frank Sparks boarded an eastbound Ohio & Mississippi train at that very depot and less than a mile down the line relieved the Adams express car of its money. The Reno brothers and Sparks, although arrested and indicted for that crime, were still free on bond as the case slowly cranked through the county circuit court.

The Ohio & Mississippi Cincinnati-bound train was on schedule—a rare event—as it started eastward at 8:00 p.m. from the Seymour depot. The dark night provided cover for two men—Walker Hammond and Michael Colleran—to run down the track after the train and then scramble aboard the back platform of the last passenger car just as the train began to pick up speed. The men walked through the passenger cars, making their way to the front of the train.

When they reached the express car, they carefully slipped around the walk plank or the running board to the express car's side door. Forcing the door open, they surprised and overpowered Mr. Dunbar, the express messenger. Although gagged and bound hand and foot, Dunbar reported he "received very little injury at the hands of the robbers." One of the men removed the safe keys from Mr. Dunbar's jacket pocket and opened the safe, quickly grabbing and distributing the bags of currency, amounting to some eight thousand dollars, into canvas satchels.

About three miles east of the Seymour depot the train had to pass over a high wooden trestle bridge that spanned a swampy ravine. In the approach to the trestle, the train always slowed down, which the express robbers knew. This would be the time to leap from the moving train as it reduced speed.

One after the other, the robbers leapt into the brush near the ravine. The second man landed badly and had to be helped to the woods by his accomplice. Outside of the injury, it seemed that all had gone well for the train robbers—the men made their escape and were eight thousand dollars richer. What they didn't know was that a brakeman caught a glimpse of the figures leaping from the express car.

Mr. Gaither, Superintendent of the Western Division of the Adams Express Company, was furious when he got the telegram that another of his express cars had been robbed in Seymour, Indiana. *That damn town!* He telegraphed Allan Pinkerton, who was on retainer to the company, and made arrangements for the detective to get to Seymour. Immediately. Pinkerton, who had warned Gaither after the first train robbery that this was just the beginning, wanted badly to say—*I told you so!*—but he didn't.

Within hours of the robbery, Pinkerton was on a special train for Seymour, where he arrived the next day. The Scotsman interviewed both Dunbar and the brakeman who caught a glimpse of the robbers. Although both had seen the robbers, neither was able to give a good description of the men.

This train robbery was almost identical to the one that occurred a year earlier, so there was reason to believe that the Reno brothers were involved. Pinkerton summoned other operatives to Seymour and had them follow up leads as they came in.

Find a man with a limp, Pinkerton told them. The hunt for the train robbers went on for weeks.

During the time Hammond and Colleran were still at large, the second annual Jackson County Agricultural Fair was held in Seymour. A reporter for the *New Albany Weekly Ledger* wrote, "We learn that the Jackson County fair at Seymour is a grand success. The attendance each day since the opening of the fair has been very large, and the display in all the various departments of stock, manufactured articles, farm products &tc, is highly creditable." It would have been a fine place for train robbers to spend their money, if they could have held onto it long enough to get there.

Reno had an on-again off-again relationship with a Rockford girl named Mollie. She definitely liked him best when he had money to spend. After losing all his farming money in the horse race, John admits that he was starting to look "seedy." He noticed that a young man, Walker Hammond, was visiting Mollie regularly and taking her on buggy rides. Reno wasn't too bothered because he knew this man and knew he didn't have any more money than he did. "Mollie loved money better than either of us," John wrote. But after Hammond robbed the express car of seven or eight thousand dollars (which Reno knew about long before Pinkerton), Reno began to think he'd better watch his girl, "or that fellow W--- would get the better of me."

An elopement was planned. Reno found out the day and the hour. When the time rolled around, Hammond picked up Mollie in the buggy at two in the morning. They hadn't gone half a mile before "W--- was brought to, and all his money taken from him," wrote John. "Then my Mollie refused to go ahead with him. I was the sweetest fellow you ever saw after that, in her estimation!"

John Reno, who had no money before the interrupted elopement, and who had described himself as "seedy," was suddenly flush. He grabbed Mollie and took her to Indianapolis, where they stayed at the Palmer House. Reno writes: "Having to pay thirty-five dollars per week for board and other comforts at that excellent hostelry, besides buying many other costly trifles, our money soon ran out."

About a month after the train robbery the *Chicago Republican* newspaper reported: "A clue was at last obtained to a couple of desperadoes, and circumstances coming to light which warranted immediate action, a young man named Walker Hammond was taken into custody on suspicion." The paper described Hammond as a "once industrious young man, but the evils of depraved companionship soon led him to dissipation and crime." On the night of the robbery a mask was found near the spot where the robbers leapt from the train, and this was subsequently identified as one made by Hammond just days before the robbery occurred.

Hammond's accomplice, Michael Colleran, was also arrested "but not without great difficulty, having made a desperate attempt to defend himself from capture by the use of a knife." Colleran had once been an apple seller and newsboy on the Ohio & Mississippi railroad. Mr. Dunlop, the express messenger, identified Colleran as the man who held a revolver on him while Hammond emptied the safe.

What's not clear is whether Reno heard about the robbery and then went after Hammond because he was eloping with Mollie or whether he knew Hammond because he convinced the young man to do the train job. The robbery had all the hallmarks of the earlier Reno Gang heist, so it's possible that John Reno found two patsies to do the hard work of actually robbing the train. Maybe he arranged the setup when he saw Walker Hammond paying attention to his girl. It is clear that before Pinkerton got ahold of Hammond and Colleran, the boys had been liberated of their money. And Hammond was badly beaten—likely by Reno. The *Chicago Republican* reported that Hammond, upon examination, "was found to be bruised in various portions of his body, and his thighs were especially abraded. He explained the ill-condition of his legs by stating that the scratches or bruises had been caused by contact with thistles." Or perhaps it was the handiwork of John Reno.

Both men were arraigned before Justice Ewing at Brownstown, and having waived examination, were admitted to three thousand dollars bail each for trial at the Circuit Court of Jackson County, at the February term in 1868. Neither could afford the bail. Hammond and Colleran were both eighteen years old.

While Hammond and Colleran were sitting in the Brownstown jail awaiting their February 1868 court date, they, and Jackson County Sheriff John Scott, had a preview of the kind of violence that would befall many of the train robbers affiliated with the Reno Gang. The Hon. Jason Brown, legal counsel of the prisoners, urged the two young men to confess. Rumors were circulating in Seymour that the vigilance committee was planning another attack on the Brownstown jail. Colleran said he'd confess, but Hammond refused. Brown told Hammond that "if he did not plead guilty, he would be hanged by a mob of lynchers." He advised Hammond to plead guilty for his "own personal safety if for nothing else." Hammond still refused, and Colleran would not testify against him, so things were at a stalemate.

When word got out that Hammond refused to confess, once again several hundred men attacked the Brownstown jail in the middle of the night. After the lynching of Talley and Brooks a year earlier, Sheriff Scott had begged the Indiana governor for more weapons. Governor Morton came through and sent, among other things, a muzzle-loading brass cannon. That night, as the vigilantes again took a battering ram to the locked jailhouse door, Sheriff Scott was behind the front door, and he was ready. He loaded the brass cannon with grapeshot, and then moved it to block the entrance. Several deputies stood nearby in the lantern light with guns leveled at the door. As the door finally began to splinter from the relentless pounding of the battering ram, Sheriff Scott yelled that he would fire the cannon and order his men to fire on the mob if any of them attempted to enter.

The mob finally busted through the door and presented a bizarre sight to Scott and the deputies, for their faces were covered with scarlet cloths hanging down from a fastening under their hats. Slits were cut in the cloth so they could see. They yelled and menaced the lawmen. Most held clubs and hammers and ropes and guns. In a tense standoff that could have easily gone either way, Scott stood behind the cannon with a lit fuse in his hand held close to the touchhole. The sheriff stood his ground, threatening to light the cannon and blow them all to smithereens if they didn't back up.

The vigilantes reluctantly withdrew, muttering threats all the way.

A decade later, an account written by Henry M. Beadle states that Colleran pleaded guilty and got a short prison term, whereas Hammond stood his trial and was awarded more years in the penitentiary. "If there is any confidence to be placed on appearances," Beadle writes, "Coleran [sic] has come out a reformed man. Hammond is also out, but is said to be engaged in practices that render any reformation doubtful."

CHAPTER TWELVE

Vigilante Fever

WHILE JOHN RENO AND MOLLIE STAYED AT THE PALMER HOUSE IN Indianapolis spending Adams Express money care of Walker Hammond, Seymour was anything but quiet. It seems that the vigilance committee was actively trying to clean up the town. First, there was the raid on the Brownstown jail and the attempt to lynch Hammond and Colleran. Sheriff Scott had put an end to that with his cannon. Now the vigilance committee was picking away at the local thieves and meting out their own judgments.

Two years earlier, Frank Reno had robbed the Gilbert's grocery and the post office in Jonesville. He was indicted for the latter, and because it was the post office, had to stand trial in federal court. A gang member and witness to the post office robbery, Grant (also called Granton and Grandison) Wilson, a black man, turned state's evidence and agreed to testify in the case. He never made it. On August 30, 1865, he was gunned down outside his home. Dr. Monroe called it a "brutal assassination."

"A colored man named Granton Wilson was brutally assassinated near his home, in Hamilton Township, a few miles above Rockford, by two ruffians about dusk on Wednesday 30th," Monroe wrote in the *Seymour Times*. "In company with a colored boy at work for him he had been in search of some hogs when near his house on their return two men, one a large one with heavy whiskers (probably false) and the other a smaller man emerged from the woods . . ." Wilson sent the boy into the house, and then the boy heard four shots. Wilson apparently crawled into the high grass after being shot and the family didn't dare go out in search of him until the next morning. Monroe believed that Wilson was murdered because Frank Reno's fate hung on Wilson's court testimony. He also wrote that Wilson was "privy to and probably an accomplice in most of the robberies, house burnings and counterfeiting enterprises perpetrated hereabout by the gang of desperadoes that have given Rockford an unenviable notoriety for years past."

No arrests were made in Wilson's murder. He had two strikes against him: he was black and he was a gang member.

Isaac Wilson, Grant's son, was seventeen when his father was murdered, and was the one who found Grant with four bullet holes in him. He wrote: "I solemnly vowed to God that I would hunt down the murderers and have them punished even if it cost me my own life to do so." Young Isaac was convinced that the Reno Gang had in some way been responsible for his father's death, so he resolved to infiltrate the gang and exact his revenge at a later time.

"Step by step I went, always carefully considering and covering my tracks. Soon I became a member but there were few, if any, outsiders who ever suspicioned that I was one of them." He was accepted by the gang and was, in particular, embraced by the entire Reno family.

Things were uneventful for Isaac until the spring of 1867 when he, his brother Lafayette, Cain D. Lamb, Cain Mitchell, and Harmon Newby ("the latter three being colored men," Isaac writes) were arrested by the vigilance committee. Lafayette and the latter three men were charged with robbing Peter Carter's dry-goods store in Seymour. Isaac wasn't charged but was brought in for questioning. They were all taken for trial to Carter's planing mill in the northern part of town near the new fairgrounds.

Carter's planing mill was owned by Travis Carter, the first person to buy a lot in the future town of Seymour from Meedy Shields in 1852. Peter Carter, his son, owned the dry-goods store. The planing mill was well known in Seymour as the "torture chamber" for culprits tried by the vigilance committee. The tortures were actually carried out at the fairgrounds after suspects were questioned and then sentenced at the mill, which served as the courtroom. Rumor had it that what was left of the Reno Gang burned the mill down in 1869. The noonday fire was spectacular in its fury and burned down the church next door as well. Both were immediately rebuilt.

The trial was held at night on the cavernous mill floor, where the air was thick with the spicy smell of drying wood and swirling particles of fine sawdust. Several lanterns lit the room, casting long arcs of light across the floor. Most of the men were sitting on benches in the otherwise dark room. All the windows were carefully covered so that people in town wouldn't get curious about the proceedings.

The robbery of Carter's dry-goods store had been committed some time before. When the mob investigated the matter, they determined that the robbing was done by Robert O'Neal, another black man, and Harmon Newby, while Cain Mitchell had concealed the goods for them. O'Neal had been hanged in a hideous manner a few days earlier by the Salt Creek Mob, another vigilance committee operating on Salt Creek, about eighteen miles west of Seymour. This left Newby, Lamb, and Mitchell in the hands of the Seymour Vigilance Committee. A committee headed by Alexander Davison was selected to fix the punishment.

Davison informed the group that they decided to give Harmon thirty-five heavy lashes and the others twenty-eight. He told the accused that they could take the punishment from the mob, or if they preferred, the mob would turn them over to the state authorities. The punishment was accepted. Peter Carter was asked if he was satisfied with the agreement between the committee and the prisoners. He was. Then a committee member told the accused that if they accepted the whippings, they were to say nothing about it. *If they breathed a word about what transpired, they would be hanged.* The prisoners nodded.

Mr. Davison, current mayor of Seymour and chairman of the meeting, called the house to order and said he wanted to ask Isaac Wilson some questions about the Reno family.

"Ike," he said. "What do you know about the Reno boys?"

Wilson looked him in the eye and said, "I know that they are all good straightforward Republicans."

Exasperated, Davison answered, "We all know that. We don't propose to make this a political matter."

"I don't understand you then," said Wilson. "You speak in reference to what?"

"To their secret life, sir," said Davison.

Wilson answered, "I know nothing more of their secret life than you do, sir."

"The devil is in him, men!" Davison shouted to the rest of the committee members. "Don't you see his horns sticking out?"

Davison had a heated exchange with another committee member for a minute or two and then was called to order and told to ask his questions in a civil way.

Davison tried another approach.

"Do you know whether Frank Reno or the rest of the Reno boys have been connected with the robberies committed about here of late?" he asked.

Wilson answered, "I do not."

"Ike, what is it you know?" Davison could see that Wilson was frightened. "Don't be afraid to tell us."

Wilson stood silently.

"Why is it that you fear to tell us?" said Davison. "If you know anything about Frank Reno spit it out and I will assure you that he will not get to kill you as he did your father."

Wilson looked down at his feet as if they were suddenly the most interesting things in the room.

"All we want to know about him is enough to have him arrested," said Davison. "We intend to hang him."

Wilson looked up and blurted out, "If I should tell you something about Mr. Reno and you would have him arrested and hang him, that would not be the end of it for he has some bold brothers."

"We intend to hang the whole family," said Davison.

"Does that include Laura and the old gentleman?" asked Wilson.

"It includes the whole damned family," Davison answered.

"I know nothing on him that would justify hanging and if I did I would hate to tell you and be the cause of having the whole family hung," said Wilson. "I am a friend to the Reno family and especially to Frank."

Davison found the last statement curious and asked, "Why are you a friend of the Reno family and especially to Frank?"

"Because I have been accommodated by them on several occasions," said Wilson.

"How have they accommodated you?" asked Davison.

"By loaning me money several times," Wilson answered.

"Why did he lend you the money?" asked Davison.

"Because he was a gentleman," said Wilson.

Davison shot back, "You call the man who murdered your father a gentleman?"

"No, sir, I do not," said Wilson. "I cannot be made to believe that Frank Reno had anything to do with the death of my father."

"Where did Frank get the $125 he loaned you?" asked Davison.

"He borrowed it from Frank Sparks," Wilson answered.

"Do you know where Frank Sparks got it?" asked Davison.

"That was about the time that Sparks got his discharge from the United States Army," said Wilson. "And I suppose the money had been paid him for services rendered in the army."

Davison, disgusted with the whole exchange, dropped his questioning, and another member of the vigilance committee took over. Wilson told him that he used the money borrowed from Frank Reno to pay a lawyer named Hoard from Columbus, Indiana, for a debt owed by Isaac's father Grant for services ". . . in what was known as the 'Jonesville' case."

This was a dramatic departure from the reasons Isaac gave for joining the Reno Gang earlier in his autobiography. It seems he had genuinely grown close to the Reno family and no longer held Frank responsible for the death of his father.

After more discussion the mob moved the prisoners outside. Everyone walked out into the night—several men carrying dark lanterns to afford light when needed. They headed across the fairgrounds and then into a clearing in the far woods.

Newby was the first man ordered to take off his coat, which he did without any grumbling. He was then ordered to take off his shirt. He wrapped his bare arms around a medium-size tree and hugged it tight. He received his thirty-five lashes. After the whipping he slumped to the ground. Several men carried him away from the tree and laid him on the grass.

Lamb and Mitchell were then ordered to take off their coats and shirts. They took too long for some of the mob, who yanked their clothes off them. Both of the men were missing their right arms—a consequence of the war. They were then ordered to the tree, where each received their twenty-eight stripes.

Members of the mob dressed the bleeding men and disappeared into the night, leaving the whipped men to stagger home on their own.

Isaac Wilson told Frank Reno what the mob said about him. Reno asked if they gave any reason why they wanted to hang him. Wilson told him that some of them seemed to think that Reno was connected with the many different robberies that had been committed in town. Reno said he didn't believe that was the real reason. Instead, he told Wilson that he belonged to a secret order and held some opinions that "Copperheads like Aleck Davison" didn't find agreeable. Reno also thought he had alienated the railroad men in town, like Robert Pattison (roadmaster for the Ohio & Mississippi throughout the 1860s), because he expressed the opinion that big businesses and wealthy people should be taxed in order to give southerners some payment for freeing their slaves.

Vigilante fever raged through the Midwest. Dr. Monroe reported the following in the November 7, 1867, issue of the *Seymour Times*: "Nine members of the Lee family, a well-known gang of burglars, inhabiting Warren county, Iowa, were arrested a few days ago, by a vigilance committee, who swung them all up and choked them until they confessed their guilt. Four of the number arrested are women."

In the following issue of the *Seymour Times*, the region sounded more like the Wild West of legend. In Seymour, "A little 'unpleasantness' occurred between Ben Kinney and Jim Hulse a few days ago, which resulted in some damage to both—it was all about a settlement—the adjustment of which required them to lie down and insert their nails in each other's eyes."

In nearby Medora, burglars entered the Post Office and Early's saloon, and made off with $30 from the saloon, and $50 from the Post Office.

The store of the Messrs. Holland, in Leesville, was robbed of over $1,000. The safe was blown open with powder.

J. W. Holmes's store, also in Medora, was robbed by burglars of some $30 in money found in the drawer.

Monroe never lost his sarcastic sense of humor, as seen in the following week's edition. He wrote that now was the time to subscribe to the paper because "an important Presidential Election is pending, and the *Seymour Times*, in this contest, as in those past, will be found among the foremost journals of the country in the defence [sic] of the vital principles and measures of the Republican party, and should therefore be read by all Republicans. The Democrats should also read it, because it continually holds up to them a faithful picture of their horrible crimes against this nation which may fright them to repentance and reform before it is everlastingly too late. Terms $2.50 a year."

A week later another store was hit. This time it was in Rockford. "Some enterprising and gentlemanly burglars went through the store of Peter & Pfaffenberger, at Rockford one night last week—The clerks sleep in the store, but had gone out in the evening to some sort of party, and during their absence the accommodating burglars, armed with a crowbar, caved in the door, went through the safe, like a dose of croton oil through a new recruit, and departed with about $250 as the reward of merit and well directed industry and crowbars. John Peff. doesn't 'fuss' much over the loss of the money, but he protests against the shocking depravity that leads men to scatter valuable deeds and papers along the railroad, as was done in this instance."

In business, pork-packing, long the stable commodity in the area, had taken a nosedive. "Pork. Nothing favorable can be said of the pork market here. Nobody with sufficient money has the nerve to buy and pack, so our farmers must seek a foreign market. The unsettled state of finances is plead as an excuse for inactivity on the part of our moneyed men. Mr. Rich the butcher, is packing a few hogs, but we presume that no considerable number will be required here. Rockford is out of the business altogether, its ancient glory as a pork mart having departed. The Messrs. Peter & Smith, now of Louisville, are packing, we understand, at Gosport and Columbus. 'Jake' Peter has got the nerve to go in every year, and we only regret that he saw fit to change the theater of his operations from Jackson county. A heavy pork-packer at this place now would be a public benefactor. The prices paid for the few hogs sold here range from $6 to $8 per head."

Various traveling shows made their way to Seymour, and Dr. Monroe, the voice of and for the people, always commented on their content. "The entertainments given by Dr. Kirbye, though of an interesting character, have been but slimly attended on account of inclement weather. Wednesday night, however, there was an appreciative audience, among which were many of our most intelligent citizens of both sexes. The doctor's powers of ventriloquism are wonderful to witness and his illustrations of this art are amusing in the extreme. Mrs. Kirbye's clairvoyant revelations are astounding and can't be explained by any known physical laws. It is a mystery that the human mind can't fathom. To contemplate it is like contemplating eternity or the infinity of space . . ."

Never a dull moment.

CHAPTER THIRTEEN

Missouri Breaks John Reno

WHILE JOHN RENO AND MOLLIE WERE HOLED UP IN THE PALMER House in Indianapolis after the Hammond and Colleran robbery, John received a letter from a friend who requested that he come over the "big muddy" river to Gallatin, Missouri. Indianapolis was five hundred miles from Gallatin. John, who knew from the letter that there must be something worth robbing in the county treasury, decided to go, stopping first in Springfield, Illinois, to pick up a friend to accompany him. Reno calls him E. (likely Volney Elliott) in his autobiography.

This would be the Reno Gang's first (but not last) out-of-state robbery.

While in Springfield, Reno and E. visited a blacksmith shop and put in an order for some tools to be made—a jimmy, four iron and two steel wedges, and a steel punch. "The jimmy was as long as an ordinary shot gun," Reno recalls. He took a large gunnysack as a carrying bag for all the tools before boarding the train for Quincy, Illinois. There the two men crossed the Mississippi on a ferry, then took passage on the Hannibal & St. Joe Railroad at Palmyra, "first filling a grip-sack with baked chicken and bread."

The two men left the train at Hamilton, Missouri, and took off—on foot—for Gallatin, the county seat of Daviess County, although it was sixteen miles from the railroad. Reno had been to Gallatin before and knew the way. Even though it was growing dark they headed out across the prairie.

The men didn't reach the town until 1:00 a.m., at which point they "reconnoitered the place," before heading down to the Grand River bottoms to camp until the following night. Their plan was to go back to Gallatin the next night, where "we would have to 'march' if we got the money that was reported as being in the country [sic] treasurer's office."

It was November 16, 1867, and the night was frigid. Reno and E. made a fire, ate their chicken, and went to sleep on the cold ground.

The next evening, they went back to the treasurer's office in Gallatin. After breaking in, they found two safes, but did not know which contained the money. They tackled the newest one first, initially trying to blow it with gunpowder (it didn't work), and then tried jimmying it open. They finally got it open after two hours, and spent another hour looking through all the papers and records and "trash hunting for the money." They found nothing. They decided to try to open the other, smaller safe. That took another hour before they were successful.

"On opening the outer door, I saw that the drawers were so swollen with money that they would not even fit in their places," wrote Reno. "On pulling out the first one, I found it to contain sixty dollars in gold, some silver, and a key . . . the key to the iron chest in the safe, which I opened and found it brim-full of big, fat packages. On tearing open one of these I found it contained green-backs . . . I spread my big handkerchief on the floor in front of the safe and went to work emptying it all of its valuables which, when counted, amounted to the sum of twenty-two thousand and sixty-five dollars, a nice haul indeed."

There was so much money that Reno had a difficult time tying his large handkerchief around the loot.

Reno and E. gathered up the tools but left behind a sledgehammer they'd "borrowed" from the blacksmith across the street, hoping this would make it look like a local job. They carried their own tools with them and about a half-mile outside of town tossed them into the tall prairie grass. By this time, it was four in the morning and bitterly cold.

Eventually they came to the Grand River, which they had to cross, but found the ferry frozen fast in the ice. And the ice wouldn't hold their weight. E. took a boat pole and broke the ice in front of them as they waded into the frozen river with all their clothes on. The water was about waist deep, so Reno held his grip-case high to protect the money. "My boots got full of water and I could not get them off, since they were tight, nor could I get the water out of them," wrote John. "So, having a light pair of shoes in my grip-sack, I cut the boots off my feet and left them by the roadside."

They were only five miles from Gallatin by daylight, so the two men moved into a cornfield. They climbed into the middle of a corn shock and lay there all day, shivering in their clothes, which were encased in ice. About two in the afternoon someone drove a wagon into the field and began gathering up the shocks. Reno and E. were terrified they'd be discovered, but their luck held out.

When darkness fell they made their way out of the field and took the road. They were very cold and their joints were stiff from their day in the cornfield. The railroad lay about twenty miles away. They hadn't eaten for over a day. After walking all night, they heard the sound of a violin wafting over the frozen field and followed the sound of the tune. They spotted a cabin, and when they entered they found an old black man sitting by the fire playing the instrument. The robbers, who looked a sight, told him they had gotten lost turkey hunting and had spent the night in the woods. Could they warm themselves by the fire and get something to eat? Reno gave the old man two dollars to get his wife out of bed to cook them a meal.

"We drank three cups of coffee apiece and ate everything eatable on that table. I have no doubt that that meal saved our lives from starvation," wrote Reno over twenty years later.

Their bellies full and their clothes almost dry, they headed out for Chillicothe, which they reached at five the next morning. Knowing the news of the robbery would have spread throughout the region by then, the two men had to be cautious. A freight train hauling cattle pulled into the station. Reno and E. "piled in" with the drovers in the caboose before the train took off. At the next station, everyone got out for breakfast, and Reno discovered that one of the drovers had five cars of cattle and no one to help him. Reno offered his and E's services, and the drover hired them. At Palmyra they went on top of the train, with poles in their hands, and guarded the cattle, "rapping the hollering beasts over the heads often, to make ourselves appear as much like real drovers as possible."

Reno and E. made it across the Mississippi and eventually back to Indianapolis, where they divided the money. Reno had been gone six days, but Mollie was waiting for him in the Palmer House. Reno counted the money in front of her "but she asked no questions; in fact, she never did on any occasion; she did not want to know anything but to have a good time as long as it lasted."

John Reno was greatly attached to Mollie, writing in his autobiography, "I fairly worshipped her."

"We occupied room No. 19 at the Palmer House, lived high, and had a chicken fight in our room occasionally by way of pastime," Reno wrote.

Mollie and John Reno's life of leisure lasted about five weeks, during which time Reno had "already nearly forgotten my trip to Missouri, except to congratulate myself on how successfully I had covered up my tracks."

One evening the bellboy came to Reno's room with a note that a "friend" wanted to see him in the hotel office. Reno sent word back that he would meet this person at breakfast. Not long after, a gang of men—including Indianapolis Police Chief Wilson—barged into his room and informed him that there were a couple of gentlemen from Missouri down at the Concordia House who wished to see him. John had anticipated trouble after the bellboy's visit and had given Mollie enough money to pay the bill and get back home to Rockford.

In the Concordia, Reno met up with John Ballinger, sheriff of Daviess County, Missouri. He was put on a train for St. Louis, in the company of Sheriff Ballinger and Chief Wilson. "I was treated very kindly by all these officers," wrote Reno. "In fact, much kinder than one would expect under the circumstances under which I was arrested."

When they reached St. Louis, Reno was shocked when Frank Sparks was brought over and shackled to him. Reno knew Sparks didn't have anything to do with the robbery, but didn't dare say so at the time. He writes that he would have said so if, in fact, they were to be tried by "Judge Lynch's Court," which he expected would happen. They were taken on the North Missouri Railroad to Hamilton.

Ballinger telegraphed ahead to Major J. H. McGee in Gallatin. "I have John Reno the great chief of Indiana and Missouri burglars—Will leave on the 10 o'clock p.m. train for Kidder, come down and meet me. I am worn out." When the party reached Hamilton there were crowds of people from Gallatin "ready to escort us over the prairie—which was very lonely—and a distance of sixteen miles." They made the journey in wagons and were escorted by about forty drunk men on horseback. The bottle was being passed around, and Sparks refused to drink. John, never one to refuse a drink, tried to remain cheerful as the night grew dark and Sparks grew more uneasy.

The party reached Gallatin at midnight, where the two prisoners were taken to the treasurer's office. Everything was in the "same disorder" as Reno had left it five weeks earlier. Joseph McGee, judge of the probate court said, "You are the men who did this work! We will hang you to the tallest tree in Grand River bottoms if this money is not returned!"

Reno and Sparks were taken to the courthouse, where they were very well guarded, the jail having been deemed too flimsy and unsafe to hold the prisoners.

"I soon found that the natives were coming in from all directions with their shotguns and coonskin caps and panther-skin coats, and with their hair hanging clear down to their shoulders," wrote Reno. "Some of them had not yet taken off the moss from their backs that had grown there while they had lain in the woods, hiding during the war."

Things were getting hot for the men. The next day, Reno wrote that Sheriff Ballinger excited the crowd by selling stray stock in the town square, making a short speech after each sale that the money was on "behalf of the little children who were behind in their schooling." Reno, it turns out, had stolen the school fund. Then Ballinger reminded the crowd of the years of schooling the children had lost during the recently ended war, "and now, when they had accumulated a small fund, it had been stolen."

Reno was getting extremely nervous. The extra guards were costing fifty dollars a day, as there were about twenty of them kept on day and night. Court wouldn't be called for another five months, and Reno knew the people would never agree to keep paying guards that entire time.

Soon Reno learned how the sheriff had found him. Clay Able, who was the friend who tipped Reno off about the treasury money in the first place, and his brother-in-law Clifton had been picked up on suspicion of knowing something about the robbery. Able was caught trying to pass some counterfeit gold coins Reno had found in the safe—coins Reno threw on the floor when he found them. Apparently Able picked them up the following morning and pocketed them, thinking they were real. Able and Clifton were released after being questioned by the sheriff, but eventually one of them broke down and confessed all he knew to the sheriff, pointing the finger at Reno.

Reno knew several families in Daviess County, Missouri, including Dan Smith's family, who had left Rockford and moved to Missouri. Dan was in jail when Reno arrived on suspicion of being involved in the robbery as well. "I had often heard of Dan praying in church while I was home, for I never attended church but my Methodist friends had told me, but I never heard so fervent a prayer as the one he offered on the night we both expected to be lynched," wrote Reno. "I never had much faith in prayer myself, but truly do believe that Dan prayed himself out of that little difficulty. He was entirely innocent of even any knowledge of the crime until committed to his cell, but of course that would make no difference at all to a mob from Missouri . . ."

John Reno confessed to the crime about five days after being placed in jail, believing he'd have a better shot of survival in prison than with the mob that was gathering outside his cell.

The December 19, 1867, issue of the *North Missourian* gave the full story of the robbery as Reno related it to Ballinger. "Frank Sparks claims entire innocence and as yet we have no positive proof against him. He is without doubt a hard character and we believe admits the fact. John Reno, the remaining prisoner, is a cool calculating burglar and admits that he with one principle accomplice whose name he will not give, broke open and robbed both safes in the Clerk's office . . . he declared himself innocent, but finding him as utterly to preclude escape, he acknowledged his guilt and divulged the affair."

Reno told Ballinger that he did all the work himself and that he blew the first safe thinking it was the one that contained the money. "He says that the report made by the explosion was no louder than that made by an ordinary linen towel were you to take it by one end and give it such a jerk as you would to crack a whip." His powder being used up, he had to cut into the other safe, "an operation which to an experienced workman like him was a short one."

The *North Missourian* article about the robbery was reprinted in the *Seymour Times* on December 27. Editor Dr. Monroe couldn't help himself. He wrote a long preface to the *Missourian* article, in which he defended both Frank Sparks and John Reno, while acknowledging his "well known position in regard to the treatment of those guilty of enormous crimes." Monroe wrote that Frank Sparks worked for him as a farmhand and "isn't to be beat in that line," and that it was impossible for him to have committed the Gallatin crime because he was gathering corn for him at that very time. "His arrest and detention are outrages that our border ruffian neighbors may have to account for, for both he and Reno were kidnapped and taken away in violation of the law." As to Reno, Monroe wrote "he has some taste for a horse race, a cock fight, or a good round bet on an election. He is a sober, quiet, self possessed courageous young man . . . we regret very much that he has turned his attention to so shabby a business." Monroe continued, "They who know him would yet take his word or trust his honor in preference to that of very many men who couldn't be induced to blow up a safe."

In other words, these might be robbers, but they are our robbers, and only we can pass judgment on their characters.

Sparks was released and sent home. Reno stayed in jail awaiting his sentencing trial on January 16, 1868. John wrote to his parents, telling them what had happened and when sentencing would occur. Laura Amanda wrote back and said that day was her seventeenth birthday.

The Circuit Court heard the case of the treasury robbery in the County Court House in Gallatin, Missouri, on January 16. John Reno pleaded guilty to the crime, and the judge issued a sentence two days later: forty years of hard labor in the penitentiary. Reno's attorney got the term reduced to twenty-five years, saying that was long enough to end John Reno's career, but even that felt like a bitter disappointment to Reno. He expected a prison sentence of no more than five or ten years at the most.

A few days before the sentencing hearing, Frank Reno came to visit his brother. The officers guarding Reno let the brothers meet, hoping to overhear something about where the money was hidden. They were disappointed. In a whispered conversation, Frank told John he'd help him escape while John was being transferred to the penitentiary. "I was in good spirits when he left, feeling that I could depend on him and that if it were possible for him to do it, this work of freeing me would be done regardless of the hazards," wrote John.

Monday morning after the sentencing, Reno was placed in a wagon surrounded by "heavily" armed guards and driven across the prairie to the railroad station to take the train to Jefferson City, Missouri. Reno was restless, watching for his brother and other gang members at every station. "I dreaded to see the time come," he wrote, "for I feared there would really be some hard fighting. The guards were all provided with long 'navies' and had the reputation of being men of steel nerves."

Whenever the door at either end of the railcar opened, Reno expected to see his brother. He both welcomed and feared the sight. "I could have felt better and I have felt worse, than I did on that trip," he wrote. "Every moment I expected 'the ball to open,' and as I was heavily ironed I could not take part, but would be compelled to stay and see it out."

It never happened. Frank Reno and his gang never showed. John Reno entered the Missouri State Penitentiary in Jefferson City through the doorway marked "The Way of the Transgressor is Hard." Visitors had to pay twenty-five cents for admission, but John was "on the list and went in for free."

A few days after John Reno arrived at the prison in late January of 1868, he received a letter from Frank saying he had a little trouble "getting the material ready" and that the gang members helping him had missed the train connections at Quincy, Illinois, or he would have been "good as his word to make the rescue."

John Reno settled in for a long stay. Ironically, this stint in prison saved his life.

CHAPTER FOURTEEN

Iowa Raids

A COUPLE OF MONTHS AFTER JOHN RENO'S INCARCERATION IN THE Missouri State Penitentiary, a "Letter from Seymour" appeared in the *Indianapolis Journal*. Written by Citizen, it might have been the work of Dr. J. R. Monroe, although the tone was a bit subdued for his writing. After slogging through much chatter about the neighboring towns of Brownstown and Ewing, the reader hit this paragraph: "The latest sensation in Seymour is the closing out of the *Times, Commercial,* and *Union* papers, to be succeeded by a new company, new editor, Mr. John McCormick, and a new paper, name not yet determined upon, perhaps *Seymour Democrat.* Mr. McCormick has purchased all the presses and materials of the three papers."

In his editorial of the April 3 issue of the *Seymour Times,* Monroe gave a brief history of his work on the *Rockford Herald* and the *Seymour Times,* stating that this would be the final issue of the paper. He added, "By the conditions of the sale we are pledged not to edit nor to publish any paper in Jackson County for one year from the 25th day of March, 1868." The Times Building was also offered for sale or rent in the same issue. "It will make an excellent business house, and occupies one of the best business localities in Seymour."

Monroe wished the editor of the *Seymour Democrat* "success in his venture "Mr. McCormick, or 'Johnny' as he is called, is a young man of fine business qualifications, industrious habits, and is possessed of rare social qualities," wrote Monroe. "He is a good scholar and an excellent writer."

Monroe, the ever nattering voice about civic duties and moral responsibilities, was leaving the paper just when things between the Reno Gang, the Pinkertons, and the vigilance committee were moving from a slow simmer to a boil.

On February 24, 1868, the United States House of Representatives began impeachment proceedings against President Andrew Johnson. On March 13 the impeachment trial of the president began in the Senate. The country was riveted by what was going on in Washington, following along in their local newspapers. People still trying to make sense of a devastating war in which 600,000 people died were now struggling to understand the intense political struggle at the heart of their government.

As the country held its breath during the impeachment trial, the people of the state of Iowa were dealing with a rash of robberies that would, in the end, net the thieves over $50,000. Between February 18 and the end of March, four county treasuries and four private homes in Council Bluffs had suffered burglaries. On February 18 the safe of the County Treasurer of Harrison County, Iowa, in the western part of the state, was robbed of $15,000. The *Indianapolis Journal* reported that the "robbers were traced to Omaha, Nebraska (just over the state line), but not caught." In the following week, the Louisa County treasury in the eastern part of Iowa was robbed of $17,000, and $1,000 was taken from the Mills County treasury. The criminals then moved on to private citizens and their biggest take yet.

The *Council Bluffs Weekly Nonpareil* reported robberies of four homes in that city on Saturday night, March 21. The following issue of the paper reported the robbery of the Howard County Treasury of $18,000. The *Nonpareil* quoted the *Dubuque Times*: "From what we learned the safe [in Howard County] was [not a] concern, warranted to be fireproof and good for everything except burglars. No one slept in the Court House and the first intimation of the robbery consisted in finding the insides of the safe alluded to blown over the public square. The officers of the law are moving hither and thither through the country endeavoring to obtain some clue to the perpetrators but as yet are unsuccessful. They are no doubt connected with the same gang whose operations we have heard of so frequently in other quarters and their detection may be considered extremely doubtful."

Meanwhile, Allan Pinkerton had been on the trail of the Reno Gang. The source for much of Pinkerton's pursuit of the outlaws is an unreliable narrator, Cleveland Moffett, who spun stories for *McClure's Magazine* in the latter part of the nineteenth century. But, Moffett did have a pipeline to the Pinkertons, being friends with William Pinkerton (Allan's son).

Several months before the Iowa crimes, and after the robbery of the Daviess County treasury in Gallatin, Missouri, Allan Pinkerton became personally involved in the search for members of the Reno Gang. Prior to that, he relied on field operatives to do the legwork. He rightly suspected they were connected to the crime. He also allowed his nineteen-year-old-son, William, to go into the field to help track down leads. The elder Pinkerton traced John Reno to Indianapolis (although Moffett says Seymour), where he stationed a "trustworthy assistant" who was to entice John Reno to the railroad platform any way he could. Once there, Reno was surrounded by half a dozen Missourians, including Sheriff Ballinger of Daviess County, who clapped Reno in irons and forced him onto the westward-bound express train on the O&M.

Reno's friends attested to the fact that Pinkerton men had kidnapped and forcibly taken John to Missouri. This was against the law, they argued, but the Circuit Court in Gallatin, Missouri, didn't see it that way. They were just happy to have John Reno in front of them and hoped to get a lead on the stolen treasury money.

In Iowa, William Pinkerton and two assistants were sent to Magnolia, the county seat of Harrison County, to run down the burglars. The detectives discovered that the thieves made their getaway on a railroad handcar heading in the direction of Council Bluffs, thirty-three miles away. In Council Bluffs, W. Pinkerton found a saloon kept by a man who used to live in Seymour and who was "known as a bad character."

The only known photograph of John Reno (left). Taken in a saloon in Seymour, Indiana, with his fellow gang member Frank Sparks. *Courtesy of Mark Boardman*

Rare photograph of Frank Reno, the oldest Reno brother and leader of the gang with his brother John. *Courtesy of Mark Boardman*

Business card of Clinton Reno, the only Reno brother not to go to the Civil War. He was only tangentially involved in Reno Gang activities. He and his brother John—when John got out of prison—owned a saloon in Seymour named the Hell Hole. *Courtesy of Mark Boardman*

Miles Ogle, master counterfeiter, member of the Reno Gang. In and out of prison, he supposedly buried his engraver's plates near Cincinnati, Ohio. *Courtesy of Mark Boardman*

Laura Amanda Reno, sister of the Reno brothers, viewed as a fiery woman, was fiercely loyal to her brothers. *Courtesy of Mark Boardman*

Meedy and Eliza Ewing Shields, founders of Seymour.

Dr. J. R. Monroe, here as editor and proprietor of the *Iron-clad Age* in Indianapolis, Indiana, in the 1880s. From *400 Years of Freethought* (1894)

The first man to buy land in Seymour, Travis Carter became one of the town's leading citizens. He was also rumored to be the head of the Seymour Vigilance Committee. *Courtesy of Mark Boardman*

Major E. J. Allen, aka Allan Pinkerton, working as head of secret service for Union General McClelland during the Civil War. *Courtesy of Mark Boardman*

William Pinkerton was a young man when his father asked him to assist on the Reno case. William later became head of the Pinkerton Agency. *Courtesy of Mark Boardman*

Jason Brown, attorney involved in all of the Reno Gang train robbery cases. *Courtesy of Mark Boardman*

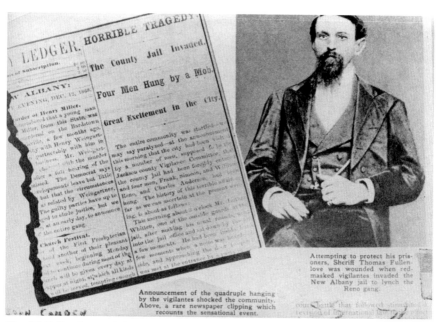

Announcement of the quadruple hanging by the vigilantes shocked the community. Above, a rare newspaper clipping recounts the sensational event.

Attempting to protect his prisoners, Sheriff Thomas Fullenlove was wounded when redmasked vigilantes invaded the New Albany jail to lynch the Reno gang.

Sheriff Fullenlove of the New Albany jail. He was shot in the arm trying to prevent the vigilance committee from hanging the Reno brothers and Charlie Anderson. *Courtesy of Mark Boardman*

The hideout of Frank Reno and Charlie Anderson in the little Canadian city of Windsor, right across the U.S. border from Detroit. *Courtesy of Mark Boardman*

Late-nineteenth-century street scene of New Albany, Indiana. *Courtesy of Mark Boardman*

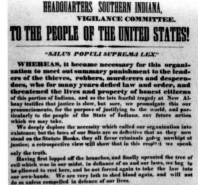

View of the New Albany cell block where the Reno brothers and Charlie Anderson were held. *Courtesy of Mark Boardman*

Vigilance committee broadside issued after the New Albany jail lynching in December 1868. It contained a clear message to remaining Renos and their friends—beware! *Courtesy of Mark Boardman*

View of the graves of Frank, William, and Simeon Reno surrounded by a cast-iron fence in Seymour's City Cemetery. *Photo by Rachel Dickinson*

The graves of Frank, William, and Simeon Reno in Seymour's City Cemetery.
Photo by Rachel Dickinson

The Colton Railroad & Express map through the midsection of the country in the 1860s. *Library of Congress*

This Ohio & Mississippi Railroad advertisement explains the Midwest runs available in 1864. This train would have gone through Seymour, Indiana.

Bird's-eye view of Seymour printed in 1870. Map paid for by the Seymour Woolen Mills, owned by Travis Carter.

Photo of the jail cell believed to have held Charlie Anderson in the New Albany jail. It now sits in the Seymour Visitor's Bureau parking lot. *Photo by Rachel Dickinson*

Pinkerton reckoned that the Renos would know the saloonkeeper and that his shop might be a rendezvous point. Two days into their surveillance, Pinkerton noticed a large man of dark complexion enter the saloon. He seemed to be conducting some kind of business with the owner. This man was Michael Rogers.

Rogers was a prominent citizen of Council Bluffs. Several newspapers reported Rogers as a trustee and faithful Methodist, which the Methodist Church in Council Bluffs vehemently and forcefully denied. Pinkerton ordered a "shadow" on Rogers and returned to Magnolia. He found out that Rogers had been seen in Magnolia the day before the robbery. Apparently, he paid his taxes that day and then hung around the treasurer's office for a while. Upon reflection, Pinkerton concluded that Rogers had been casing the joint. But no one would cast any aspersions on Rogers. He was viewed as a respectable member of the community.

William Pinkerton returned to Council Bluffs, where Rogers's shadow reported he had seen several strange men going into the Rogers house. They had not come out.

The detectives watched the house for four days, and finally Rogers emerged accompanied by three strangers. One of these men, "a brawny, athletic fellow nearly six feet tall, and about 28-years of age," Pinkerton suspected to be Frank Reno (although he could not be certain since he had never seen Frank Reno before). The men headed to the train station, where they took a westbound train.

Pinkerton figured the men would ultimately find their way back to Rogers's house, so he decided they should keep watch rather than follow them. Pinkerton's hunch paid off. Early the next morning the four men, covered in mud, came back to the house from the direction of the railroad. Pinkerton found it all quite curious, as no train was due into the station around that time. The men also looked sweaty and exhausted, like they had been working hard.

Within hours, news that the Mills County treasury in Glenwood had been robbed flew around the city. The similarity to the Harrison County robbery was remarkable, right down to the escape by handcar. Detectives discovered the missing handcar lying beside the tracks, a short distance from the Council Bluffs station. This evidence—an abandoned handcar and the muddy, exhausted men—was enough to convince Pinkerton that the men in the house were his prime suspects. The local authorities laughed at him. Rogers was one of the most respectable citizens in the state, they said.

Pinkerton resolved to attempt an arrest. He placed guards at the front and back doors, then entered the house with a couple of detectives. The first person they met was Rogers.

"Who have you in this house?" asked Mr. Pinkerton.

"Nobody but my family," answered Mr. Rogers.

"We'll see about that," answered Mr. Pinkerton.

The detectives searched the house and came upon the three strangers, who were just sitting down to breakfast. The men offered no resistance. Pinkerton figured out that he had Frank Reno, Albert Perkins, and Miles Ogle in front of him, the latter two being the best-known counterfeiters in the country.

While securing the men, one of the detectives noticed smoke curling out of the kitchen stove. Pinkerton pulled off the lid and found several packages of banknotes, already on fire. Fortunately, the packages were wrapped so tightly that only the outer notes had burned. The notes were later identified as having come out of the Mills County safe. The detectives also turned up two sets of burglary tools.

Reno, Rogers, Ogle, and Perkins were taken to the railroad station in cuffs, and the detectives escorted them on the train the thirty miles to Glenwood. Pinkerton wrote that an excited crowd met them at the Glenwood station and "for a time they were in a danger of lynching." The detectives managed to get them secured in the jail on March 31, 1868, to await trial.

The next morning—and no one really knows how this happened—the cells were empty when the sheriff of Mills County went to check on the prisoners. A big hole was sawed through the back wall of the jail. Scrawled in chalk on the walls and floor was "April Fool."

A large reward was offered for capture of the escaped robbers. Two of them would next show up a couple months later much closer to home.

At this point the story runs up against the vagaries of history. The Pinkerton account via Cleveland Moffett via William Pinkerton appears to be a compression and conflation of what really happened if one reads and believes the newspapers of the day. According to the *Council Bluffs Weekly Nonpareil*, Mike Rogers and three other men were picked up on February 28, 1868, the morning after the Mills County Treasury had been robbed. Dan Ludy, who was down in the river bottom hunting for his mules early in the morning, saw four men go into Mike Rogers's house. Ludy went to town and reported what he saw. Marshal Bump led a posse out to the Rogers' place.

"They found a large package of money, partly burned, in the stove," according to the *Nonpareil*, "and one behind a picture hanging on the wall. Mr. Rogers and the other three men, whose names are not yet disclosed, were brought to town and placed in the Pacific House for several hours. After they were brought to town it was thought best to make further search in Mr. Rogers' house. A company went back and instituted a search, which resulted in finding five thousand dollars, in a belt, under the clothing and around the body of Rogers' wife." The men arrested with Rogers were not Reno, Ogle, and Perkins.

Another Iowa paper reported: "Quite a quantity of good and counterfeit money was recovered—more, perhaps, of good money than was taken from the Mills county safe."

Angry men gathered around the Pacific House in Council Bluffs, where the criminals were being held until a preliminary trial the following morning. It seemed as if the locals were determined to take matters into their own hands, perhaps fearing that justice would not be served. The anger was focused on Mike Rogers, one of their own, who had duped and betrayed them.

The *Nonpareil* also reported that Rogers was not a prominent member of the Methodist Church as reported by the *Omaha Herald*. "Whether the effort of the *Herald* to bring reproach upon the church will elevate it in the estimation of the good people of Omaha, we cannot say," wrote the *Nonpareil*. "Mr. Rogers has lived in this city many years, and we repeat, was never a member of the Methodist Church here."

The robberies continued in Iowa despite the arrest of Rogers and some of the gang—four houses in Council Bluffs were hit and then the Howard County Treasury was robbed of $18,000. More of the gang were apparently arrested—including Frank Reno, Miles Ogle, and Albert Perkins—but the details are murky. What is clear, however, is that a couple of months later, Frank Reno and Albert Perkins were back in Jackson County, Indiana.

There was a spectacular jailbreak on April 1, 1868, but it occurred in the Fremont County jail in Sidney, Iowa. It's true that Mike Rogers was one of the escapees. The *Nonpareil* reported: "The excitement of our citizens, yesterday, on hearing the news that Mike Rogers and his confederates had made good their escape from the Sidney jail, was so intense as to paralyze nearly all kinds of business. Knots of men congregated at street corners, anxiously awaiting full particulars and discussing the probable manner in which they effected their escape." The reporter added, "After mature deliberation, the unanimous decision of the citizens was that they would all go down to Finley Geesaman's drug store, where the finest assortment of drugs and fancy goods ever brought to the west, could be found."

Miles Ogle was later recaptured and arraigned at Glenwood, Iowa. He was brought into the upstairs courtroom in the two-story courthouse heavily chained, ironed, and manacled. Sometime during the hearing, Ogle made a dash for the window and leaped out, bursting through the sash and glass and hurtling two stories down to a sand bank below. He gathered up the irons and ran.

Ogle was recaptured many months later.

Records of the Secret Service, under the Department of the Treasury, described Ogle as being hideously scarred, no doubt the result of his dramatic courtroom exit.

Chapter Fifteen

The Third Train Robbery

It was a hot, humid Friday night—so humid that the smells of the earth, the dung, the animals, and the people sweating were almost overpowering. In other words, typical early summer Indiana weather. The northbound Jeffersonville & Indianapolis train left the Jeffersonville station at 9:30 p.m. on May 22, 1868. Around 10:45 the train was scheduled to stop at Marshfield in Scott County to take on water. Marshfield was about seventeen miles south of Seymour.

The train traveled through the darkness, but most of the passengers were local and knew well the landscape of trees with an occasional pasture carved out of the forest. There was nothing in Marshfield except thickets and trees and swampy lowlands. There were no houses; no bustling reminders of civilization. Yet this was a good place for a train stop, because there was plenty of water available to fill the engine's boiler. There was also wood for the taking to top off the tender. The railroad had built a wooden water tower and Marshfield became a regular refueling station for the Jeffersonville & Indianapolis Railroad.

It was closer to 11:00 p.m. when the train pulled into Marshfield. The engineer hopped off the train to oil the engine when he was "knocked in the head with a billet of wood." The fireman, caught off-guard when a man climbed up into the tender, was thrown from the train. According to the *Indianapolis Daily Sentinel* the train boy told the conductor that several men were getting on the express car. Mr. Whedon, the conductor, rushed to the front of the passenger cars and found men cutting the bell rope and unhitching the express car. "He ordered them to desist, and as they did not do so, he drew a small four-barreled pistol and began firing at them. They returned the fire, one bullet passing through his coat, and another through his hair by his ear," reported the paper.

The robbers successfully detached the engine and Adams Express car from the rest of the train. One of the robbers commandeered the engine, built up a head of steam in the boiler, and started up the tracks toward Seymour. In a show of ruthlessness that had not been apparent during the first train robbery, "They beat the [Adams Express] messenger, Mr. F. G. Harkins, until he was senseless, and threw him headlong from the train, going at a speed of at least twenty miles an hour, inflicting injuries from which it is thought he will not recover."

While under steam, the express car was ransacked and the three safes opened with crowbars.

When but a mile from Seymour, whoever was in charge of the locomotive slowed it to a stop. Under cover of darkness the robbers left the train on the tracks and took off with their booty by way of horses that had either been tethered nearby earlier or were brought to the location by an accomplice.

Meanwhile, Conductor Whedon, "as soon as he recovered from the astonishment of this unheard of proceeding," took the passengers from the cars, and placed signals on the tracks on the lonely road in Marshfield so the abandoned cars would not be hit by approaching trains. Whedon walked six miles to the next station, where he learned that the missing engine had "whizzed by like a streak of lightning." He then telegraphed Jeffersonville to have another train sent to pick up the stranded passengers, who were waiting near the mosquito-infested swamps of Marshfield.

At this point, no one knew how much money the robbers stole from the express car. Estimates ranged from a high of $170,000 to a low of $42,000. The *Daily Sentinal* noted "The neighborhood in which the robbery took place is known to be infested with a gang of as shrewd, bold, and unscrupulous scoundrels as exist on the face of the globe, who are banded together in a regular organization, and have reduced villainy to a science." Of course the editor was referring to the Reno Gang.

The story hit the front page of the *New York Times* under the headline "Bold Robbery of Adams Express on the Jeffersonville Railroad, Ohio."

The paper got the state wrong, but it was clear that the Adams Express robberies were now considered real news. The *Seymour Democrat* added: "[That night] some parties at the Depot seeing the headlights so long stationary, supposed the train was off the track, and going down discovered the true state of affairs."

The Indianapolis paper pointed out that this "extraordinary robbery is calculated to unsettle railroad business, and will probably necessitate the employment of railroad guards. Now that the thing has been successfully done, everybody can see how easy it is, and imitators of the Marshfield robbery will not be slow to repeat the operation on that and other roads as occasion may offer."

E. S. Sanford, president of the Adams Express Company, wasted no time in getting the Pinkertons involved. Yet again. He ordered a special train sent from Chicago, and on Sunday a detachment of detectives landed in Seymour. Allan Pinkerton, who was in Pittsburgh, was ordered to Indiana himself to head the investigation. Seymour was again full of detectives looking for express robbers and stolen money—a state of affairs the little city was getting used to.

The third train robbery in May 1868 had been carefully planned and executed by Frank, Sim, and William Reno and fellow gang member and counterfeiter Charlie Anderson. In the final accounting, the robbers grabbed $96,000 from the three safes in the express car. The robbery was stunning in its simplicity and went off without a hitch in the minds of the robbers. After dividing the money, the group decided to split up and head in different directions, at least for the time being. William and Sim wound up in Indianapolis, where they were soon apprehended by the Pinkertons and hauled off to side-by-side cells in the New Albany jail—fifty miles southeast of Seymour—under the watchful eye of Sheriff Fullenlove of Floyd County.

Frank Reno and Charlie Anderson headed to Windsor, Canada, near Toronto, a town that counterfeiter Anderson liked immensely and considered home. Windsor had a reputation as a haven for crooks, bandits, and thugs from the United States. It lay just a mile or two across the Detroit River and was the southernmost town in Canada. John Larney, aka Mollie Matches (so named because of his penchant for dressing in old women's clothing and selling matches as a ruse for pick-pocketing), and the Garrity Gang had established themselves in Manning's saloon in Windsor to work the busy railroad and the ferry stations. When the trains and ferries pulled in, disgorging hundreds of passengers at a time, the pickpockets and thieves had an easy time of it in the jostling crowd.

In 1868, Windsor was a border town of several thousand people. During the Civil War, it had come under the close scrutiny of the Federal government because Michigan feared a cross-border attack by Confederates who had moved into Canada for just that purpose. Such an attack never materialized. Post-war Windsor was thriving. Windsor officials and entrepreneurs built sturdy stone churches and schools and hotels. They had a jail and a courthouse. There was both a ferry platform for the boat that shuttled back and forth between Detroit and Windsor and a railroad station for the train that brought Canadians to the little city. A bit later in the century, a local businessman would convince town leaders to let him drill for oil, and he hit a geyser, but it was of mineral water. Soon Windsor became popular with people wishing to seek the healing properties of H_2O with a high concentration of sulfur.

Frank Reno and Charlie Anderson settled down among the toughs of Windsor, ready to give themselves a little vacation before heading back to Seymour.

Allan Pinkerton was knee-deep in work in the autumn of 1868. He had offices in several big cities, including New York and Philadelphia, but the headquarters of Pinkerton's National Detective Agency was in Chicago, where he was based. When Pinkerton and his operatives weren't shadowing suspected criminals, inserting themselves into operations under disguise, or following up on leads, the boss was likely in court testifying.

In early October of 1868, J. S. Love was arrested in Chicago on a charge of stealing government bonds. It turns out that Love was a detective (although it's never been established for whom), and in a Keystone Kop or Monty Python–esque turn, the man Love was trying to entrap, Samuel Felker, was also in the "detective line."

At that time, Felker worked for the United States Department of Treasury's Secret Service under Director William P. Wood. Wood, as detailed earlier, was hired as the first Secret Service director in mid-1864, his task to ferret out counterfeiters and try to put a dent in the enormous flow of boodle entering the market. Wood was serving as superintendent of the Old Capitol Prison in Washington, D.C., at the time. He was a curious choice in some ways. He was known as a shady character in some circles, and the way he chose Secret Service detectives or agents was the opposite of how Pinkerton chose his operatives (he would never hire thieves because he could neither trust nor control them). But Wood knew counterfeiting. He went to the prisons and rounded up several well-known counterfeiters to work for him, believing that it took a thief to know a thief. His agents skimmed off the top when making arrests, took payments for looking the other way, and engaged in scams that stretched the concept of legality. Felker, as one of Wood's agents, seems to have setup a number of stings, many of which backfired.

In court Love testified that he offered Felker a number of bonds purported to have been stolen in New York. Felker, "getting into confidential relations with Love," confessed to him that he had "$25,000 of bonds which the New York boys had made," and somehow a deal was arranged. Love delivered a package to Felker, who then had Love arrested.

The package from Love to Felker was opened in court and instead of stolen bonds, there were one hundred and nine large-size envelopes. The tables had turned. Felker was taken into custody in the courtroom, where he had been summoned as a witness, and charged with grand larceny. The next part of the story is where Pinkerton comes in. The courtroom reporter from the *Chicago Tribune* wrote, "the scene that ensued was one to which no description can do justice."

Felker seemed as if he intended to pay no attention to the arrest, but then handed over his pocket book and some papers to his brother. Pinkerton, "regarding the attempt as an unwarranted one," hit the brother's arm and the papers fell to the floor. "Then ensued a fight," wrote the *Tribune*, "but the reporters, being behind the table, while the affray took place near the door, could not tell what blows were struck." In the middle of the melee, Pinkerton's pockets were emptied of five United States bonds: two for one thousand dollars, two for one hundred dollars, and one for fifty dollars. The bills were handed back to Pinkerton at the end of the fracas. In spite of the courtroom upheaval, the presiding justice decided that Felker could not be taken from the room as long as he might be called as a witness. The trial continued.

The counselor for Mr. Love called Pinkerton to the stand.

Felker looked at Pinkerton and said, "You old thief, you."

Pinkerton then "moved forward to resent the insult, but was prevented by the crowd, and in the scuffle several more blows were struck. Mr. Pinkerton then seized an inkstand from the table, but did not throw. He did succeed in spilling the ink liberally around, and the coat of Mr. Hervey was well spotted. The Justice instantly ordered Felker under arrest, and he was conveyed to the central station and locked up. Mr. Pinkerton then apologized to the court for trouble which had been occasioned, and was assured the court had no desire to assess a fine under the circumstances."

At the close of court, Love was acquitted.

Felker was taken from the central station to the depot of the Pittsburgh & Fort Wayne Railroad, where he was placed on board the train in irons.

"The affair is an intricate one, and may yet develop many incidents now unknown," wrote the reporter. "Pending this it is not judicious to speculate."

Pinkerton hated Felker, and the feeling was mutual. Was it professional jealousy? Felker worked for the very agency that Pinkerton tried to establish several times while in Washington during the war. But Pinkerton was never taken seriously. The choice of Wood for the first director must have seriously rankled Pinkerton. Then Wood's reliance on criminals to do the same job Pinkerton's handpicked operatives did was an insult. To Pinkerton, the good work of his detectives reflected back on his agency. Pinkerton's ego and financial future were completely tied up in the reputation of the detective agency he founded. Then along came a character like the lying, cheating Felker, who also called himself a detective. *Here is the reason why detectives get a bad reputation*, Pinkerton must have fumed. Criminals like the Reno Gang didn't muse on the reputation of detectives. They just tried to stay one step ahead of the hired guns in their increasingly elaborate game of cat and mouse.

CHAPTER SIXTEEN

The Fourth Train Robbery

FRANK SPARKS, JOHN MOORE, AND HENRY JERRELL HEADED OVER TO Mattoon, Illinois, to lie low after the awful experience they had trying to rob the O&M train in the middle of the night outside of Brownstown, Indiana. *Goddamn son of a bitch engineer turned on us,* John Moore might have thought, for he had no one to blame but himself, because he'd made all the arrangements for the heist.

While the remaining Reno boys—Frank, William, and Simeon—and Charlie Anderson were cooling their heels out of town after stealing $96,000 from an Adams Express car two months earlier, John Moore had decided to do his own train job. He'd copy the last one, a train job so successful that Moore was sure this fourth train robbery would yield enough riches to keep him set for the rest of his life. Some say John Moore did not come up with this idea on his own—that the Reno brothers selected these six gang members to replicate their most lucrative train job—but given the outcome, that seems unlikely.

The timing was right. If Moore did set up this job on his own he knew he wouldn't run afoul of the Reno brothers. Will and Sim had left town and were spending their money in Indianapolis, while Frank Reno and Charlie Anderson made their way to the criminal harbor town of Windsor, Ontario. The oldest brother, John Reno, was doing his twenty-five-year stint in a Missouri prison. Moore got word to railroad engineer James Flanders of the Ohio & Mississippi and suggested they meet in front of the Harvey House in Seymour. Moore had briefly been an engineer for the O&M, so he thought he'd use his own connections to try to pull the train job.

"He had never spoken to me direct on business before, but had thrown out hints and had been given to understand that I was a safe man to deal with," Flanders told a newspaper reporter for the *Cincinnati Enquirer* in 1878, a decade after that initial conversation. What Moore didn't know was that Flanders immediately told his boss about the fourth proposed heist of the Adams Express car, which then brought the Pinkertons into the picture.

"He was a young fellow, not over twenty-five years old, but an old stager in crime, and one of the boldest men I ever knew," said Flanders. "He said he wanted to stop the express train some night at the water tank at Brownstown and wanted me to get off the engine with my fireman. He would be there with some boys from Cincinnati and would tend to all the rest. He said I couldn't be blamed for just stopping at a water tank and that he would do the square thing by me. I said: 'all right; let me know when you're ready.'"

The next time Flanders saw Moore in person was on a hot, humid summer night in the wee hours of July 10, 1868. Earlier that evening John Moore, Charlie Roseberry, Volney Elliott (the same Volney Elliott that accompanied John Reno to Gallatin, Missouri), Henry Jerrell, and Frank Sparks boarded a westbound train in Seymour. They purposely didn't buy tickets. They knew once the conductor checked for tickets and found they didn't have any, they'd be thrown off at the next stop—Brownstown—which was part of the plan. After the inevitable happened, the robbers walked through town and followed the tracks to the Brownstown water tower on the outskirts of town. Then it was just a matter of waiting for the eastbound O&M to come through.

As planned, Flanders pulled the engine of the O&M in for an unscheduled water stop at Brownstown at about 1:30 a.m. The county seat of Jackson County, Indiana (in spite of Seymour's repeated attempts to wrest county-seat status from them), Brownstown was a dying-on-the-vine town of no more than nine hundred people. The water tower was a good half-mile trek from the train station and town, and at that hour in the morning Flanders and the robbers knew it was unlikely there would be onlookers to see what was about to happen.

After the engine stopped, several men who had been lurking in the shadows of the trees under a still-bright waning moon, ran to the coupling between the first passenger car and the express car. One of them lifted the pin holding the cars together. Another unhooked the bell cable between the cars. Vol Elliott got on the engine. Moore, Sparks, Roseberry, and Jerrell climbed onto the rear platform of the express car—the car that held the safes and valuables. Unbeknownst to Elliott—who didn't know anything about engines and wouldn't be able to tell if something was amiss—Flanders had fixed the engine so it wouldn't run more than half a mile. He had drained the boiler nearly empty of water. When Elliott got on, Flanders and the fireman got off, as planned.

Elliott threw some wood in the firebox, then pushed the throttle to open. The engine and express car started rolling down the track, leaving behind passengers sitting in the dark railroad cars by the water tower. The men on the back platform of the express car called through the door—*come out, you son of a bitch! We won't hurt you if you get out now!* The messenger opened the broad side door of the express car and jumped from the slow-moving train, disappearing into the Indiana night.

Moore, Sparks, Jerrell, and Roseberry made their way from the back of the car to the express car's side door. They entered and were instantly greeted with a barrage of bullets. Pinkerton guards, who had barricaded themselves into one end of the car so as not to shoot each other, fired wildly in the dark as the robbers pushed through the side door. Within seconds, thick smoke filled the express car. The sound of the guns firing was like cannons exploding in the confined space. Several of the thieves were hit. Yet they all managed to jump from the moving train and run down the dark tracks toward the sixth member of the gang, Theodore Clifton, who was holding the getaway horses about a hundred yards away. They quickly mounted the horses, which were wheeling and snorting from the commotion, and rode away from their failure.

Up in the engine, Elliott pulled on the brakes as soon as he heard the gunfire and turned to see what was happening. Just then a Pinkerton, who was hiding in the tender, stood up and opened fire. Elliott writhed on the floor with a shoulder wound.

The Pinkertons choked and gasped on the acrid smoke filling the express car—smoke that curled up and then hung like a curtain in the still summer night. The detectives' eyes burned and watered as they rushed to the side door. One by one they also jumped from the car and headed down the track in pursuit of the robbers. All of the operatives had been soldiers in the war and had experienced the chaos, smoke, and sounds of battle before. Yet everything went wrong. They had reacted too quickly when the robbers entered the car. Even with the element of surprise on their side—the Pinkertons fired over a hundred rounds in the railroad car—they hadn't managed to kill any of the thieves.

As the robbers leapt from the train and disappeared into the southern Indiana night, the Pinkertons heard the cries and moans of the wounded. Later in the morning, when the sun had risen and the smoke finally cleared, people from Brownstown came to view the express car abandoned not far from town. It looked like a bomb had exploded—the walls were splintered by the bullets, leaving gaping holes in the siding. No one could understand, when looking at the destruction in front of them, how the Pinkertons managed to miss their marks.

The Pinkerton guards had been hired to thwart this robbery. They had been hired to put an end to some of the members of the noxious Reno Gang. Everyone was disappointed at the outcome. All they had to show for their effort—for the hours of planning and then waiting, crammed into the end of a sweatbox of a railcar—was the wounded Elliott.

Allan Pinkerton would be angry when he heard the news. Because they had seen his reaction before when things didn't go as planned, the operatives knew the stocky Scotsman would get red-faced and fume and wonder why he had to do everything himself if he wanted the job done right. One of the operatives waited in Brownstown and took the next train east to escort the wounded Elliott to Cincinnati to be questioned at the regional Adams Express company office.

After rendezvousing with Clifton and the horses on the night of the failed robbery, the five outlaws galloped northeast toward the swampy lowlands of the Muscatatuck River. Brownstown was in the hilly part of Jackson County, where the limestone weathered into knobs and ridges. The gang members knew that once they were able to dip down into the river valley and the swamps, they could easily lose their pursuers. They were all local boys who knew every creek and hollow. The woods of sweet gum and maple and tulip poplar were their woods. And once they disappeared into the dense thickets of the lowlands, the gang knew the Pinkertons would have an extremely difficult time rooting them out.

The next morning the detectives joined a posse of about a hundred men that formed in Seymour. They all headed toward Old Rockford, where they suspected they'd find members of the gang holed up in the decaying houses. They entered the burned-out village and immediately heard the *pop pop pop* of shots being fired from one of the abandoned buildings. The gunfire scared the horses, which snorted and reared and had to be reined in by the riders.

The posse—shopkeepers, farmers, railroad men, and the Pinkerton detectives—raised their pistols and rifles and opened fire in the direction of the building. Bullets entered the punky wood of the half-charred house—a victim of one of the many fires that ravaged Old Rockford—blowing holes in the walls and spraying splinters. In a matter of minutes Roseberry and Clifton staggered out to the weeds beyond the house, both wounded. Moore, Sparks, and Jerrell managed to get to their horses, swing into the saddles, and lose themselves in the thicket. The Pinkertons gathered up the wounded men—Roseberry and Clifton—not caring about their moans and cries as they were manhandled onto horses, and took them back to Seymour. Later that day the prisoners and some of the Pinkertons boarded the train and headed east to Cincinnati for questioning.

The next morning, as the sun burned off the morning mist and the day promised to be as hot as the day before, hundreds of men from Seymour tramped into the boggy bottomland thicket that hugged the river in search of the three remaining would-be robbers.

In a special to the *Cincinnati Commercial*, dateline "Seymour, Ind., July 12, 1868," a reporter wrote: "Great efforts have been made, today, to capture the three remaining express robbers, but without success. A force numbering from three to four hundred have been scouring the country for miles around. There seems to be a determination on the part of our citizens to secure them, and if they do, there is not much doubt that they will stretch them up on the first tree, as an abundance of rope, was taken along for that purpose." The lawlessness raging through southern Indiana was now a familiar news story.

The reporter continued, "It is supposed that the robbers made their escape out of the thicket, which they had been in for twenty-four hours; last night, however well it was guarded, and from last accounts they were making their way northward. It seems impossible for them to holt [sic] out much longer. It is expected that their capture will be effected tomorrow."

But capture was no sure thing. The Pinkertons had cornered them in the express car, then let them all get away. They had surrounded them at Old Rockford, yet most of the gang had managed to reach their horses and head for the woods, unscathed. The frustration of the operatives must have been almost unbearable with pressure coming from Allan Pinkerton and from the Adams Express company office in Cincinnati. They had been hired to get the job done. This, and the whispering chants, real or imagined, of *hang them hang them hang them* that ran through the bars and businesses and through the crowds that gathered at the train station in Seymour must have added to the resolve of the detectives.

The attempted robbery of the Adams Express car of the O&M train near Brownsville was all anyone could talk about. The regional newspapers were chock-full of information and speculation about the robbery and the robbers. Among certain members of Seymour's citizenry, it's likely this was the tipping point—Seymour was being dragged through the mud because of the Reno Gang. In the end, the town would be the biggest loser. This kind of news would have a decidedly negative impact on the town's development. The town leaders felt they had been pushed and poked and taunted by the Reno Gang long enough, and like a dog worrying a burr caught in its paw, they finally felt it was time to get rid of the source of their problems.

In a dispatch to the *Cincinnati Commercial*, a reporter, most likely Dr. J. R. Monroe, wrote, "Frank Sparks, Volney Elliott, Charles Roseberry, and John Moore . . . are petty thieves, and this is, no doubt, their first attempt at so big a job. Henry Jerrell, who was also connected, comes from Williamsburg, Clermont County, Ohio, and has always been regarded as an honest boy. How he came to be in such company I cannot account for, as he is the last person, in my opinion, who would engage in committing such a crime."

Elliott and Sparks were described as "honest and industrious," with respectable relations, whereas John Moore and Charles Roseberry were "constitutional thieves." It continues, "They can't help stealing if they have half a chance. Roseberry is also something of a desperado, and would not hesitate to stab a man in the back. Moore's disposition runs rather to fun and deviltry. Not long since he stole a locomotive on the Jeffersonville railroad, at Seymour, and ran it about sixteen miles, by which time he had pumped the boilers full of water, and could proceed no farther. Numerous are the wicked and humorous jokes told of him by his fellow soldiers, some of which are exceedingly ludicrous. He is just the opposite of a desperado."

The reporter offered a solution to Seymour's problem: "The best thing that could be done for Seymour would be to hang the leading scoundrels and drive the others away, which, we are glad to see, the citizens are now likely to do."

Monroe must have been twisting and turning and pounding the table not to have his own paper at this time. However, his characteristic style of writing, featuring an overabundance of commas and snarky comments, could not be disguised in the anonymous dispatches and reports showing up in papers from Cincinnati, Ohio, to Louisville, Kentucky. He would not be silenced.

On the night of July 20 the three robbers in custody in Cincinnati—Roseberry, Clifton, and Elliott—were taken aboard an O&M westbound train under heavy guard. They were to be delivered into the custody of Sheriff John Scott of Jackson County at Brownstown.

It was 10:00 p.m. on a Monday night as the westbound O&M train approached the Seymour station. The engineer clanged the engine bell, and the sound of steel against steel broke the still night air—tons of metal and wood shuddering to a stop. Steam hissed from the idle engine as it stood next to the platform. Passengers getting off the train were approached by boys willing to carry their bags to one of the several hotels adjacent to the tracks. The sound of a piano came from the open door of the Rader House, where men were drinking at the bar and playing in the perpetual poker game at the corner table. The atmosphere felt still and heavy with the ever-present southern Indiana humidity and the smells of horse manure, coal and wood fires, and body odor lingering on the platform without a breeze to freshen the air.

Roseberry, Clifton, and Elliott were in the baggage car with two Pinkerton guards. Although all three men had been shot—Elliott during the holdup and the other two while being captured—their hands were tied behind their backs. The guards and the robbers were nervous. And the rank air in the baggage car wasn't helping. All of them had heard the rumors about men in Seymour who were more interested in seeing vigilante justice prevail than letting the case against the Reno Gang members drag through the court system.

The engine took on water while stopped in Seymour, then started up again with another clang of the engine bell and a final *All Aboard!* from the conductor. The train moved slowly at first. The fireman threw pieces of wood into the firebox, and the train picked up speed as it moved west along the railroad tracks toward Brownstown.

About a mile after leaving the Seymour station, as the fireman was working hard to raise a full head of steam in hopes of reaching a top speed of forty miles per hour at some point during the journey, the engineer saw a red lantern on the tracks ahead. It seemed to be just past the railroad crossing of the Brownstown Road. The engineer yelled to the brakeman, *Stop the train!* The brakeman ran the length of the train wrestling with the dinner-plate-size brake wheels on top of each railroad car. At last the brakes gripped and the train shuddered to a stop.

Out of the darkness and the swirl of smoke and steam released from the locomotive appeared hundreds of masked men. Witnesses reported at least two hundred, perhaps as many as four hundred. They surged toward the engine and the express car. The side door to the baggage car was wrenched open. The Pinkerton guards took one look at the size of the crowd and then stood aside. Several men climbed into the car, jerking Clifton, Roseberry, and Elliott to their feet and then pushed them out the door. The engineer was ordered to move the train on quickly, leaving the three gang members with the masked men next to the tracks.

Clifton, Roseberry, and Elliott were dragged along the ground, then lifted and thrown onto the back of a wagon. A huge, lone beech tree—black and menacing in the dark evening—rose at the edge of a nearby pasture. A beech tree wouldn't normally have been the best choice for what the masked men had in mind, because its limbs were not as sturdy as, say, an oak tree. But location was everything in this case. The wagon was driven beneath its widespread limbs. The outlaws were yanked to their feet on the wagon bed. Hands passed three heavy hemp ropes forward through the crowd, which were then handed to the driver of the wagon. He placed nooses around the necks of Clifton, Roseberry, and Elliott.

Clifton fell to his knees and begged for his life, saying he was not guilty of any crime since he actually hadn't robbed anything. He was only holding the horses, he cried. He then asked to be allowed to speak to his mother for a few minutes before his death. Incredibly, Clifton had buried his father the day of the robbery attempt, leaving the Seymour cemetery and his grieving mother to join up with Elliott, Roseberry, Jerrell, Sparks, and Moore to go over last-minute plans for that evening's heist. The mob ignored Clifton's request.

The three men were given time to pray and confess. None did either, or if they did, no one heard them. Roseberry stood stoically on the wagon bed awaiting his inevitable execution. Clifton sobbed.

Elliott's only reply to the mob was reported as, "Confess hell, you've got me here, thousands of you, now do your damnedest." Elliott's declaration made the mob angry, and the man on the wagon threw the ends of the ropes over three different limbs, pulling them taut. He then grabbed the horses' reins and drove the wagon forward, leaving three bodies jerking and twitching and slowly twirling on the ends of the rope. The mob stood silently until the quivering bodies became still. Then they returned to their wives and children, carrying home whatever pangs of guilt they felt, whatever thoughts they had about the enormity of what had just transpired.

Early the next morning, an old German farmer, whose house stood not too far from the great beech tree, was almost petrified by the sight of the three men dangling, swaying gently in the early morning breeze, with thick tongues protruding from their blackened, swollen faces. The terrified old farmer hitched up his wagon and drove into town with the news, which spread through Seymour like a prairie fire. Soon a crowd had converged on the scene of the hanging. The county coroner was telegraphed and summoned from Brownstown to investigate.

The coroner didn't arrive at the beech tree until around noon, and it was only then that the bodies were cut down, placed on a wagon bed, and examined. In each case, the coroner determined that the cause of death was "hanging by a rope around the neck—supposedly done by a group of men for robberies the deceased had committed."

The Coroner's Inquest was published the following day in the *Seymour Democrat*. It provides the only surviving physical description of the three members of the Reno Gang killed in the incident, for no photographs of them exist. When Thomas Volney Elliott died, he was twenty-four years old and wearing "black cloth pants, striped calico shirt, boots and cotton socks." He was described as having a dark complexion, brown hair, gray eyes and was about 5 feet 10 inches tall and weighed approximately 140 pounds. Valuables on his body were listed as "three brass door keys, one iron door key, one padlock key—all on a key ring, and one wood pencil."

Charles Roseberry was the youngest of the group at twenty-three years old. He was wearing, "one cotton shirt with linen bosom, low crown black fur hat, one pair gold mixed dark cassimere pants, one pair calf boots, white cotton socks, and one pair suspenders." Roseberry was short at 5 feet 4 inches tall with black eyes and dark hair. He weighed about 135 pounds. Valuables found on his body included "one white linen pocket handkerchief, one pocket comb, one wood pencil, one satchel key, and smoking and chewing tobacco."

Finally, Theodore F. Clifton, the young man who wanted to speak to his mother before his death, was listed as being about twenty-four years old. He was wearing a "white cotton shirt, steel-mixed cassimere pants, white cotton drawers, brown cotton socks, and elastic garters." He was 5 feet 11 inches tall, weighed about 160 pounds, and had light hair, a light complexion, gray eyes, and a sandy goatee. The valuables found on Clifton's body were "one pocket book, a newspaper, a gold breastpin, a gold ring on his finger, a Police whistle, buttons, and other trinkets."

Over a decade later, James Flanders, the engineer on the bungled last robbery attempt, gave an interview to a reporter from the *Cincinnati Enquirer*. In it, he solved the Clifton mystery. "A discovery was made which shortly afterward gave a new meaning to Clifton's dying prayer. Soon after his death his mother moved away from Seymour, and the house in which she had lived was rented by a poor German, whose name I have forgotten. He plowed up the yard about the house and found buried in the ground a two-and-a-half gallon fruit can filled with money. The amount was very large. I had lived in that same house before Clifton's mother moved there, and had plowed up every foot of the ground without making such a discovery. There is no doubt that this money was Clifton's share of the Marshfield booty, and that his anxiety to see his mother before he died was caused by his desire to tell where the treasure was buried. She was, of course, ignorant of it, or she would not have left it there when she moved. The poor but lucky German who found it removed to Madison, Ind., and is now one of the wealthiest men in that place. The amount found by him must have been nearly $20,000, as Clifton was entitled to one-sixth of the money stolen at Marshfield. The Adams Express Company tried to get the money back, but of course they failed, as they could not identify it or prove that it had ever belonged to them."

Chapter Seventeen

Hanging, Redux

THE NIGHT FOLLOWING THE LYNCHING, BROADSIDES APPEARED AROUND the town of Seymour, plastered to the sides of buildings, on store windows, and in all the obvious public places. The posters confirmed that the vigilance committee meant business. Crowds of people gathered around the posters. Those who couldn't read listened while others read them aloud. The words brought chills to those who didn't know about the vigilante committee's existence, and knowing smiles from those who did.

ATTENTION THIEVES

The attention of all thieves, robbers, assassins and vagrants, together with their aides, abettor and sympathizers, is called to the doings of the Seymour Vigilance Committee last night.

We are determined to follow this up until all of the classes above named, whether imported or to the Manor born, are driven forever from our midst.

Threats have been made of retaliation, in case we should resort to Capital Punishment. In answer we say, should one of our committee be harmed, or a dollar's worth of the property of any honest man be destroyed by persons unknown, we will Swing By the Neck until they are dead every thieving character we can lay our hands on without inquiring whether we have the proper persons who committed that particular crime or not. This applies not only to Seymour but along the line of the two roads, and wherever our organization exists.

LAW AND ORDER MUST PREVAIL.
By order of the Committee
Seymour, Indiana July 21, 1868

Three of the train robbers were still at large—Jerrell, Sparks, and Moore. After escaping from the posse that rounded up Roseberry and Clifton in Rockford, the three headed north to Mattoon, Illinois, about 180 miles away. There they quickly found work on a farm and would have probably remained undetected were it not for Jerrell's desire to have his clothes sent to him. Jerrell, who was quite the ladies' man, but lacked a certain amount of common sense when it came to women, sent a telegram to one girlfriend in Louisville asking her to write to another girlfriend in Seymour. She was to ask the Seymour girlfriend to send his clothes to the Louisville girlfriend, who would then send the clothes on to him. The girlfriend in Seymour couldn't read, and had to have the telegrapher read the telegram aloud. The telegrapher promptly informed the Pinkertons.

Newspaper accounts don't agree on the above story. The following might be just a bit more plausible. Jerrell wrote to his girlfriend in Louisville asking her to tell his friends and his brother in Seymour that he had died from his gunshot wounds. He instructed her to write to him under the alias "George Hudson." There was already a Pinkerton operative shadowing the girl's home, and when the letter from Jerrell arrived the operative watched her closely. The girlfriend was unable to read and had a friend read Jerrell's letter to her. The operative was listening at the keyhole. Jerrell's brother, after getting the news of Jerrell's unfortunate demise, wrote to "George Hudson," but sent the letter via the O&M train rather than through the local mail. The Pinkertons, who were also watching Jerrell's brother, located the letter and noted the destination.

A year earlier, Allan Pinkerton had enlisted R. J. "Dick" Winscott to be an informant for him. He set Winscott up as a barkeep in a saloon near the Rader House, the Reno Gang hangout in Seymour. Winscott was already friendly with the Reno brothers—he was a local boy, and he had seen action in the Civil War with John. The only known photograph of John Reno was taken by Winscott, at the behest of Allan Pinkerton, and it was taken in his saloon. The picture shows a small man, slightly hunched forward, perched on the edge of a chair with his legs crossed. He holds a glass mug of what is likely beer in both hands, which rest on his lap. His dark coat is buttoned right up to his chin, and a brimmed hat is pulled down on his head. There is something about the set of his mouth and the look in his dark, close-set eyes that suggests a kind of intolerance. Maybe his face was just registering impatience at having to sit and wait while the photograph was being taken.

When Allan Pinkerton heard that the three fugitive gang members were in a tiny town outside of Mattoon, he contacted Dick Winscott. Winscott had recently been elected Seymour city marshal, but that was a job with no real power. Winscott was deputized by Jackson County Sheriff John Scott to go to Mattoon, Illinois, and arrange for the arrest and return of Jerrell, Moore, and Sparks. This job appealed to Winscott, who had designs on John Scott's job and the office of county sheriff. He delivered a warrant for the arrest of the trio to the Coles County (Illinois) sheriff. The sheriff sent a posse with Winscott, who quickly located Moore and Jerrell in a tavern. Moore and Jerrell knew they were caught, so they didn't make a fuss. They also told Winscott that Sparks was working on a farm on the outskirts of town and pointed him in the right direction. When the posse approached the farm, Sparks recognized Winscott and took off on foot. The chase lasted for about a mile until Sparks fell in a ditch and was captured. The three prisoners were taken to the Coles County jail.

Winscott returned to Seymour without the men. The Coles County sheriff told Winscott the outlaws would not be delivered to Seymour until he received half of the reward money offered by the Adams Express Company for their arrest. Winscott contacted Pinkerton, who told him to withdraw one thousand dollars from the express company office in Seymour. Winscott returned to Coles County and handed the sheriff $750 (he presumably pocketed the rest), at which point the three prisoners were placed in Winscott's and deputy Ben McKinley's custody for extradition to Indiana.

On Friday morning, July 24, Winscott, McKinley, and their three prisoners boarded a train in Terre Haute, Indiana, for the journey to the county jail in Brownstown. They took the Jefferson & Indianapolis train south to Seymour. There they would catch the westbound O&M train that would take them on to Brownstown.

As the J&I train approached the Seymour station at 10:30 that night, Winscott, McKinney, and the three prisoners were nervous. They all knew what had happened five days earlier on the edge of town. Upon reaching the depot, they found that they had just missed the last westward-bound O&M train for the evening. Winscott knew there was no place in town where he could safely guard the prisoners overnight, so he rented a wagon and a team of horses from the livery adjacent to the station. The prisoners were ordered to get in the wagon bed and lie down and be still. Winscott then scattered several layers of hay over them.

Two mounted Pinkerton detectives joined the group, and they headed out of town along the Seymour-Brownstown road. They approached and then passed the gigantic beech tree with the spreading branches—already known as the Hanging Tree. It seemed all the more eerie under a sliver of moon blinking through the clouds on the hot Indiana night. Just when Winscott and McKinney thought they were clear of the terrible specter of a repeat of Monday night, hundreds of men appeared before the wagon, encircling it and the detectives.

A small group of masked men pulled Winscott and McKinney from the wagon and held them with the detectives. The wagon was driven back a couple hundred yards to the beech tree, and the prisoners, who hadn't dared breathe until then, were told to get up from the wagon bed.

An immense crowd circled the beech tree and the wagon and called for vengeance. *Hang them! Hang them! Hang them!* they shouted.

Perhaps John Moore felt particularly strange, for the hanging tree was but 150 yards from the house he grew up in on the edge of Seymour. He likely couldn't see the dwelling through the darkness of the Indiana night, but he knew it was there.

When Moore was told to remove his hat, he said he would meet his Maker with his hat on. Ropes were thrown over the "hanging limbs" and then fastened around the prisoners' necks. After the ropes were pulled taut, the driver urged the team of horses forward with a crack of a whip, and for the second time in a week, three men met a grisly fate, jerking at the end of their ropes. The crowd watched in silence until the bodies stopped moving, then the vigilantes began making their way back to Seymour.

The next morning, when the old German farmer discovered the latest set of limp bodies hanging from the beech tree, John Moore was still wearing his hat. The coroner arrived at about noon, cut down the bodies, and laid them on planks. He then declared they were hanged by the neck until dead by unknown person or persons. A train, chartered in Seymour, pulled nine carloads of "curiosity-seeking people" to the scene. They arrived at the Hangman's Tree—only two miles from Seymour's O&M railroad station—as if on an excursion train. There the passengers disembarked and gawked at the bodies.

Several days later, a letter was printed in the *New Albany Weekly Ledger*, signed by T. H. C. It was from Seymour and could have been written by Travis Carter, who many believed was the leader of the vigilance committee. It said, in part, "People at a distance must not condemn us; under the circumstances, others might have done even more."

Sparks and Jerrell were buried in Seymour, and Moore in a family burial plot on Chestnut Hill. Services for Moore were held upstairs in the Rader House before the burial. Ben Carter, son of Travis Carter and supposedly a member of the vigilance committee, came to view Moore in the Rader House. Nellie Jonas, Moore's sister, attacked Carter, pushing him down a flight of stairs. She also attacked Joseph Kling, a Seymour merchant, in his own store, claiming he was also a member of the vigilance committee that killed her brother. "You dirty Jew, you dirty Jew!" she screamed as he took refuge behind his counter. He yelled, "You are a hussy, and you should have been hanged with your brother!" She then tried to cut him with a knife but was dragged out of the store before she could do any damage.

Frank Sparks was about twenty-five when he died and according to the paper, "kept bad women at Rockford." He was buried at Seymour, with six hundred in attendance. "For three years he served in the 89th Indiana Infantry, and was a 'frequent deserter,'" wrote a local reporter. He was five feet four inches tall, had black hair, and a dark complexion.

CHAPTER EIGHTEEN

Will and Simeon Reno's Day in Court

BEFORE THE BODIES OF THE LATEST VICTIMS OF THE HANGMAN'S TREE were even laid in the ground, Pinkerton operatives caught Will and Simeon Reno in Indianapolis. The two brothers were arraigned before Judge Jewett on July 22 in Lexington, Indiana, at the Scott County courthouse. A week later the two Reno brothers, in the company of the Scott County sheriff and his deputy, arrived at the Floyd County jail in New Albany, Indiana. They had traveled by horseback all night, in a driving rain, to reach the relative safety of the stone fortress of the two-story New Albany lockup. Things had gotten way too hot in Lexington for the young robbers. New Albany was almost sixty miles from Seymour, a distance the sheriff hoped would discourage the Seymour Vigilance Committee from going after their prey.

Simeon and William were charged with participating in the Marshfield Robbery, where $96,000 had been nabbed from the Adams Express car while the locomotive was stopped and taking on water. The Renos were arraigned in Lexington because it was the county seat of Scott County, where the robbery took place. Judge Jewett set bail at $63,000—apiece—an outrageous sum that the Reno brothers could not pay. They were remanded to the Scott County jail to await trial by the Scott County Circuit Court.

The jail in Lexington was built of brick but was very flimsy. The fear was twofold—that the brothers could escape, or that the vigilance committee would be able to easily apprehend the Renos and lynch them. Laura Amanda Reno, sister of the Reno brothers, fearful for her brothers' lives, said her family would pay the expenses of housing them back in the jail in New Albany if the court would okay the move. The Scott County sheriff was more than happy to get the Renos out of his county, because he had been receiving threats from the Seymour Vigilance Committee and he knew they were poised to act.

All of southern Indiana was in an uproar over the robberies and the hangings. Threat of attack by the Seymour Vigilance Committee was taken very seriously, putting tremendous pressure on local lawmakers to keep the Renos safe so that justice could be served. Adams Express didn't want them lynched either—at least until they had disclosed what happened to the stolen money. Even Lyle Levi, a Reno confederate and notorious counterfeiter, sent threats to the O&M railroad saying he would switch off all the trains going in and out of Osgood (thirty-five miles east of Seymour) if "any of his friends the Renos are hanged by vigilantes."

Sheriff Fullenlove of Floyd County took custody of the Reno brothers after the all-night ride from Lexington. He then told the brothers of the most recent lynchings at Hangman's Crossing. Both of the Renos were unnerved by the news. William became defiant while "Simeon shook with fear."

The preliminary hearing for William and Simeon Reno was held on the following day, meaning the brothers had to turn right around and travel the thirty miles back to Lexington. Fullenlove decided to move his prisoners by steamboat on the Ohio River. They landed fifty miles upriver at Madison, Indiana, and then had to travel another eighteen miles to Lexington. The Scott County Sheriff William Wilson and five heavily armed deputies met the Renos at the landing in Madison and decided to move them under cover of darkness, thinking it would be safer. They headed out for Lexington at 7:00 p.m., which meant they'd arrive in the early morning.

Once Sheriff Wilson knew the Renos would be tried in the Scott County courthouse, he appealed to Governor Baker for more arms for use during the court hearings and trials. The governor, also fearful of another violent outburst by the public, sent forty rifles and his Adjutant General Mansfield down to Lexington to help preserve the peace. A reporter from the *Cincinnati Times* remarked on the company of "old veterans" guarding the jail. "The moment I saw the men tramping up and down, I knew that they were former soldiers, accustomed to obeying orders at all hazards," wrote the reporter. "No matter what their private feelings were, they would protect the prisoners under all circumstances."

The Scott County courthouse was full for the Reno brothers' hearings. Judge Jewett had found it inadvisable to search the spectators before they entered the courtroom and many were believed to be carrying concealed knives, pistols, razors, and other deadly weapons. It was feared that if the Renos didn't plead guilty to the charges, the courtroom rabble would grab the robbers and do their worst.

The crowd of mostly men sat cheek to jowl in the sweltering, stifling Scott County courtroom. The ripe smell from the spectators filled the air as many sat on the benches with their coats on so as not to call attention to the weaponry they carried.

"After sitting there about half an hour, a considerable stir was visible in the yard: a moment more and a squad of ten men, with guns at their shoulders, came marching in," wrote the reporter, who had snagged a good seat in the front row of the courtroom. The squad surrounded William and Simeon Reno as they entered. The young robbers were dressed in black and wore broad-brim plantation hats. Both were clean-shaven. "Sim is the older, being 28 years of age, and is far from being a bad looking person; he has a very full and large gray eyes and a Websterian forehead; his compressed lips and finely chiseled nose would mark him as a man of great determination and will," wrote the reporter. "Bill, the younger brother, is only about 20 years of age but while a youth in appearance is a giant in action. He is a man who would never swerve at anything—thin, spare made, he is the beau ideal of a desperate man and this is saying much, when it is told that he was never arrested before on any charge."

The bailiff called *Hear ye, hear ye!* and everyone settled down. The first affidavit was read stating that Samuel A. Jones, under oath, did solemnly swear that William and Simeon Reno had participated in the express robbery at Marshfield on May 22, 1868.

How do you plead? asked the judge.

The crowd leaned in to hear the answer.

The Reno brothers pleaded *Not guilty*, in "clear, firm voices."

At that moment a number of "rough-looking men" surged toward the prisoners. The judge banged his gavel on his desk, ordering the sheriff to clear the aisles.

Everyone sit down! he thundered. As a tense quiet filled the court-house, the prosecutor read a warrant signed by Allan Pinkerton, charging the two Reno brothers with conspiracy to commit a felony on May 22 and naming Frank Reno, Charles Anderson, Albert Perkins, and Charles Spencer as their accomplices.

How do you plead? asked Jewett.

Not guilty, your honor, answered the Reno brothers.

With this, the audience burst into an uproar, men leaping up from their benches and heading toward the table where the Reno brothers sat. The sheriff and his deputies pushed against the crowd while the militia-men shouldered their guns and encircled the Renos to protect them from the vigilante justice that would have surely rained down on them had the court not been prepared.

Judge Jewett bellowed *Get those men out of here!* as he banged his gavel so hard that those watching feared it would split the desk.

The wedge of militiamen with the Reno brothers at their center cleaved the crowd, kicking and punching anyone who didn't move fast enough. They managed to enter the back passage leading to the side entrance to the courthouse. The sheriff slammed the door behind the militiamen and stood in front of it, blocking the way, as angry men yelled and sputtered and otherwise vented their frustration.

The reporter from Cincinnati was allowed into the Scott County jail, where he crossed paths with Laura Amanda Reno. "As the family have now a national reputation, a short description of her might not prove uninteresting," he wrote. "She is of rather medium size finely molded form . . . hair quite dark, and short ringlets all over her head. She is in fact as handsome a girl of seventeen as I ever saw and has a look of the most intellectual character." The reporter heard her say to her brothers, "Be cheerful boys; if all the world deserts you there is still one left who will stand by you, at all hazards—your sister." As she left the jail, the crowd peppered her with insults. She yelled back, "Can you blame me, a sister, for standing by my brothers?"

Judge Jewett let the reporter interview the Renos in jail. The reporter reassured the two young men that the danger of being hanged by vigilantes that day had passed—"each of the brothers gave vent to their relief in words showing how great had been their suspense and fear." The Renos also talked about the trips going back and forth between Lexington and New Albany, expressing their fear that every time they came near a stretch of woods, an unruly group of armed men would emerge and string them to the nearest tree.

On August 4 William and Simeon Reno were once again sent back to New Albany, where it was hoped the fortress-like county jail would prevent vigilante action. The Renos did the reverse of the trip that brought them to Lexington the last time—horseback to Madison, then steamboat to New Albany—this time in the company of the militiamen sent by Governor Baker.

The August 5 issue of the *New Albany Daily Ledger* carelessly reported that the Reno brothers "will be taken to Scott County on September 7 for trial."

On Saturday evening, September 5, about forty men boarded a train in Seymour. The train was running dark—no lights, blinds drawn, no unnecessary noises. After a twenty-five-mile trip, the locomotive slowed and finally stopped at the depot in Vienna, Indiana. While a handful of men stayed with the train to detain anyone from town who got too curious about what was happening, most of the band split into small groups and headed into the village. It was after midnight, and the day had slipped to Sunday.

The men were dressed in their now recognizable vigilante garb: coats turned inside-out, and red flannel cloths that hung down in front of their faces with holes cut for eyes and mouths. Some coats had numbers chalked on their backs; the number one designated the leader. The groups headed to houses that had been handpicked for their purposes. The vigilantes burst in, rousing the families that lived there, herding them into one room, and then threatening them with violence if they didn't cooperate. They wanted to "borrow" the family horses and wagons for a couple of hours. A vigilante stayed with each family to keep them quiet while another held a pistol to the head of the man of the house, encouraging him to get dressed and then hitch the horses to the wagon as quickly as possible. The vigilantes piled into the half-dozen commandeered wagons, and the owners drove them—at gunpoint—toward the town of Lexington, about eight miles away.

The Seymour Vigilance Committee had a plan. A well-thought-out plan. And they believed they had the element of surprise on their side.

Lexington was dark when the vigilantes arrived. No lights burned in windows. No one was on the streets. There wasn't a hint that the committee had been found out. The men driving the wagons pulled the horses to a stop outside the brick jail. Number One motioned for several men to join him in waking up the jailer, Mr. Amos, who lived nearby.

Amos, woken out of a sound sleep, was terrified at the bizarre sight of the men with the scarlet cloths flapping over their faces.

Give us the keys to the jail, said Number One as several men held pistols pointed at Amos's head.

I know who you want and they're not there, said Amos. *Don't hurt me! I'm telling you, they're not there! There's no one in the jail!*

We know the trial starts tomorrow so give us the goddamn keys, said the leader. One of the men pulled back the hammer on his pistol to drive home the point. Number One slapped Amos hard across the face.

Now terrified, Amos got out of bed, took a ring of keys from a nail by the front door, and, still in his bedclothes and bare feet, walked next door to the jail. The three-dozen vigilantes waiting by the jailhouse door were quiet but menacing—most of them carrying pistols, knives, or clubs. A few men held knot torches, and in the flickering light the vigilantes looked like demons from a nightmare. Someone, in anticipation of the main event, had already thrown a rope up and over the limb of a large tree that stood near the jail.

Although his hands were shaking so much he had a tough time fitting the key into the lock on the jailhouse door, Amos finally pushed the door open. Several men shoved him aside and charged into the jail. They ran from cell to cell, thrusting torches forward to light the insides of the metal boxes. Nothing, nothing, nothing. Amos was telling the truth. No one was there.

What does this mean? demanded the leader. *We know they got trial tomorrow.* Amos whimpered and looked pathetic. Number One knew he didn't know anything.

The vigilantes got back in the wagons, which scattered in different directions. Number One had given explicit instructions to each driver. He ordered wagons to block the entrances to town and sent one wagon toward Madison in case the Reno boys and their captors were coming in from the east. He told each driver to be back at the depot in Vienna by 6:00 a.m.

The wagons reported back to the Vienna train station in the morning. No one had seen a thing. Either the September 7 trial date was deliberately false information given to the New Albany paper, or there was a change of plans and no one bothered to tell the vigilance committee.

This just fanned the fire that already burned within the vigilantes. They waited at the railroad station until the westbound morning train came in. A couple of the vigilantes had already silenced the telegrapher, holding guns on him to prevent him from sending messages from the station. The rest of the vigilantes stormed through the passenger cars, looking for the robbers who they already knew would not be aboard. Terrified riders huddled together to avoid attracting attention as the vigilantes began to rampage, yelling and throwing bags and parcels on the floors of the cars before leaving the train. Several vigilantes ripped the telegraph wires from the poles and damaged the telegraph receiver before getting back on their own train, which was waiting on a nearby siding.

It seems that the hearing in Lexington never took place because of Allan Pinkerton. The detective had caught Frank Reno and Charlie Anderson in Canada about a week earlier and was waiting for extradition papers to the states. In the meantime, Pinkerton advised Adams Express to try the four robbers together, thereby saving the expense of two trials. Judge Jerrett in Scott County agreed, although he might have been thinking that two trials could cause twice the chaos in Lexington. William and Simeon's necks were spared . . . that night.

Local papers reported mass hysteria in Vienna and Lexington after the vigilantes' midnight visits to their towns. "Nearly all normal business activity was suspended as immense crowds poured in from outlying districts, excited and curious to learn the details," wrote one reporter. Laura Amanda Reno was in Lexington on Monday and Tuesday waiting for the trial that was not to be. Supposedly, when she heard about the attack she was horrified and infuriated and shrieked, "If they touch my brothers, God will punish them!"

Chapter Nineteen

Extradition from Canada

Allan Pinkerton and a small cadre of handpicked detectives were sent to Canada to chase after Frank Reno and Charlie Anderson. The outlaws knew they were coming and were not concerned. Blending in with the other riffraff working out of saloons and bars along the waterfront, Reno and Anderson decided they liked Windsor and planned to stay for a while.

The Adams Express Company, meanwhile, was frantic to get its money back. They had lost a couple hundred thousand dollars to the Reno Gang over the past two years and were in danger of losing more than the money: the trust of their clients was imperiled. The company encouraged the Pinkertons to work the case hard. At that point, the detectives knew the outlaws were in Canada but didn't know exactly where.

They caught a lucky break in August during a raid with the Toronto police working the case of Morton and Thompson, two fugitive train robbers who had held up a Hudson River railroad train near Garrison, New York, also in May of 1868. They'd made off with $11,000 from the Union Express Company safe. Morton and Thompson were "known to have been consorting with the Renos," and it's likely that the Pinkertons learned of the Reno hideout at that time.

Pat O'Neil, one of the Pinkerton detectives shadowing Frank Reno and Charlie Anderson in Canada, described how he then arrested the Indiana outlaws in a saloon in Windsor. O'Neil said that when he entered the waterfront saloon, one of the Garrity Gang smashed him in the face with a pool cue. Others quickly joined in, kicking and punching

O'Neil, who managed to stay on his feet and found himself fighting off the attackers with his back against the door. He was rescued when the Windsor police chief and a local judge pushed through the door and into the saloon. Jack Friday, the man who struck O'Neil with the pool cue, saw the police chief and dived through the closed back door, taking its panels with him.

Jack Friday was a pal of the Renos. In fact, the Renos were his paying customers. Friday owned a carriage and often drove the American outlaws about town.

"Mollie Matches and the Garrity gang put up another job at Manning's saloon to do away with me," remembered O'Neil, who went back to the saloon still looking for the Renos. At that point, the saloon owner interfered and told everyone to leave O'Neil alone. He told the riffraff that if anything happened to O'Neil, Mr. Pinkerton would never let any of them rest until he ran all of them down. Mollie Matches and the Garrity Gang agreed to stand down.

O'Neil finally caught up with and arrested Frank Reno and Charlie Anderson in that same saloon. O'Neil wired to Allan Pinkerton for extradition papers. Pinkerton, as the representative of the Adams Express Company, got in touch with U.S. Secretary of State William H. Seward.

In his letter to Seward dated August 2, 1868, Allan Pinkerton first described the Marshfield robbery, where the Reno Gang made off with $96,000, then wrote, "A part of the gang concerned in that high handed outrage escaped to Canada where they are residing. We have the evidence clear and conclusive against them and they are the most lawless and desperate characters in the Section of Indiana."

He further described the train robbery, which included throwing the messenger, Mr. Harkin, off the train while it was going at least twenty miles per hour and "taking possession of the treasures contained in the safe." Then he told of the assault on poor "George Fletcher the Engineer of the train who was beaten with clubs and the engine taken away from him." Pinkerton wrote, "I believe that all these charges of assault with intent to kill and also the Robbery come within the treaty. I send this by the Bearer and hope it will be in your power to issue the President's requisition on the Governor General of Canada, for the parties named, at the earliest possible moment."

And so the stage was set for the battle for the extradition of members of the Reno Gang from Canada. What followed were months of misinterpretation, almost daily cables, diplomatic runaround, and ultimately failure on the part of the U.S. government to follow through on a promise it made to the British government.

Just a year earlier, Great Britain and Canada had ironed out the terms of the British North America Act, which passed the British Parliament in February 1867. In March, Queen Victoria issued a royal proclamation reading, "We do ordain, declare, and command that on and after the First day of July, One Thousand Eight Hundred and Sixty-seven, the Provinces of Canada, Nova Scotia, and New Brunswick, shall form and be One Dominion, under the name of Canada."

This brought all of Canada (except Prince Edward Island and Newfoundland—they would sign on later) into a confederation. However, the confederation—or the new dominion of Canada—did not have control over all aspects of government. Great Britain maintained responsibility for foreign policy and military protection of Canada. As a dominion, Canada was essentially a self-governing colony of Great Britain. This meant that requests for extradition from Canada also had to be cleared by the Crown.

On August 6, 1868, in response to Pinkerton's cable to Seward, Acting Secretary of State William Hunter wrote to Edward Thornton, minister to the United States from Canada, requesting that "Her Majesty's authorities will, in compliance with existing treaty stipulations, cause the necessary warrant to be issued for the arrest and delivery of the above named fugitives into the custody of either of the following named persons: Allan Pinkerton, Frank Warren or L. C. Weir, or to such other person or persons as may be duly authorized to receive them in order that they may be brought back to the United States for trial." The next day Thornton replied to Hunter saying the warrant would be issued and Governor-General Viscount Monck would be informed.

The Webster-Ashburton Treaty between the United States and Great Britain governed, among other things, extradition between the United States and British North America. The treaty was originally written in 1842 to resolve border disputes (including conflicts between lumberjacks along the Maine, Quebec, and New Brunswick borders known as the Aroostook War).

Article 10 of the Webster-Ashburton Treaty identified seven crimes subject to extradition: "murder, or assault with intent to commit murder, or piracy, or arson, or robbery, or forgery, or the utterance of forged paper." It did not include slave revolt or mutiny—already a sticky topic in 1842 as the United States headed toward a national conflict in which slavery played a central role. Additionally, the United States did not press for the return or extradition of an estimated 12,000 fugitive slaves who had reached Canada.

It was under Article 10 of the Webster-Ashburton Treaty that Pinkerton, and then Hunter, made their case for extradition to the Canadian government. The Scott County Grand Jury (Marshfield was in Scott County) in Indiana returned three indictments against the Reno Gang on August 6 and issued warrants for their arrest. Bail was set at $60,000.

Two days later, on August 8, Frank Reno and Charles Anderson were arrested in Windsor. On August 12, the *New Albany Weekly Ledger* printed, "If Reno is extradited, the last male member of this family of villains will be safe for some years to come. Anderson, who was arrested with Reno, is a noted English burglar, and has figured in some of the boldest burglaries in the States." Two days later, an article in the *Louisville Journal* stated, "Of the two, Anderson is the sharpest, and is regarded by the detectives as one of the shrewdest and most efficient burglars and robbers in the country."

During this time, Allan Pinkerton also decided to pick a fight with Jason B. Brown, a Seymour attorney, who would later be elected to two terms in the Indiana Senate and then serve as Secretary of the Wyoming Territory from 1873 to 1875. Brown was hired by the Adams Express Company to prosecute the Reno Gang for the first train robbery in December of 1866. John Reno, Sim Reno, and Frank Sparks all made bail and, because Brown and the Adams Express Company were not ready to prosecute the case when it came on the docket of the circuit court, Brown requested and was granted a continuance.

In August of 1868, Pinkerton was furious that two years had passed since the Reno Gang made bail for that first train robbery. Since then these same people had committed a number of robberies. Pinkerton accused the lawyer, in essence, of defending the Renos, which infuriated Brown and prompted him to write a response in the local paper, ". . . in no case have I been counsel for the Renos. . . . not that I don't have the right to defend the Renos, or anyone else charged with crime, whenever I see fit to do so."

Because Brown was the prosecutor in the first train robbery, the Adams Express Company asked if he would represent the company in the second robbery as well. When Brown told them what he would charge, the company balked. Although Brown was technically correct—he never did defend the Renos—he did defend the accused robbers of the second express company holdup, Michael Colleran and Walker Hammond, who were more than likely mixed up with the Reno Gang. As their lawyer, Brown suggested the young men plead guilty because of the whispered threat of lynching. Brown was ultimately involved in all four train robbery cases, as the prosecutor for Adams Express Company three times and once as a defense attorney.

While Frank Reno was waiting for extradition from Canada, his mother, Julia Ann Reno, died on August 28, 1868. In her will, witnessed by Dr. J. R. Monroe and his daughter Julia, the Reno matriarch left her daughter Laura Amanda Reno the piano and the sewing machine, and all of her real estate. "To have and hold said Real Estate to the said Laura A. Reno during the term of her natural life, without any control over, or interference with the same by her husband, if she should marry . . . if [she] should die without any heirs the issue of her own body the said Real Estate goes in equal portions to my Sons, who are now living, or their children if any of them are deceased." Then she gave all of her personal property to her son Clinton Reno—the only Reno brother never to be involved with the Reno Gang—except for the "Said Machine and Piano."

In a strange turn of events, a short dispatch in the *New Albany Daily Ledger* published on September 15, 1868, said, "Allan Pinkerton and

L. C. Weir, two detectives, who have been in Canada watching the case, were arraigned on Saturday at the insistence of the Reno brothers for perjury. They were released on $400 bail." Attorneys for John Reno and Charlie Anderson claimed that Pinkerton and Weir lied on the stand.

Attorneys for Reno and Anderson worked every angle possible and obtained a writ of *habeas corpus* on the grounds that train robbery was not an extraditable crime. While Pinkerton and the Adams Express Company fumed, the writ was argued in the Canadian courts and would not be resolved until early October. Eventually, the Chief Justice of the Dominion ruled that the prisoners were eligible for extradition under the Webster-Ashburton Treaty between the United States and England.

On September 16, 1868, Mr. C. A. Seward (Secretary of State William Seward's nephew) of the Adams Express Company wrote both a formal and an informal letter to William Hunter, assistant secretary of state of the United States. The subtext in his formal request was to ask Hunter to speed up the process because the Adams Express Company had lost a great deal of money in the robberies and was anxious to have it returned to them and their clients. He also requested that additional agents be assigned to bring the criminals back across the border. In his informal letter he further explained this last request.

"The two in Canada [Reno and Anderson] were examined before a magistrate, under threats on the part of their friends to assassinate Allan Pinkerton, who is conducting the case on behalf of the Express Co. [Pinkerton] appealed to me by telegraph to request the Department to authorize Gen. Averill of Montreal to protect him. A telegram received from Pinkerton yesterday, advised us that the protection was promptly acourse [sic] took the somewhat forceable [sic] appearance of a Gunboat. So far it is all right. After the case had been submitted to the examiner, his son was offered $6,000 if he would persuade his father to liberate the prisoners. This clenched the nail against the prisoners & the justice yesterday decided to hold them. . . ."

The circus around extradition of the two Reno Gang members now included a gunboat and an attempted bribe of a Canadian judge.

The State Department acted immediately. On September 16, Secretary of State William H. Seward signed a letter on behalf of President

Andrew Johnson to authorize the extradition of Frank Reno and Charles Anderson to the State of Indiana and to surrender them to the proper authorities.

Almost a month later—after elections in Indiana in which Conrad Baker was elected governor, John Scott was re-elected sheriff of Jackson County, and Robert M. Weir was re-elected prosecuting attorney of the Jackson circuit judge—William H. Seward received a letter from Thomas M. Pomeroy, an attorney for Adams Express Company connected with the extradition. Pomeroy indicated he didn't want to gum up the works but was very concerned about what Frank Reno and Charlie Anderson might be walking into. He worried that "summary execution of the parties arrested in Indiana was the work of a regularly organized 'vigilance committee' rather than of a mob."

He thought the governor of Indiana should move the venue outside of Jackson County to avoid potential violence against Reno and Anderson. He also suggested that, "It might be well also instead of having the parties surrendered to Pinkerton or any of his detectives that the Governor should designate some suitable person or persons in whom he had entire confidence to receive them."

In a telegram sent to Seward two days prior, Pomeroy wrote, "I have personal connection with Extradition of Reno and Anderson and cannot therefore answer positively. I apprehend however that the same public indignation which caused the Execution of their accomplices would endanger their safety in Indiana." Pomeroy knew that Reno and Anderson's lives were in danger if they were to be extradited to Indiana.

On October 13, Reno and Anderson were moved from the Windsor jail to the jail at Sandwich, Canada, a neighboring town, to await extradition.

C. A. Seward of the Adams Express Company sent a telegram on October 14 to the assistant secretary of state (his cousin and William H. Seward's son) and asked him not to change the U.S. agents who had been "Appointed to receive Express Robbers in Canada until you hear from the Company, which will be tomorrow."

That same day William H. Seward sent a telegram to Conrad Baker, the governor of Indiana, saying, "Apprehensions prevail of mob violence to Reno & Anderson when delivered in Canada and brought into Indiana. Please answer by telegraph whether proper care will be taken." Seward wanted an assurance that the lives of the gang members would not be endangered by sending them back to Indiana.

Governor Baker replied immediately, stating, "If informed in advance when Reno & Anderson will be delivered I will see that they are properly escorted to Scott County and delivered to the local authorities of that County. *I have no authority and no military force or means to guard them after they are thus delivered* [italics added]. This duty divorces on the local authorities & I can only use my influence to see it properly performed. I am not entirely free from apprehension that an attempt may be made to take them from the jail by violence after they're delivered. Cannot their delivery in this state be delayed until I can communicate with the local authorities of Scott County and make arrangements?" Even the governor of Indiana was worried that Reno and Anderson could not be protected once they reached the state.

While diplomats and judges were determining whether the Reno Gang members could be extradited, Reno and Anderson were not passively waiting in jail. On October 15, Pinkerton and the judge from Windsor were summoned to the jail in Sandwich where Reno and Anderson had been behind bars for two days.

What they found shocked them. There was a hole—six feet long by fourteen inches wide—in the flooring of the jail. The prisoners would have escaped in a short time if the police had not discovered it. It seems that the jailor, who was not in favor of the extradition (and who likely was influenced by sums of money changing hands), had permitted people from the United States, identifying themselves as detectives, "with other thieves and prostitutes" to visit the prisoners at will. Reno and Anderson were immediately clapped in irons.

Later, on that same day, an attempt was made to assassinate Allan Pinkerton. On his return to Windsor with the judge, their coach was passed by a speeding carriage. Pinkerton saw a man in the other vehicle pointing a pistol at him, which he then lowered when he saw he was being watched.

Hours later Pinkerton noted that the same man was following him around Windsor. At noon, Pinkerton took the ferry for Detroit and when he landed the same man stepped off the boat beside him and placed a revolver to his head. Pinkerton grappled with the would-be assassin and threw him to the ground, and Pinkerton operative L. C. Weir—who was there to meet his boss—rushed over to assist. Once in police custody the man gave his name as George Johnson and stated that he did not aim to kill Pinkerton. Johnson was sent to jail to await extradition back to Canada and held for a $20,000 bail. Not long after the event, Pinkerton was furious when he found out that Johnson had escaped that same day. When Pinkerton demanded to know what happened, a deputy sheriff told him that Johnson had escaped from a buggy that was taking him on a tour of the city.

Ambassador Edward Thornton wrote to Secretary of State Seward on October 16: "I received last night from Lord Monck a telegram in answer to mine of the morning and to the effect that no warrant should be issued until he hears from him. In the meantime, you will see from the morning papers that Reno and Anderson have been trying an attempt to escape from prison, and that two attempts have been made to shoot M. Pinkerton. It would therefore be very desirable that preparations should be made for the reception of the prisoners as soon as possible. Believe me, Very truly yours, Edw. Thornton."

The general superintendent for the Adams Express wrote to William Seward a few days later saying that Governor Baker of Indiana had changed the venue to Floyd County. He suggested the criminals be taken to New Albany via Cincinnati by river or by some secret route. A day later Thornton told Seward that Lord Monck gave the go-ahead but said that the extradition request needed to go to Ottawa for final approval, which could take up to a week.

Finally, after months of negotiation and with the assurance of the federal government and President Andrew Johnson that gang members would be delivered safely to Indiana, and then with further assurances from Governor Baker of Indiana that the local authorities had been informed and would guarantee their safety until legal proceedings against them could occur, Frank Reno and Charlie Anderson were placed in irons and taken from the Sandwich jail by Allan Pinkerton and his detectives. The gang members were to be delivered to Sheriff Fullenlove and placed in the fortress-like New Albany jail, about sixty miles south of Seymour.

In 1951, James Horan and Howard Swigget combed through the Pinkerton detective agency files and published a book about their more famous cases. The first section in *The Pinkerton Story* was devoted to the Reno Gang. Dates and details are wrong—whether they were written into the agency case files this way or misremembered by a descendant is unclear.

In their retelling of the extradition story, Horan and Swigget wrote that Frank Reno, Albert Perkins, and Charles Spencer were transferred from Canada to Indiana, while in reality it was Frank Reno and Charlie Anderson. They also wrote that the day of extradition was October 7, 1868, which would have been impossible, because the governments of Canada, Great Britain, and the United States were still negotiating the terms until late October. However, some details, while questionable, are too interesting and perhaps too fanciful not to include.

They wrote that when extradition was approved, Allan Pinkerton wired to his son William at the head office in Chicago to send a seagoing tug to Windsor. Captain Patrick Foley, head of the Patrol Service of Pinkerton's Chicago office, and John Curtin, later to become a famous San Francisco detective, were in charge of the craft.

The prisoners, in irons, were led down to the dock by Allan Pinkerton, his detectives who had been working the case in Windsor, and Windsor police, who "undoubtedly heaved a big sigh of relief when the American detectives said good-by."

The detectives, who were all heavily armed, sat in the cabin with their prisoners, smoking and chatting. Suddenly the tugboat gave several sharp warning whistles, then swerved to one side. As Pinkerton and his men leaped to their feet, the bow of a steamer sliced the boat in two. Miraculously, neither the detectives nor the outlaws were injured. Weighed down by their irons and handcuffs, the Indiana robbers were helpless in the water, but "Pinkerton, Curtin, and Foley desperately clung to their floundering, gasping charges, as the rammed tug sank like a stone."

The steamer, its bow crumpled but still watertight, swung around, and the detectives and bandits were taken aboard. The steamer limped back to Detroit, where a large posse of Pinkerton detectives and Detroit police met the six dripping men. Although the tug incident came on the heels of the numerous threats made by the underworld at Windsor, William Pinkerton claimed the ramming of the tug was nothing more than a strange coincidence. He called it "an accident caused by a mistake in signals."

Finally, by late October, five months after fleeing to Canada, Frank Reno and Charlie Anderson were on their way back to Indiana to stand trial. They would be taken to the Floyd County jail in New Albany, where they'd join the other Reno brothers, Sim and William. They were likely relieved to end up in New Albany, where the lockup resembled a two-story stone fortress. Less than two months later, on a bitterly cold December night, they would have some unwelcome midnight visitors.

CHAPTER TWENTY

Cutting Off the Head of the Snake

BRING A ROPE, ORDERED THE LEADER TO TWO MEN STANDING ON THE balcony. They went to Frank Reno's cell first.

Henry Clark, who was in the New Albany jail for murdering a man in Salem, witnessed the whole affair and gave an interview filled with disturbing details several days later.

At first Frank said nothing, according to Clark. Then he heard the words, "Frank Reno, No. 24," and then, "pull him out." Reno must have resisted some, because he then cried, "For God's sake, gentlemen, what are you going to do?" They told him to dry up and tied his hands.

Clark, who had to stand close to the metal grate on the front of his door on the second floor of the cell block in order to see, said that a couple of the vigilantes grabbed Frank by the throat and pushed him along. As they got to the top of the stairs, Frank clutched at the banisters but made no noise. They threw him over the balcony railing so that he dangled just above the cold stone floor of the large jail.

"He died very hard," said Clark.

After hanging Frank, they went to No. 7, a double cell housing both Simeon and William Reno. As the vigilantes opened the door, someone spoke up and said, "What do you want here?" Then, said Clark, "I heard something fall, and afterward heard that one of them had been knocked down by Simeon, who had seized the sink lid to defend himself. I then heard the fall of another body as they rushed into the cell. Simeon had been knocked down. I heard him groan. Then they pulled him out by his feet and carried him round and hung him. I heard him make no noise."

Next was William, who they took downstairs, and Clark saw them put a rope around his neck. "An order was given for 3 and 5," said Clark. "Every man seemed to be called by a number instead of by name. They were told to go up and catch the rope. William said, 'I am innocent gentlemen, never done the robbing—Oh, Lord protect my father and sister!' Two men pulled him up—William struggled very hard."

When Anderson was taken out of his cell, he asked for time to pray, but was told to "shut his mouth and that they did not want anything out of him." They strung him up, but the rope broke. It was tied again and he was again pulled up.

Anderson didn't have it so easy. When the rope broke, he crumpled to the floor. He moaned while a vigilante on the first floor fastened another noose around his neck, then threw the end up to his compatriots looking over the balcony railing. Anderson didn't have the luxury of a quick death; his body was hauled up and left dangling as it was tied off on the balcony.

All the members of the vigilance committee gathered on the first floor, and, in the murky darkness of the cavernous room lit by only a few lanterns, they looked up and watched as the bodies of Frank, Simeon, William Reno, and Charlie Anderson swung slowly, the ropes twisting and untwisting. The vigilantes stared in silence and didn't even wait for them all to die.

One by one the vigilantes left the darkness of the old jail and walked slowly back through the dark, frozen streets of New Albany to their waiting railroad car. The leader brought along County Commissioner Perrette, who was in his nightshirt and boots, telling him he could fetch the doctor for Sheriff Fullenlove as soon as the train left. Vigilantes who had been standing guard on street corners, ready to sound the alarm if anyone in the dark town awoke and took notice of them, joined the silent parade. At the train station, the leader told the engineer, who had been under guard with the telegrapher, to fire up the engine. He warned the terrified telegrapher and the county commissioner not to say a word until the train had left the station. He didn't tell the telegrapher that they had already pulled down the wires leading out of town.

Before boarding the two railroad cars, the leader put his hand into his pocket and took out the ring of keys, handing them to Perrette. "Here, these belong to Floyd County," he said before getting on the train. The locomotive hauling its mystery guests left the station and slowly headed in the direction of Jeffersonville.

No one seems to know how the vigilantes got back to Seymour. They abandoned their train about five miles outside of New Albany and scattered in every direction. They must have made plans ahead of time for this evacuation—maybe there were horses and wagons waiting in the dark to pick them up. It was a good plan, for within minutes of their leaving the New Albany station, a posse was already forming in New Albany to go after the vigilance committee.

This was the final major act of the Jackson County Vigilance Committee, a group of men that arose in response to the Reno brothers and their gang's stranglehold on their town of Seymour, Indiana. There would be smaller menaces in the upcoming years resulting in warnings and beatings, but the hanging in the New Albany jail was their masterpiece.

The Reno Gang thugs had terrorized Seymour for years. The vigilance committee took care of the problem by cutting off the head of the snake. The hanging of the four members of the outfit—including the three Reno brothers—in the New Albany jail in 1868 brought the number of Reno Gang members hanged by the committee during the previous eighteen months to ten men.

The news of the lynchings spread like wildfire. A thousand rumors were afloat, plunging the little city of New Albany into pandemonium. Thousands arrived by early morning and milled about the scene of the catastrophe. Curiosity seekers jammed the area around the jail, pushing up against its metal fence hoping to get a glimpse of something ghastly. Policemen had to fight a passage through the milling thousands for Coroner Sinex, who arrived and impaneled a coroner's jury of twelve. The men filed into the death chamber and witnessed the cutting down of the Reno brothers and Anderson. U.S. Army Chaplain Lozier helped the coroner place the bodies on the stone floor of the main part of the jail for the coroner's inquest. The three Reno brothers, arranged side by side, were about the same height; Anderson was stretched at their feet. The victims all wore plaid shirts and denim pants. None of them had on socks or shoes. None of them wore underclothing. Frank's and Simeon's faces were clotted with blood, while Anderson's and William's complexions were described as pallid. William had a hideously swollen, purplish neck.

Dr. Anderson Lee of New Albany examined the corpses one by one. Frank had died of a broken neck, he declared, while William Reno and Charles Anderson had suffered strangulation. Simeon Reno's face, inhumanly distorted, was thrown back, revealing his raw, chafed throat. The doctor bent over him and exclaimed, "The rope did not even compress his jugular! He must have lived for at least a half an hour!" The jury was horrified.

The other prisoners held in the jail, who had all been removed from their cells and were being contained under guard in the courthouse across the street, were called in for questioning one by one. Each had snippets of information to tell, based on what they witnessed or heard through the grates on the front of their cell doors, compounding the hideousness of the event.

The crowd outside had grown even larger. They pushed and pushed against the cast-iron fence, and the sheriff's department, jail guards, and deputies were having a terrible time keeping the throng out of the yard. Even reporters, who could usually push or sweet-talk their way into any situation, were being kept from the jailhouse.

Afraid the crowd was going to storm the jail and create uncontrolled chaos, the coroner's jury decided the bodies should be moved across the street into the courthouse so that people could catch a glimpse of the lynched robbers. That, after all, was what they were clamoring for. Coffins were brought into the cell block and the bodies dumped inside. The coffins were carried through the crowd, which reluctantly parted, and taken into the courthouse lobby, where they were set upon the floor.

Thousands filed into the courthouse to satisfy their curiosity.

"This is the God-awfullest thing I ever seen," wept one old woman. "I cain't stand it."

Frank was the only one of the Renos who was married. His wife, Sarah, was the daughter of Dr. John L. Ford, a well-known citizen of Seymour and former member of the state legislature from Jackson County. "She is represented as a most estimable lady," wrote the reporter for the *New Albany Daily Ledger.*

Sarah Reno came to the impromptu viewing with her daughter Appelina in her arms. "The little baby screamed with fright at the pushing mobs." Mrs. Charles Anderson and her child were right behind Sarah Reno. The two young women were led by two big officers, who elbowed their way through the crowd. The women had been living in New Albany for the past couple of months pending the trial of their husbands, "which," said one reporter, "had been moved up unexpectedly by the masked men from Mules Crossing."

Jargo Nethliz, reporter for the *Indianapolis Journal,* was in town to cover a convention. The convention was quickly cancelled because of the disaster, so Nethliz grabbed a front-row seat near the dead men. As the wives approached the bodies, "the scene that meets these ladies is beyond description," he wrote. "Their screams and moanings are heard above all the din and clamor of the people."

Laura Amanda Reno, the Renos' sister, joined the wives at ten o'clock. She came from the Catholic school she had been attending in Louisville. "Terrible was the sight of her three brothers stretched out in death," opined the reporter. "There in the Floyd County Courthouse, almost before the very seat of justice lay the mutilated victims of mob law.

"Her agony could not be translated into words. She uttered a violent shriek, covering William's drawn face with her tearstained handkerchief. Desperately she turned to those about and swore an oath of vengeance on the Seymour lynchers. 'The blood of this innocent boy is on all your heads!' she cried," wrote Nethliz. Apparently she called on God to punish the men from Seymour in so terrible a manner that none of the newspapers reporting on the lynchings would print it.

William, the youngest of the Reno brothers, was Laura Amanda's favorite. Reporters made much of her pitiful screams as she bent over him. She flung herself repeatedly over his corpse, screaming: "Oh, my brother! My baby, baby brother!"

The *Nashville Union and American* and many other newspapers around the country picked up the wild story in the *New Albany Companion*. It was lurid with details about the wives' and Laura Amanda's reactions to the sight of the bodies. They shrieked and wailed and tears gushed "like rain, bursting from overflowing fountains." The women moaned, "then followed that quiet, almost stolid look, a sort of blank, purposeless agony, that tells that hearts are breaking."

The vigilance committee demanded anonymity. Although one of the newspapers reported that the leader of the vigilantes was a large man who wore a diamond on his pinky, no one would identify who that might be. And if there was a large man who at one time wore a diamond pinky ring, after the New Albany hangings, no diamonds were seen on men's hands, at least in public.

Later that month, a *New York Times* reporter trying to get to the bottom of the story wrote, "[M]any people know by this time . . . who the leading Regulators are (especially in Seymour, where everybody is familiar with everything connected with the wretched Vigilance Committee business, but where strangers, upon inquiry about it, are regularly met by shrugs and the invariable reply 'We don't know anything about it')."

On Monday morning, December 14, 1868, the train from Jeffersonville brought the bodies of the Reno brothers back to Seymour. Charlie Anderson had been interred in New Albany in a secret location in hopes that grave robbers and medical students wouldn't find his grave. All three of the Reno brothers had been placed in one pine box. At the Seymour depot, friends of the Renos took charge of the overly large coffin. At the funeral (it's not clear where the funeral was held), the Seymour correspondent for the *Indianapolis Journal*, likely Dr. J. R. Monroe, wrote: "The attendance was quite large, and among other persons, a resident of Seymour, whose name we have forgotten, dropped in. He had scarcely made his appearance, before Miss Reno rose from her seat, and walking across the room fiercely told him that that was no place for him, that she recognized in him one of the murderers of her brother, and if he did not leave immediately it would be the worse for him. The fellow slunk out of the house like a whipped cur, frightened almost to death. Unless a great mistake has been made in the estimation of Laura Reno's character, the Jackson County Regulators will find that the oath of revenge she took over the dead body of Will Reno, was no mere empty threat, to be forgotten in an hour, but a promise of terrible meaning."

On Tuesday, after a sermon by the pastor of the Methodist Episcopal Church, the bodies were interred in the cemetery north of town. Fearful of grave robbing, headstones were not placed on the gravesite, but rather, were put at another location in what is now known as the old City Cemetery.

"I may mention another story which circulated here on Saturday of last week, and on Monday of this, and it is given for just what it is worth," wrote the *Indianapolis Journal* reporter. "It is to this effect, that some time since the thieves held a convention at Fort Wayne, and resolved, that if the Reno brothers were hung, Seymour would be laid in ashes. There are also stories afloat of threats having been made by persons in this vicinity, but as to the truth of the stories I cannot vouch. The people here do not seem to be alarmed."

After the burial of the Reno brothers, the newspapers grabbed hold of the story about the Adams Express money. Where was it? The *New Albany Daily Ledger* wrote that only Frank Reno knew where the money was, and that when Laura Amanda came to visit him a couple of days before he was lynched, she asked about its whereabouts. He reportedly answered that, "if he could not live to enjoy it, no one else should."

One of the New Albany newspapers wrote, under the title "Absurdities" that "Madame Ross, a well-known astrologist of Cincinnati, was consulted a few weeks ago by superstitious persons as to the hiding place, and described a piece of ground so nearly like the bluff bank southeast of Lafayette Junction, that some gentlemen visited the spot and made an examination. A new tea kettle, answering the description of one bought by Reno at a country store, was found buried near the spot indicated, but it was empty, and had probably been stolen from the Junction Hotel by some boys who were roasting tender-loins and boiling pig's feet behind the bluff a few days before."

Many thousands of dollars had been spent on the legal defense of Frank Reno while he was in Canada. The Reno family had also spent a great deal of money, having hired extra guards for the New Albany jail in the attempt to keep the brothers alive while they were incarcerated there. If the family hadn't been using the Marshfield money for the defense of the brothers, then they didn't know where it was. It's also possible that the Marshfield robbers handed off the money to an accomplice and never saw it again.

"We suspect, therefore, that it will require a wiser seer than Madame Ross to discover the whereabouts of the $90,000," wrote the *New Albany Daily Ledger*. "Indeed, if that amiable lady knew where it was hidden, she would be most likely to go and get it, instead of confiding the secret to a 'superstitious person.'"

Several days after the murders of the three Reno boys and Charlie Anderson in the New Albany jail, a broadside nailed to buildings in Seymour appeared. It read:

To the People of the United States
Salus Populi Suprema Lex
Headquarters Southern Indiana, Vigilance Committee

Whereas it became necessary for this organization to meet [sic] out summary punishment to the leaders of the thieves, robbers, murderers and desperadoes, who, for many years, defied law and order, and threatened the lives and property of honest citizens of this portion of Indiana, and as the late fearful tragedy at New Albany testifies that justice is slow, but sure, we promulgate this, our prounciamento, for they who need not justifying to the world, and particularly to the people of the State of Indiana, any future action which we may take. We deeply deplore the necessity which called our organization into existence; but the laws of our State are so defective that, as they now stand on the statute book, they all favor criminals going unwept [sic] of justice; a retrospective view will show that in this respect we speak only the truth.

Having first lopped off the branches, and finally uprooted the tree of evil which was in our midst, in defiance of us and our laws, we beg to be allowed to rest here and be not forced again to take the law into our own hands. We are very loath to shed blood again and will not do so unless compelled in defence [sic] of our lives.

A Warning

We are well aware that at the present time, a combination of the few remaining thieves, their friends and sympathizers, have been formed against us, and have threatened all kinds of vengeance against persons whom they suppose to belong to this organization. They threaten assassination in every form, and that they will commit arson in such ways as will defy legal detection. The carrying out in whole, or in part, of each or any of these designs, is the only thing that will again cause us to rise in our own defence [sic]. The following named persons are solemnly warned, that their designs and opinions are known, and that they cannot, unknown to us, make a move toward retaliation.

Wilk. Reno, Clinton Reno, Trick. Reno, James Greer, Stephen Greer, Fee. Johnson, Chris. Price, Harvey Needham, Meade Fislar, Mart. Lowe, Roland Lee, William Sparks, Jesse Thompson, William Hare, William Biggers, James Fislar, Pollard Able.

If the above named individuals desire to remain in our midst, to pursue honest callings, and otherwise conduct themselves as law-abiding citizens, we will protect them always. If, however, they commence their devilish designs against us, our property, or any good citizen of this district, we will rise but once more. Do not trifle with us, for if you do we will follow you to the bitter end, and give you a "short shrift and a hempen collar." As to this, our actions in the past will be a guarantee for our conduct in the future.

We trust this will have a good effect. We repeat, we are very loth again to take life, and hope we shall never more be necessitated to take the law into our own hands.

By Order of the Committee
Dec. 21, 1868

The newspapers had a field day with the Seymour Vigilance Committee's final lynching. Many used the term Judge Lynch for the extra-legal system. A reporter for the *Cincinnati Gazette* wrote, "Judge Lynch is without a court, sentences without a trial, and hangs without benefit of clergy." Members of the vigilance committee were referred to as "murderers," and the lynching was a "lawless procedure disgraceful to the State."

"Indiana is deeply disgraced by this act," opined one out-of-state newspaper. "Which ranks the State with Kentucky in barbarism, only Kentucky does not pretend to be civilized."

Most newspapers saw it for what it really was—a deep failure of the legal system, at least in this part of Indiana. For years the people of Seymour had tried to rid itself of the Reno Gang. The legal systems that were supposed to protect and look out for the greater good were in place. There were sheriffs, marshals, lawyers, judges, and juries. It had stabilizing institutions like churches and schools and social clubs. All of these institutions were supposed to protect against the kind of lawlessness brought on by the Renos.

The judges and lawyers and juries of Seymour and Brownstown would not convict the Reno brothers and throw them in jail. No matter what the bail (until the high amount set for the Marshfield robbery), the Renos could pay. Proceeds from burglaries and robberies funded bails and sometimes went to line the pockets of weak jurists, witnesses, railmen, and lawmen. Everyone had a price, and the Renos were not shy about trying to buy their way into and then out of situations. If money didn't work, the Renos were not afraid to use force, cultivating a culture of fear around them. Witnesses disappeared or were gunned down. Many of the Reno Gang stayed in Rockford, where saloons, gaming houses, and whorehouses were the only thriving businesses. But the Reno brothers themselves liked to come into town and invade the saloons near the depot. They liked to be where the action was. They wanted to watch the trains come in bringing strangers—and money—to the little town.

No one could have foreseen the impact the Civil War would have on this band of brothers. Prior to the war, they were annoying petty thieves, and eventually the local legal system could have taken care of the problem. However, during the war, if John Reno's autobiography is anywhere near accurate, the Reno brothers met and were attracted to characters like themselves—young men who preferred outlaw behavior. Men who deserted. Men who made money by bounty jumping. Men whose moral compass was permanently knocked askew by the chaos of killing and disease and death surrounding them. Men who could never go back to life on the farm, or in the small town, and be content.

The Reno brothers surrounded themselves with their Civil War pals. They provided these men, who might otherwise be drifters, with a place to live and work. Although many were minor thieves and cutthroats, at the core were a number of trained safecrackers and safeblowers, and some of the best counterfeiters and shovers in the business. The Reno brothers were the leaders, the brains of the operation. Then there was the brawn. Men who liked being on the edges. Men who would do as they were told using brute force.

The amount of actual money that went through the hands of the Reno Gang from county treasury and Adams Express robberies numbered in the hundreds of thousands. The amount of counterfeit money—the best boodle in the business—could have been in the millions.

The Reno Gang members were the spiders at the center of a five-hundred-mile web of crime.

Chapter Twenty-One

Fallout from the New Albany Hangings

THE LYNCHINGS OF CHARLIE ANDERSON AND RENO BROTHERS FRANK, William, and Simeon in the New Albany jail on December 6, 1868, caused a diplomatic kerfuffle on an international scale. An editorial in the *Boston Evening Post* of Massachusetts hit the nail on the head. "The lynching will seriously embarrass the cabinets in Washington and London, and will complicate negotiations already pending. Seward gave the British Ambassador every assurance that the United States would do 'its whole duty.' Thornton bluntly replied that we had already failed to do our duty, and could not see what might be our duty now that we had already violated our national pledge. Mr. Seward evidently has another nice diplomatic question to settle before he retires from the Department of State."

The editor of the *Indianapolis Journal* took umbrage with the impertinence of the *Boston Post*'s assumptions and wrote: "A government is not responsible for a trial that a mob makes impossible. The blame lies upon the New Albany community. Every precaution was taken—a strong jail and a strong guard were ready until apprehension died away. A guard was kept outside to arouse the populace. At least eighty were in the mob, and they could have overcome many more guards than Mr. Whitten. A small army would have been needed. Twenty men could never have stopped the Seymour lynchers. England's assumption that they can supervise our law-enforcement agencies is impertinent. England surrendered her jurisdiction to Canada; she cannot follow here. [British diplomat Edward] Thornton's implications are ridiculous and preposterous, and an insult to our country. No government's pledge can add force to the assurance of fair trial for accused persons. That is to be understood by the very fact of its existence."

Secretary of State William Seward had promised safe delivery of the Renos to the Indiana authorities who were to try them. This is what was stated in the presidential warrant for their extradition. The horrified Canadian authorities believed they had been misled and deceived. Frank Reno and Charlie Anderson had never been arraigned in Scott County. In essence, the Canadians believed the gang members were still under federal custody when they were lynched in the New Albany jail.

William Seward understood the sticky situation the United States was in with Britain. He sent a note to British diplomat Edward Thornton that read, in part, "In view of the recent shocking and indefensible proceedings at New Albany, Indiana, I think it not improper to give you herewith a copy of a Bill which has been recently introduced into the Senate of the United States."

Within five days of the lynching, U.S. Senator Lyman Trumbull from Illinois introduced the bill in the third session of the 40th Congress. On March 3, 1869, President Grant officially endorsed the bill after it had passed both the Senate and the House. Entitled "An Act to Further Provide for Giving Effect to Treaty Stipulations Between This and Foreign Governments for the Extradition of Criminals," the bill consisted of three parts. Part one stated that the president's responsibility is to protect all such accused persons against "lawless violence" until the trial and for a "reasonable time thereafter." The president can use land, naval, or militia forces if necessary. Part two provides that those who take custody of extradited persons be accorded the status of U.S. marshal and that this shall be recognized in every district through which they pass. Part three states that any person who obstructs a marshal, rescues a prisoner, or attacks a jailor is to be fined and jailed.

The British government was appeased by the passage of the law and no more was said about the matter.

The *Indianapolis Journal* ran a piece about this law under the title "A Law to Punish Lynch Law."

Wilkinson Reno and Laura Amanda Reno went to Indianapolis to visit Governor Baker on Christmas Eve in 1868, asking for protection from the lynch mob.

Two more things came out of the lynching of the Reno brothers in December 1868. The people of Seymour scared themselves—their citizens had taken power into their own hands and meted out justice when they felt frustrated by the broken legal system. Now the stain of vigilante violence was forever stamped on their community. Seymour could now be used as the morality tale told to children about what happens when people lose control. The second outcome was that the people of Seymour and Jackson County decided they weren't going to talk about what happened. It was as if collective amnesia spread across the land. The names of the members of the Seymour Vigilance Committee, aka The Scarlet Mask Society, aka the Jackson County Regulators, would never be revealed. The citizens closed the circle, and if one of them was found guilty of lynching, they were all guilty.

To most people in Jackson County, and particularly in Seymour, the end did justify the means. Over the course of six months they had rid themselves of a gang that had such a grip on their livelihoods and, many felt, their lives. Should members of the Reno Gang have been brought to justice through the court system? Absolutely. But the citizens of Seymour believed the court system was broken and corrupted by the very people they were trying to prosecute. They felt caught and, to them, there was only one way out.

CHAPTER TWENTY-TWO

Dr. Monroe Moves On

DR. J. R. MONROE, THE VOCIFEROUS SPOKESMAN FOR MORALITY IN SEY-mour, Indiana, because of the sale of his newspaper in March of 1868, was quieted during the last year of the Reno Gang and the Seymour Vigilance Committee's reign of terror. His voice peeked through the editorial scrim in some of the regional papers, but the loss of his direct voice was felt. His sarcastic, caustic, pointed observations of the events swirling around him—whether about discussions in the city council over when and where to build a bridge across the White River or the rampant lawlessness pressing in on the heart of the community—could not be duplicated. His silence during this period was deafening.

In July 1869 Monroe again assumed the editorial mantle at the *Seymour Times*. The paper hadn't been published since April of that year, probably because the former editor had too much to handle, trying to edit and print several Seymour papers at the same time. After selling the paper a year earlier, Monroe left town for several months. When he returned, "with no intention of renewing the *Times*," he found "the want of a Republican paper here so manifest—the want of a paper that dares to have some opinions in regard to the local questions agitating the people of the county, and that has the will and the ability to do battle for the interests of Seymour and its mechanics, laborers and business men, is so plain that we have to yield to the general and pressing demands of the people to revive the *Times*."

It wasn't until several years later that Monroe even brought up the Reno affair. The *Indianapolis Journal* printed a story about the Ku Klux

Klan in Kentucky and took a jab at Seymour and the lynching of the Reno Gang. Monroe took the bait, and his response is worth quoting at length:

"The grand juries of Jackson county had become accustomed to the farce of indicting the members of the Reno gang, and when the time for their trial came, the Democratic Sheriff of Jackson county invariably packed a jury of Democrats, who gave the Renos the benefit of the reasonable doubt, and acquitted them. The result was the Renos were growing rich, their attorney was thriving on fat fees, the Democratic Sheriffs were enabled to accumulate handsome fortunes, the Democratic juries were well paid for the time consumed in trying the cases, while the Democratic majority waxed larger and larger every year. Meanwhile, the respectable Democrats and Republicans were leaving the county, the price of real estate was declining, and a general state of lawlessness pervaded the county, encouraged, backed and defended by the Democratic politicians. The laws were annulled. The robbers had seized upon and suborned the instruments and ministers of justice, the jury box the Sheriff, the bar of the county were controlled by them. This was borne for years, until in a moment of wrathful indignation the better people determined to band themselves together, and measure strength with the villains. They made quick and thorough work, and the result is known. If lynch law was ever right, it was right in that case . . ."

That he was wrong about a fundamental fact—several of the Renos were outspoken Republicans, which he surely knew—didn't stop Editor Monroe from taking the opportunity to rail against the Democrats.

Sometime in the mid-1870s, Jasper Monroe made the leap from outspoken critic-at-large (but particularly of Democrats) to bona fide freethinker. He published a book of poems and plays, creative writings that seemed to be the catalyst for his change. God no longer had a capital G in his paper. Organized religion was mocked. There were lots of small items—jokes, really—throughout the paper that were akin to "a priest, a minister, and a rabbi walk into a bar . . ." Nothing was sacred. Literally. Soon the reading public knew he didn't believe in heaven. They knew he didn't believe in hell. And it seems odd that in this midwestern town in the third-quarter of the nineteenth century Editor Monroe's words were tolerated.

For a centennial issue published on George Washington's birthday in 1876, the paper was full of profiles of the town's movers and shakers. Seymour was just a couple of decades old, but it was prospering and the town fathers were ready to be lauded. Once Seymour got rid of its gang problem, it settled into being the quintessential small city in the heartland of America. A place worth celebrating.

Perhaps because Monroe felt awkward about profiling himself, the editor of the *Brownstown Banner* sent in a lengthy biography of Monroe, which took up several columns of the paper, at least twice as much as the other profiles. Early on in the piece the editor wrote: "Dr. Monroe was taught to read by his mother and while yet a child he read the bible through and aloud at her knee, believing every word of it then, as he says, though we are sorry to say he rejects its divine origin now, and seems to regard it as a blundering and contradictory history of doubtful authenticity, or a 'cunningly devised fable.' In this the writer sees nothing to commend except the Doctor's boldness and candor and evident sincerity, which the writer freely concedes."

Eventually Dr. Monroe went too far. By 1880, the *Seymour Times* had morphed into a paper with the subtitle "A Paper with Few Principles." The fancy, engraved masthead said "Justice, Mercy, Truth, Forbearance," illustrated with an engraving of a women handing a baby to a man under the heading "Our Trinity." To the left of that was a drawing of a sour-looking preacher pointing to devils leaping through hellfire. The words "Theology at Work" were printed above it, and the phrases "The Darkness of Superstition" and "The Dead Past" to the side. To the right sat an engraving of a woman feeding the poor with the words "Humanity at Work" above it and the phrases "The Light of Reason" and "The Living Present" to the side. The date of the paper was May 1, 1880, but read "Saturday, May 1, 104. J. R. Monroe, M.D., Proprietor, A Weekly with few Wants."

At this point Dr. Monroe had rejected what he calls the "christian" calendar.

Within two years Monroe packed up his steam-operated printing press and relocated to Indianapolis with his wife, Mary, and five children. He took the paper with him, renaming it the *Iron-Clad Age*, a paper by and for freethinkers. He wrote about politics and women's equality, and the bonds of marriage and free love. His wit and sarcasm were as sharp as a fish knife, and he had over seven thousand subscribers from around the world. When he died in 1891 at the age of sixty-eight, letters and tributes poured into the weekly paper and covered its pages for months. Robert Green Ingersoll, the country's best-known freethinker and the first Attorney General of the State of Illinois, gave an oration at Monroe's funeral. The *Iron-Clad Age* outlived Monroe and would continue to be edited and published by his children.

Monroe—Whig, Know-Nothing, American Party, Republican, and finally freethinker—helped define for the people of Seymour what it meant to live in a community. When seemingly unstoppable forces threatened the young town, Monroe took a very vocal stand. He knew he was poking a hornet's nest as he railed week after week about robberies and murders and justice, justice, justice. Where was it? Who was going to make it happen?

The good doctor certainly printed the broadsides for the Seymour Vigilance Committee, because at that point he had the only printing press in town. Based on the phrasing, and the liberal use of commas, he also likely wrote the announcements. Whether he was involved in any of the lynchings or stayed behind the scenes almost doesn't matter. He hated bullies and went after them with his most powerful instrument, his writing. To him, surely, the end justified the means.

CHAPTER TWENTY-THREE

John Reno—Last Man Standing

IT TOOK JOHN RENO TEN YEARS AND TWO MONTHS TO FINALLY BUY HIS way out of the Jefferson City penitentiary in Missouri. It was 1878, and by this time both his parents were dead as were three of his brothers. In his autobiography he wrote: "These awful tidings came very near to dethroning my reason, but I was kept so hard at work that it may have saved me, although my mind was not with my hands. On this subject [the lynchings of his brothers] I have been as brief as possible, for however great my sins have been against society, my feelings are as sensitive as those of the least guilty."

The prison years were hard. Reno described escape attempts—once by digging under the wall, and the other by stuffing himself in a pork barrel—that were both thwarted by "treacherous" guards. He spent his days working in the quarry, where he learned the craft of stone masonry. He spent his nights writing letters to prison officials and the governor begging for his sentence to be reduced from twenty-five years to ten.

The autobiography is an interesting look at prison life in the mid-nineteenth century. Reno was in an institution run by a private company, and, as a policy, spent no more money than they had to. At one point, the management changed and the conditions went from bad to worse. "[T]hey began to economize in the way of supplies—such as clothing and food—and got it down so fine that they fed the men on nine and ¾ cents each per day! They also enlarged the tasks in some of the shops, making extra work for everyone, and this finally got so bad it brought on a revolt."

One day at dinner, fifteen or twenty prisoners took the lead and raised above their heads large knives they had secretly made in the blacksmith shop. They said they would not return to work until they had better food to eat and more of it. The leaders of the revolt posted prisoners at the doors so the guards couldn't get out, and soon the revolt became a riot

"I never heard such yells and screams," wrote Reno, "nor such a throwing of tin cups and tin pans, in all of my life. Everybody was completely demoralized. A herd of wild buffalo on the plains would have been easy to control compared with these men, numbering as they did about eleven hundred, cursing, shouting, throwing things round, and breaking up tables."

The warden and more guards came to the door, and the warden promising better food if the prisoners would return to their work places. "But in a few minutes the men from one of the shops came out in the yard halooing and cursing, and going to the engineer of the prison, told him to stop the engine in a hurry. Then they went from shop to shop, until all the work in the whole prison was brought to a stop. There were five or six hundred men running all around the yard, howling and yelling and swearing, 'More grub, or death!'"

The militia was called in and the prisoners barricaded themselves in the shops, threatening to burn the place to the ground. They hesitated attacking because, Reno reckoned, the contractors didn't have any insurance on the place.

This "grub riot" lasted for six full hours and ended with a conditional surrender—the prisoners would not be charged with anything, and they were also to receive more food during the day. Reno wrote that these terms were upheld.

John Reno, the hardened safe blower and express car robber, had another side to him that emerged in his autobiography. He was extremely kindhearted toward animals. While in prison he kept "pets." The first was a fledgling robin that stayed with him through the fall and winter and finally flew off in the spring. Next was Tommy, the opossum, which could never be tamed and so was "never a very agreeable pet." One night it took off and Reno suspected it became someone's dinner.

Next Reno stole three eggs from a nest of the warden's game chickens. He wrapped the eggs in flannel and snuck them into the sickroom, where there was a radiator, a regular source of heat. He hid them behind the radiator and then turned them faithfully every twelve hours "as he had seen an old hen do." On the nineteenth day he was rewarded with a chick! (The other two eggs didn't hatch.) Reno slept with the chick under his shirt to keep it warm, and then the half-grown chicken took to roosting on Reno's pillow at night. He trained it to defecate on the floor and not on his bed. He named the chicken Dick, but Dick grew up to be a hen. He mated her with a neighbor's rooster and in the next eighteen months raised over a hundred chickens. When he left prison, he left old Dick behind. "A young room-mate of mine became so attached to her that I did not want to separate them," Reno wrote, "for no one but he who has been there, knows what a comfort and pleasure the company of such a pet is to a man in prison."

His favorite pet was a baby squirrel he bought from a guard for half a dollar. As the squirrel grew, it would come and go freely, slipping through the grates, but it always came back to Reno. In his washstand drawer, Reno kept nuts that he fed one at a time to his pet. It became a game. When the squirrel had eaten his fill, he'd store the nuts under the bed covers, which Reno would then take out and place back in the drawer.

Soon the squirrel became too big to fit through the grating. Reno smuggled in a mallet and chisel from his stone mason job and cut a hole out of the stone step beneath the door so that the squirrel could come and go at will, "for I would not have a pet that I would have to confine in a cage or in a cell, for I knew what that was like for me. I thought too much of them to restrain them from their liberty."

One night the squirrel didn't come back from his day's wanderings. The following morning Reno found him drowned in a water barrel, where he had likely attempted to get a drink and fell in. Reno took the death hard. "No parent ever grieved for a little child much more than I did my dear pet," he wrote. "For months afterward, whenever I heard a little noise in my cell, I would at first think it was him."

The governor of Missouri finally pardoned John Reno after evidence of graft and wrongdoings at the executive level surfaced. So after serving ten years and two months—much of it at hard labor—Reno walked out of the Jefferson City prison in February 1878. He was promptly taken into custody by John Hazen and Larry Egan, the two detectives who had nabbed John Reno on the Seymour train platform many years earlier for the first train robbery. Reno had skipped bail on that first train job twelve years earlier. Detectives Hazen and Egan accompanied Reno to Brownstown, where he was under bond for the train job. While waiting for a train in St. Louis, Reno telegraphed his brother Clinton and his brother-in-law Elisha Goudy to bring money to the courthouse so he could post bond.

A *St. Louis Republican* reporter talked with the detectives and John Reno while they were waiting for their next train. The reporter was charmed by Reno. "The celebrated crook here opened a cigar box in which were two Bibles beautifully cut in stone and a pair of gaffs with which the game chickens which the owner had raised in the Penitentiary had been heeled," he wrote.

"'There is a man,' laughed Eagan, 'who came out of the "quay" with two bibles and a pair of spurs,' and nobody appreciated the joke more than the person at whom it was aimed." When the two detectives and Reno left for Indiana on the morning train, the reporter, who met them there, wrote, "Seen as a group it would be extremely difficult for a stranger to pick out the prisoner, who, dressed in a neatly fitting black coat and vest, gray pants, and dark hat looks far more like an honest commercial traveler or clerk than the notorious criminal which he is said to be. He is accorded perfect liberty of action, handcuffs or shackles being superfluous ornaments which the officers in charge do not deem it necessary to use. The prisoner, apparently, has not the slightest desire to escape, but is extremely anxious to again view the scenes of his boyhood."

John Reno had to wait in the Jackson County jail for three days for the judge to return from a convention before he could post an $18,000 bond for the Adams Express robbery. Within a year, Reno was acquitted of the robbery, and the case was never tried in a court.

When Reno left the Jackson County courthouse he wrote, "I stepped forth a free man, for the first time in ten years and two whole months.

The change was so delicious, yet so bewildering withal, that I have but an indistinct recollection of what I even said or did that day."

In an afterword to his autobiography, Reno spun the cautionary tale. He figured he'd lost at least $75,000 on cards over the years. In a funny aside he wrote, "An 'honest' gambler could not live in this climate, it is too cold. He might live in South America or some other tropical clime, where he could wear a linen duster the year around for clothes, and where he could get his grub by picking it off trees. But he would soon starve to death in Indiana."

He blamed his parents for his and his brothers' failings. The memories of the beatings with sumac switches were somehow still fresh after decades. "I am satisfied that their troubles had a great deal to do with demoralizing my brothers and myself; and believe that if they had lived together peaceably and not separated and squandered their properties, that the boys would have been living and been good citizens of society today."

Finally, he wrote that his friends were "filling felons' graves" or in prison. Or they'd squandered their ill-gotten gains. Andy McKay of Springfield, Illinois, once in possession of $200,000 gotten by burglary, was sent to prison in Cincinnati for want of $100. Long John Welsh, another high roller, was in prison. Jack Nelson, aka Tom Dunn, aka California Jack, "who wore ten thousand dollars' worth in diamonds," was in prison. Then there was his buddy counterfeiter Joe Rittenhouse, who made millions of dollars. Reno wrote that when Rittenhouse was finally released from Joliet prison, "he will be a pauper, with nothing for his thirty year's labor but gray hairs and a very ruined reputation."

Everybody had a John (or Jack, as he was sometimes called) Reno story after his release from prison. Someone writing to the *Indianapolis Journal* from Seymour, two weeks after his release, felt sorry for the man and described a more poignant scene. "There seems to be a decided feeling to 'give the young man a chance' to become a law-abiding citizen if he is acquitted of the charge for which he is under bail. John Reno is a man of mark-intelligence, is a pleasant talker, speaking in a low tone of voice, and always very earnestly, as if in the strictest confidence, and bears every appearance of being cool and deliberate. He served near three years in army, was a member of thirteenth Regiment Indiana volunteers and claims to have been the sixteenth man who enlisted from Indiana. His prison life has agreed with him, for he looks like the same Jack Reno of twelve years ago, when he used to figure among the boys at Alec Burke's and Fitz and Boney's saloon. He has been rather secluded since his return. He occasionally wanders about the streets, in the role of a Rip Van Winkle, and what a change since he left ten years ago, to fill a felon's cell. Upon his return he was bewildered in the streets of his native town; instead of the old fireside he found the homestead deserted; instead of the family circle, the marble monument over the graves of his father, mother and three brothers met his gaze. To see him talking to some of his schoolmates, and hear him recall incidents of boyhood days upon the playground, one would hardly take him to be a desperado of national reputation, and one of the most skillful safe-breakers in the United States."

Almost as an afterthought, the reporter quoted Reno as saying: "The charges pending against me cause me no anxiety, and I have no fears of being lynched, though Allan Pinkerton sent word to Missouri that the only way to try me was under a tree."

John Reno didn't play Rip Van Winkle for long. Just a week later the *Indianapolis Journal* reported on a telegram they'd received from someone in Seymour. It read, in part: "It is thought there is a conspiracy afloat to murder James Flanders, an engineer of the Kankakee Line. It will be remembered that Flanders took a very prominent part in the capture of the Reno boys in 1868, near Seymour, he being the engineer in charge when the train was attacked, and it being through Flanders's representation of a 'fat express' that the Renos were induced to fall into the trap prepared. Today a friend of Flanders made affidavit before Esquire Weaver that on the 8th of the present month, he being in a room over a saloon owned by John Reno's brother at Seymour, Indiana, heard John Reno say, 'I will give a thousand dollars if that son of a b----is put out of the way,' meaning Flanders. Then one Jack Semple said: 'You dare not give me the money.' Reno replied: 'I will put it up.' At the same time counting out one thousand dollars and placing it in a man's hand whom they called Font.

"The affiant's name is withheld, as giving it would endanger his life. Flanders says he has reason to believe there is one or two of the Seymour gang in the city watching him.

"Should any trouble occur, especially in the vicinity of Seymour, John Reno would be held responsible for it, and would probably suffer. The Jackson County Regulators, the organization which cleared out that part of the State ten years ago, has not yet been disbanded, and Mr. Reno and his new confederates will conserve their own interest and safety by pursuing a discreet course of conduct. Any efforts of theirs in the direction indicated in another part of the State, will be viewed with much the same disfavor as is expressed in Seymour."

John Reno. Up to his old tricks.

In August of 1880 John Reno married Sarah (Sadie/Sallie), his brother Frank's widow. "John and Mrs. Sade Reno matrimonied with success a few days ago," read the short piece in the *Seymour Times*. "They will lead an agricultural life on their farm near town." Some believe John married Sarah to keep her quiet because she knew too much about the family business. A wife could not testify against her husband in court.

But why did she marry him? Perhaps to get her hands on some of the Reno estate. She and her daughter, Apple, never received a cent from Frank Reno's estate after he was lynched in New Albany, although it was not for lack of trying.

The marriage between the two didn't endure. "John Reno, the 'queer shover' has been arrested and taken to Indianapolis on a charge of passing counterfeit money-bills on the Third National Bank of Cincinnati," read a news report in the *Brownstown Banner* in 1885. He got sentenced to three years in prison. When John was doing time in Michigan City on the counterfeiting charge, Sarah divorced him. Sarah, who was never able to tap into the brothers' ill-gotten fortunes, must have hated the Renos.

John Reno didn't change after being released from jail. He loved cock fighting and gambling as much as he ever did. He loved counterfeiting. He spent most of his days in his brother Clinton's saloon—a shack near the intersection of the train lines called the Hell Hole. "Honest" Clint had to pay one hundred dollars to the county court in 1880 for "keeping a gaming house." The year before John Reno died he was also charged with "keeping a gaming house." Dallas Tyler paid the twenty-five-dollar fine and kept John Reno out of jail.

John Reno died as he lived. On January 31, 1895, after an all-night poker game that was still going strong (although Reno was losing, according to one source), he proclaimed: "I will beat you, damn it! Or die doing it!" Reno keeled over headfirst onto the table. He was dead at the age of fifty-six. John Reno was buried in the old City Cemetery near his three brothers.

Chapter Twenty-Four

Allan Pinkerton Writes His Books

Bringing Frank Reno and Charlie Anderson back from Canada was just about the last on-the-ground investigative work of Allan Pinkerton, the great detective from Chicago. Although only in his late forties, Pinkerton suffered a stroke in 1869. Built of strong stuff, the detective taught himself how to walk again, which took almost two years, but his days of chasing counterfeiters and murderers were behind him. Pinkerton's two sons—Robert and William—took over many of their father's duties as the agency expanded and established offices in other cities around the country. But it was always clear (at least in his own mind) that the old man was in charge.

Just before his stroke, Allan Pinkerton suffered another loss. Kate Warne, the first female detective, died of pneumonia in January of 1869. Allan Pinkerton was at her side when she took her last breath. She's buried in the Pinkerton family plot in Chicago's Graceland Cemetery under the name "Kate Warn." Kate was cryptic and private to the end; it's said that even the Pinkertons didn't know her actual name. Her death was a real loss to Allan Pinkerton, who had hired her in the late 1850s. She proved to be an excellent operative and was involved in several high-profile cases. There were whispers that Pinkerton and Warne were romantically linked—the two frequently traveled together—and this could be the case, as the Pinkerton sons never hired another female detective.

In 1871 the Great Chicago Fire swept through the city and the Pinkerton Detective Agency lost all of its files—photographs of criminals, detailed reports written by operatives, and financial statements. So they started over. It's a shame that all of the Pinkerton reports about the Reno Gang were lost at that time.

After their success with hunting down members of the Reno Gang, Pinkerton operatives chased after many of the West's best-known desperados, including Butch Cassidy and the Sundance Kid, and Jesse James and his gang. They had a terrible time with Jesse James in particular. At one point operatives threw a bomb into the James' family house, killing Jesse's little brother and leaving his mother with one arm. Jesse James was not there at the time and went on to rob more banks and trains and to taunt the Pinkertons at every turn.

In the early 1870s a Pinkerton operative "embedded" himself with the Mollie Maguires in a coal-mining region in Pennsylvania. Historians continue to debate who the Mollie Maguires really were and what role they played in the anthracite coal region of Pennsylvania. The most powerful coal-mine owner in the area hired the Pinkertons to spy on the Mollies and other troublemakers in an attempt to bust the growing move toward workers' unions. One of Pinkerton's operatives, McParland, testified against the Mollies in a series of trials in the late 1870s, leading to the execution of dozens of Irish immigrants. This shifted the focus (and reputation) of the Pinkertons; they would now be viewed primarily as a security company, rather than a detective agency. Even the word Pinkerton morphed in meaning from hard-boiled detective to hard-nosed security guard protecting the property of the wealthy.

In the mid-1860s Allan Pinkerton bought 254 acres in Onarga, Illinois, a small prairie town 85 miles south of Chicago on the Illinois Central Railroad line. In 1873, while still struggling with partial paralysis from his stroke, Allan Pinkerton began work on Larch Farm (aka The Larches, aka The Villa). The main house was low-slung with a cupola on the roof and verandahs surrounding all four sides. There were eight rooms divided by a central hallway fifty feet long. Pinkerton brought an artist from Scotland to decorate the walls in the hallway with scenes from his life, including Civil War battles and a picture of Pinkerton surrounded by his Secret Service operatives.

The property was called Larch Farm or The Larches because Pinkerton had 85,000 larch trees imported from Scotland. They were planted—

six rows deep—around the perimeter of the estate. Massive flower beds lay along each side of the drive from the three entry gates to The Villa. Guards dressed in bright blue uniforms were posted at each gate. They warned visitors to slow their horses to a walk because Pinkerton did not want dust stirred up and settling on his flowers.

Constructed near The Villa were barns (Jumbo 1 and Jumbo 2 held "Indian" and Shetland ponies), outbuildings, a small lake, and a wine cellar (called the Snuggery). The Snuggery had large paintings on the walls celebrating heroic Scottish figures. A pet cemetery for Pinkerton's beloved Scotch terriers was at the edge of the lawn.

Accounts vary on how much time Pinkerton spent at Larch Farm. Some sources say he used it as a weekend retreat (one source called it a "Whoopee House") and entertained writers, artists, and wealthy industrialists at The Villa. Other sources vehemently deny the implication that the old man used this property as a weekend hideaway for shenanigans.

Timothy Webster, Pinkerton's operative hanged by the Confederates in Richmond, is buried on the grounds of Larch Farm. While his name is engraved on a memorial stone in Graceland Cemetery in Chicago, his body is actually interred at Pinkerton's beloved estate.

The old man spent the last fifteen years of his life writing books. Or, rather, he collaborated with ghostwriters to tell the stories of the exploits and successes of the Pinkerton Agency. It's presumed that much of this writing was done at Larch Farm. Pinkerton dictated his story to a collaborator, who then smoothed out the narrative and typed it up. Dozens of books came out under Allan Pinkerton's name. Much of what we think we know about the early Pinkerton cases comes from these books and from newspaper accounts of the day.

Allan Pinkerton died in 1884 and is buried between his wife and Kate Warne in the family plot in Graceland Cemetery in Chicago. The circumstances of his death are murky. Some say it was his heart. Others say he took a fall on the sidewalk and bit his tongue, which became gangrenous, and that's what killed him. Either way, the bulldog of a man at the center of the demise of the Reno Gang was no more.

Larch Farm—once a showplace in the 1870s and 1880s—quickly fell into disrepair. Allan Pinkerton's will stipulated that each of his sons take care of the country estate in successive seven-year terms. The Pinkerton boys were busy with their own lives—William running the Chicago bureau, and Robert in New York—and the elder Pinkerton's beloved Larch Farm was neglected. The buildings fell one by one. The last time anyone took note of the paintings in the Snuggery, they had been cut from their frames and rolled into a barrel that sat in the corner of the damp cellar. The property has variously served as tenant housing and an orchard, and today, 140 years after Allan Pinkerton sat by the cemetery and enjoyed the view of the lake, it's not much more than a ruin.

Chapter Twenty-Five

Seymour after the Reno Gang

ON A HOT SUMMER'S DAY IN 1869, TRAVIS CARTER'S PLANING MILL burned to the ground and took most of the new adjacent Christian Church with it. All that was left was one tool chest. Some said this wasn't an accidental fire—it started at noon—and under-the-breath comments suggested that perhaps it was set by someone loyal to the Renos. This was, after all, the supposed site of the vigilantes' courtroom. After the New Albany hangings various newspapers mentioned Travis Carter as the probable leader of the vigilantes. The description fit. He was a big man and he did own a diamond ring, which he never wore after the New Albany lynchings. Carter had no insurance on his massive building, but friends and neighbors helped him rebuild.

That same year, business in the little city seemed to be thriving. Seymour had "a woolen mill, three planing mills, six dry goods stores, two first-class hotels, six boarding houses, ten saloons, four drug stores, three tailors, three dressmakers, six carpenter and joiner contractors, two brickworks, two saddle and harness makers, two jewelers, three butchers, three cigar makers, one tombstone maker, eight physicians and surgeons, two justices of the peace, two barbers, a photograph gallery, a tannery, and two breweries."

The 1870s were prosperous years. The Seymour Manufacturing Company began making spokes, hubs, scythe snaths (handles), and grain cradles in 1872. Doctor Monroe built a handsome new home on Chestnut Street the following year.

Seymour, like all nineteenth-century cities, was never far from its agricultural roots. An article in the *Seymour Weekly Times* reported on "the buzzards holding high carnival over the mortal remains of a defunct porcine in the roaring branch west of Chestnut Street." Another hog incident was reported. This time a porker was killed by the "Jeff cars" in front of the Harvey House near the tracks. "When the hot sun came out on Sunday the air was filled with a perfume anything but delicate."

Laura Amanda Reno married Elijah Goudy in 1870, and they moved to Indianapolis. They had one daughter, Effie. Wilkinson Reno, the patriarch of the Reno clan, died in 1877, a year before John Reno was released from the Jefferson City penitentiary in Missouri. At some point, after John Reno came back to town, brother Clinton Reno moved west. It was reported that he went insane.

Six years after the lynchings at Hangman's Crossing, an article in the *Seymour Times* stated: "The celebrated beech tree upon which several persons were hung by unknown men some years ago burned down the other night. It had been a very strong and thrifty tree before it became famous. It had a large, stout body with numerous strong and heavy limbs jutting out low and at right angles with the trunk. The top was large and the foliage dense in summer. Numerous names had been cut upon it, including several of the supposed lynchers. It was cut and haggled a good deal, but its decay was so rapid as to be observable, and it became an easy prey to fire which some person in whose bosom perhaps it excited unpleasant emotions may have applied to its root."

Several years after the beech tree burned, an article in the *Seymour Democrat* claimed that a sister of the lynched John Moore had the tree girdled and then set on fire.

The dying beech tree, the very symbol of citizens run amok, had been obliterated. The site was not marked, and within generations Hangman's Crossing, per se, disappeared.

Other western train robbers would capture the public's imagination far more than the Renos ever did. Jesse James was good-looking, articulate, and an unrepentant Confederate guerilla. He corresponded with newspaper editors who, in turn, gave him a lot of ink. Butch Cassidy and the Sundance Kid were also charismatic figures about whom newspaper reporters spun romanticized tales. The one surviving photo of John Reno shows him to be anything but charismatic. Hunched over in his chair, a slouch hat pulled low, and a scowl on his face, Reno looks more like a barfly than the mastermind of a gang.

As we've seen, the Renos had a formidable opponent in Dr. J. R. Monroe. The newspaperman was able to rile up the community with his constant haranguing about anything—be it the Renos, politics, or, later, atheism and free thought. In his early days in Seymour, Monroe frequently wrote about the inadequacy of the legal and judicial system in rural Indiana. He often pointed out that those involved in the local legal system could not handle the pressures the Reno Gang exerted upon them through briberies, threats, and lawless behavior.

When the Reno Gang shifted their sights from the robbery of county treasuries to robbing express cars, they also incurred the wrath of Adams Express Company, who brought in Allan Pinkerton. Pinkerton and his operatives took on the Reno Gang and doggedly pursued them across four states and into Canada. In addition to Adams Express and their clients losing large sums of money from the express robberies, the extensive counterfeiting ring the Renos were part of wrought havoc on the regional banking system. Pinkerton, with a single-minded focus that became especially apparent when chasing Frank Reno and Charlie Anderson in Canada, persevered in his pursuit of the gang. Ultimately, the Renos could not win against Allan Pinkerton because he would not give up.

The railroad companies themselves suffered consequences of the Reno Gang's activities. Threats of robbery or some kind of violence against the railroads put a real dent in the train-riding public. Seymour was full of men whose livelihood rested with the two railroad companies that brought trains through the town several times a day. They worked at the depots hauling and loading freight, and on the trains as brakemen, firemen, and engineers. A team of mechanics worked in the massive roundhouse where the locomotives were stored and overhauled. If the railroads felt threatened, that could lead to fewer trains, and consequently, less available work for the men who lived in Seymour. No one wanted that.

All of these factors led to the rise of the vigilance committee, but Monroe was certainly the most visible and vocal critic of the gang. The *Seymour Times* called for vigilante action repeatedly. It was clear to Editor Monroe that if anything was going to be done about the rampaging Renos, it would have to be a local initiative. By casting the Renos as unrepentant amoral characters, who were taking advantage of a legal system they could easily bully and outmaneuver, Monroe was giving the community permission to take the law into their own hands.

Seymour . . . lying on the shortest route for all criminals to their destination.

We have no law in this place.

Let a vigilance committee be formed.

Vigilante justice was not unknown in the West. It was understood that lawmen couldn't do everything; that their jurisdictions were too large and there weren't enough of them.

Crimes are committed with impunity in our county.

Organize in self-defense.

As the work is at last begun . . . it will be continued until the country is rid of thieves and cut-throats.

And in the end, everyone who whispered and then acted on these thoughts put forth by Monroe was not wrong. For even though there was widespread condemnation of the hangings, no one was ever charged with the murders of the Reno Gang members. In spite of an international incident with Canada and Great Britain, the little community of Seymour would not betray its own. Members of the vigilance committee were neither literally nor figuratively unmasked. The town went about its business building bridges, fixing roads, and encouraging manufacturers to settle in the little city that exhibited what became known as solid midwestern family values.

Dr. Monroe died in 1891. A decade later, with the death of Travis Carter and the city perched on the front edge of the glorious twentieth century, all thoughts of the Reno Gang and the Seymour Vigilance Committee were pushed aside. The complicity of the citizens of the town in the most violent episode in the county's history—and a notable episode in the history of lynching in America—was all but forgotten.

Chapter Twenty-Six

And in the End

THE OLD BROWNSTOWN ROAD HEADS OUT OF TOWN AND SWINGS briefly south to cross Route 50, the new road to the county seat. Even if you squint hard and look beyond the weedy patches and the low-slung houses, it's tough to conjure up the old beech tree that stood on the edge of a German farmer's field.

Former Jackson County historian Charlotte Sellers wrote: "Today interest in the Reno Gang when not openly aflame always smolders just below the surface." One of the jail cells from the old New Albany jail—they think the one Charlie Anderson was incarcerated in—sits in the parking lot of the Seymour Visitor's Bureau. It's painted matte gray, and a piece of Plexiglas covers the grate opening in the heavy iron door. It's a small metal box, not much bigger than a couple of phone booths pushed together. What a visual reminder of the events that took place 150 years ago between 1866 and 1868.

The great roundhouse where the locomotives were repaired is gone, as are the railroad depots from the nineteenth century. Travis Carter's planing mill is gone, as is the woolen mill. The crossing of the railroad tracks—the reason for Seymour's very existence—is still there, but the hustle and bustle of freight being loaded and unloaded and passengers milling about train platforms are gone. The sounds of the saloons with the plink of piano music spilling out into hot Indiana nights are gone. There are no cockfights or horse races to bet on. The Agricultural Society's fairgrounds, where once prize-winning pies and dahlias were shown, and where Isaac Wilson witnessed a flogging, are gone.

The Reno homestead is gone.

Once a fairly common name in the area, there are now no Renos in Seymour.

After all these years, we still don't know who the members of the Seymour Vigilance Committee were.

Frank, William, and Simeon Reno are buried in the old City Cemetery in Seymour. It's not a quaint old burying ground with worn headstones leaning this way and that amid large trees. It's not even a particularly nice nineteenth-century graveyard. There are no rows or clusters of granite or marble headstones telling the truncated stories of entire families. Oddly, there are very few headstones at all in the cemetery. It's a desolate place. No one wanted to be buried with the Renos, at least in the nineteenth century, and many of those who had family members already interred moved them to the new Riverside Cemetery on the edge of town, where they would rest for eternity under cool trees, within sight of the river.

In 1930, not long before Sarah V. Ford Reno died at age eighty-six, she had the Reno brothers' headstones taken down and buried just above their caskets. When she herself was buried, her headstone read "Sarah V. F.," obliterating the Reno name from her personal history. Years later, no one even knew where the Renos were buried. There was a rumor that a student, while on a field trip in the early 1960s, sat somewhere on the one small knoll at the back of the City Cemetery, placed his hand down into the grass, and felt the coolness of a headstone. That appears not to have been investigated further.

In the early 1980s, Seymour's Chamber of Commerce decided to spruce up the town. They paid the Boy Scouts to clean up the City Cemetery on the corner of Ewing and Ninth Streets, noting its disgraceful appearance. The following year the Beautification Council of the Chamber supported the Jackson County Genealogical Society's efforts to clean up the cemetery. Local restaurants donated four hundred dollars to the cause. An iron fence was erected around a spot in the cemetery near Ewing Street, and although it wasn't where any of the Reno brothers were buried, it allowed the genealogical society to erect a small plaque noting that the Reno brothers slept there. A couple of days after the fence was put in place, the Fellowship of Jackson County Clergy, opposed to the veneration of the Reno Gang, sent a letter to the city council asking them not to "lift up as a tourist attraction something so unattractive as the Reno Brothers."

That same year, the director of the Jackson County Public Library in Seymour uncovered a tombstone in their collection. Apparently it came from the estate of Edwin J. Boley, who died in 1984. Boley was a high school history teacher and a Reno Gang aficionado. He compiled *The First Documented History of Jackson County, 1816–1976*, and *The Masked Halters* (the latter about the Reno Gang and the Seymour Vigilance Committee). Both books are compendiums of newspaper accounts. They are wonderful resources. The executor of Boley's estate said that for several years Boley displayed the tombstone (which was given to him by someone who knew he liked the Reno Gang) and conducted historical tours in his home.

"I think everybody in town knew he had that headstone in his house," Boley's executor told the newspaper. "I gave the stone to the library because I thought it could pursue and promote the history of Jackson County more so than a cemetery could."

The headstone, which reads "W. R. Renno," a common alternate spelling of Reno, likely once marked the remains of William Reno. The head of the cemetery commission—who also happened to be president of the historical society—said that he wanted that stone back and intimated that he would take legal action.

"The question is, do we have a legal obligation to give it back," the library director said. "The library has got no use for a tombstone. But we don't feel the appropriate response to these threats is to turn it over [to the cemetery commission]."

According to rumor, at some point the headstone was stored out of sight in the library director's bathroom.

The headstone did end up back in the cemetery, cemented into place within the fenced-off area dedicated to the Reno brothers.

But it seems that even long after their deaths, the Renos are still stirring up trouble. In 2009, that same headstone—W. R. Renno—was found among other stolen items during a vehicle search. Two fourteen-year-olds and one eighteen-year-old were picked up for the crimes. No one seemed to know how long it had been missing from the cemetery. The president of the Jackson County Cemetery Commission said, "It's a sad day when people do those things. There's more of it going on than you think."

An op-ed in the *Seymour Daily Tribune* said: "William Reno's stone was stolen from a fenced area at the cemetery that includes much newer markers for the Renos, all of whom are reportedly buried elsewhere in the cemetery. The brothers' graves over the years have been targets of vandalism because of infamy. Other graves, of course, are vandalized simply because they're there and stupid people do stupid things."

Nearly 150 years after the death of the Reno brothers at the hands of their neighbors, the relationship between the gang and the town is still fraught. It's curious, in a way. The Reno Gang rarely displayed the viciousness of the James Gang, yet a whole tourist industry has sprung up around the latter. Every moment of the James Gang's deadly Northfield Raid has been documented and written about—more than once. Seymour doesn't really know what to do with their infamous antecedents, so what they've come up with is a freestanding prison cell in the visitor bureau parking lot and a fenced-off area in a neglected cemetery. Even those who know their local history equivocate on whether or not the Reno Gang *really* committed the world's first robbery of a moving train. *There was that one in Kentucky* . . . they'll start to say, then trail off because the place where that robbery supposedly took place can't be found on a modern map. The fact itself seems to be as lost as the spot on a nineteenth-century map.

Like a boa constrictor, in the mid-nineteenth century the Reno Gang encircled the town and squeezed tighter and tighter for several years until the gang's activities seemed to threaten the very future of the community. It was then that the townspeople took matters into their own hands. Perhaps Seymour seems so ambivalent about examining this part of its origin story because the real crime is that none of the vigilance committee members was ever prosecuted for murder. Maybe, on some level, all of Seymour's community members feel complicit in a 150-year-old wave of violence that ended with ten men swinging on the ends of ropes.

Acknowledgments

THE NOTORIOUS RENO GANG BEGAN AS AN MFA THESIS IN CREATIVE nonfiction at Goucher College, where I received invaluable help and encouragement from my mentors Webster Younce, Jacob Levenson, Phillip Gerard, and Diana Hume George. I'd also like to thank classmates Kristina Gaddy, Neda Semeni, Memsy Price, Ginny McReynolds, and Jean Guerrero for their readings, writings, and friendship. Leslie Daniels, Amy Reading, and Jan Smith are my hometown posse of readers and writers and I've always valued their friendship and input.

Marian Van Loan, Marcia Eames-Sheavly, Heather Sheridan-Thomas, Jane Boursaw, Kristin Ohlson, Bobbi Dempsey, Gwen Moran, Barbara Benham, Pam Oldham, Kathleen Conroy, and family members Jan Smith, Nancy Carver, Lorraine Buonviri, Amy Dickinson, and Anne Dickinson kept me sane after my seventeen-year-old son committed suicide in 2012. Without them I would still be huddled in the green chair under an old red quilt unable to do anything except watch a lot of bad television.

Thanks to agent John Rudolph at Dystel & Goderich Literary Management for selling this book, and to senior editor Keith Wallman at Lyons Press for making this jumble of words coherent.

Finally, I'd like to thank my husband, Tim Gallagher, and children, Railey, Clara, and Gwen, for their unwavering support.

Bibliographic Note

THE HISTORIAN HITS A WALL WHEN CONFRONTED WITH CENTRAL characters, in this case the Reno Gang, who left no writing behind. There are no letters, diaries, or journals penned in the hand of the Reno brothers (with one exception). Everything is hearsay. The desire to hear them speak—to hear their voices (were they high or low, nasal or clear?)—is immense. This desire, and then failure, to be able to capture the rhythm and cadence of their language, is the pinnacle of frustration. The problem then becomes how to create three-dimensional characters whose voices you can't hear.

A second, and maybe more serious problem, is the reliability of the available sources. A wonderful secondary source is the thesis manuscript written by Robert Volland for completion of a master's degree in history from Indiana University. The problem is that the Indiana University's department of history has no record of Mr. Volland attending the university and receiving a master's degree from their department. Volland's thesis is, oddly, edited by Robert W. Shields, a name that crops up several times in what little Reno literature is extant.

Robert W. Shields, whose life spanned most of the twentieth century, was born in Seymour and became a preacher and high school teacher who lived and worked in various states. He also kept the world's longest diary—37.5 million words—which covered a quarter of a century at the end of his life. Every four hours, Shields sat in an office chair surrounded by typewriters arranged in a horseshoe shape around him, typing his thoughts and the minutia of his life during that block of time. This diary is under seal in the University of Washington's archives until fifty years after Shields's death. According to his obituary in the *New York Times*, Mr. Shields also wrote an unpublished account of a train-robbing gang. Is this a reference to Volland's thesis or something else? No one seems to know.

Within Robert Volland's thesis are long quoted sections from a small book written by Isaac Wilson. I could locate no extant copies of *Four Years in a Home-Made Hell* (Siloam Springs, Arkansas). All I have from Wilson are the words quoted in Volland's mysterious thesis. Wilson's book was provided to Volland by Robert W. Shields.

Volland also quotes extensively from John Reno's autobiography, written and published in 1879 and sold for fifty cents around Seymour. I have not seen an original copy of this book. All that seems to exist, at this point, is an edited and illustrated version published by Indiana's Jackson County Historical Society in 1940, edited and illustrated by Robert W. Shields. The problem becomes one of trying to determine which layers and words belong to Volland/Reno/Wilson and which belong to Shields. At this point, it's impossible to really know.

To contextualize the Reno Gang, I've relied heavily on contemporaneous newspapers, particularly around southeastern Indiana. Dr. J. R. Monroe's newspapers—the *Rockford Herald*, and the various iterations of the *Seymour Times*—are integral to the story. Mid-nineteenth-century newspapers are fascinating because factual information is always embedded and surrounded by opinion. Scenes are imagined or embellished, and consequently, must be taken with a grain (or many grains) of salt (as in Laura Amanda's theatrical outburst over the bodies of her dead brothers). Edwin J. Boley's books about the history of Jackson County and the events surrounding the Reno Gang were a great starting place for the newspaper research. Many archival newspapers can be viewed remotely through an aggregate service like newspaperarchive.com, something that allowed me to spend far too much time sitting at my desk.

Charlotte Sellers, the former Jackson County Historian, was invaluable. We met when I was visiting the Jackson County History Center in Brownstown, Indiana. Someone mentioned I was working on a thesis about the Reno Gang, and Charlotte, who was sitting at a computer in the corner, turned around and began quizzing me about what I did and did not know. I could tell she was testing me, and apparently I passed muster. Charlotte was a researcher's researcher. I could send her an e-mail beginning "What do you know about . . ." and receive an answer, complete with bibliographic references, within hours. This book could not have been completed without my friend Charlotte's encyclopedic knowledge of nineteenth-century Jackson County, Indiana.

Bibliography

Abbott, Karen. *Liar, Temptress, Soldier, Spy*. New York, NY: Harper, 2014.

Barbour, C. "Two Vigilance Committees." *Overland Monthly & Out West Magazine*. 10, no. 57 (1887): 285–91.

Berg, Manfred. *Popular Justice: A History of Lynching*. Lanham, MD: Rowman & Littlefield, 2011.

Bird, Isabella L. *The Essential Isabella L. Bird Collection*. Electronic. Public Domain.

Bogardus, Carl Robert Sr. *The Scarlet Mask*. Austin, IN: Carl Bogardus, 1960.

Boley, Edwin J. *The First Documented History of Jackson County, Indiana*. Seymour, IN, 1980.

Boley, Edwin J. *The Masked Halters*. Seymour, IN: Graessle-Mercer, 1977.

Bonansinga, Jay. *Pinkerton's War: The Civil War's Greatest Spy and the Birth of the U.S. Secret Service*. Guilford, CT: Lyons Press, 2012.

Brant and Fuller. *History of Jackson County, Indiana*. Chicago, IL, 1886.

Brown, Dee. *Hear That Lonesome Whistle Blow: Railroads in the West*. New York, NY: Holt, Rhinehart & Winston, 1977.

Brown, Richard Maxwell. *Strain of Violence: Historical Studies of American Violence and Vigilantism*. New York, NY: Oxford University Press, 1975.

Capuzzo, Michael. *The Murder Room: The Heirs of Sherlock Holmes Gather to Solve the World's Most Perplexing Cold Cases*. New York, NY: Gotham, 2010.

Cox, E. T. *Sixth Annual Geological Survey of Indiana: made during the year 1874*. Indianapolis, IN: Sentinal Company printers, 1875.

Craughwell, Thomas J. *Stealing Lincoln's Body*. Boston, MA: Belknap Press, 2008.

Dickerman's United States Treasurey Counterfeit Detector and Banker's & Merchant's Journal. John Holler Publisher. Vol. XVIII, no. 1, 1901.

Dillon, Mark C. *The Montana Vigilantes: Gold, Guns and Gallows*. Boulder, CO: University Press of Colorado, 2013.

Distler, A. David. *Anarchy in the Heartland*. Lexington, KY. POD, retrieved October 21, 2013.

Dunlop, Richard. "The First Train Robbery." *Inland: the magazine of the Middle West*. No. 10, pp. 16–18.

Faragher, John Mack. *Sugar Creek: Life on the Illinois Prairie*. New Haven, CT: Yale University Press, 1986.

Faragher, John Mack. *Women and Men on the Overland Trail*. New Haven, CT: Yale University Press, 1979.

Ferguson, Andrew. *Land of Lincoln: Adventures in Abe's America*. New York, NY: Atlantic Monthly Press, 2007.

Fishel, Edwin C. *The Secret War for the Union: The Untold Story of Military Intelligence in the Civil War*. Boston, MA: Houghton Mifflin, 1996.

Floyd, William Jr. "Allan Pinkerton: A Far from Ordinary Life." *History Magazine*. 17, no. 4. (2016). 8–12.

Friedman, Lawrence. *A History of American Law*, 3rd revised edition. New York, NY: Touchstone, 2005.

Gardner, Mark Lee. *Shot all to Hell: Jesse James, the Northfield Raid, and the Wild West's Greatest Escape*. New York, NY: William Morrow, 2013.

Garland, Hamlin. *A Son of the Middle Border*. New York, NY: Grosset & Dunlap, BF Collier & Son, 1917.

Goodwin, Doris Kearns. *Team of Rivals: The Political Genius of Abraham Lincoln*. New York, NY: Simon & Schuster, 2005.

Gordon, Sarah H. *Passage to Union: How the Railroads Transformed American Life, 1829–1929*. Chicago, IL: Ivan R. Dee, 1996.

Greenhow, Rose O'Neale. *My Imprisonment and the First Year of Abolition Rule at Washington*. London, 1863.

Hansen, Ron. *The Assassination of Jesse James by the Coward Robert Ford*. New York, NY: Alfred A. Knopf, Inc., 1983.

Hargrave, Frank F. "Rivals and Rails: a Documentary History of the Ohio and Mississippi Railroad." West Lafayette, IN: Purdue University, 1957. Manuscript.

Hogg, Wilgus Wade. *The First Train Robbery: being an enhanced narrative treating the Nation's first such endeavor and its bloody aftermath*. Louisville, KY: Data Courier, Inc., 1977.

Holland, Cecelia. *Vigilante Wars: Gang Democracy and the Collapse of Government in San Francisco's Gold Rush Years*. Kindle Single: Now and Then, accessed 2015.

Holzer, Harold & Craig L. Symonds (eds.). *The New York Times Complete Civil War, 1861–1865*. New York, NY: Black Dog & Leventhal Publishers, Inc., 2000.

Horan, James D. & Howard Swiggett. "Gold, Guns, and Gallows." *The Pinkerton Story*. New York, NY: G. P. Putnam & Sons, 1951. Chapter two.

Hough, Emerson. *The Story of the Outlaw: A Study of the Western Desperado*. New York, NY: The Outing Publishing Company, 1907.

Lamon, Ward H. *The Life of Abraham Lincoln from his birth to his inauguration as President*. Boston, MA: James R. Osgood & Co., 1872.

Lawler, Steph. "Rules of Engagement: Habitus, Power & Resistance." *The Sociological Review*. Vol. 52, October 2004, 110–28.

Madison, James H. *The Indiana Way: A State History*. Bloomington, IN: Indiana University Press & Indiana Historical Society, 1986.

MacKay, James. *Allan Pinkerton: The First Private Eye*. New York, NY: John Wiley & Sons Inc., 1997.

McCord, Shirley S. *Travel Accounts of Indiana, 1679–1961: A Collection of Observations by Wayfaring Foreigners, Itinerants, and Peripatetic Hoosiers*. Bloomington, IN: Indiana Historical Bureau & Indiana University Press, 1970.

Melanson, Phillip H. *The Secret Service: The Hidden History of an Enigmatic Agency*. New York, NY: Carroll & Graf, 2002, 2005.

Mihn, Stephen. *A Nation of Counterfeiters: Capitalists, Con Men, and the Making of the United States*. Boston, MA: Harvard University Press, 2009.

Moffett, Cleveland. *True Detective Stories: From the Archives of the Pinkertons*. New York, NY: G. W. Dillingham Co., 1893.

Morn, Frank. *The Eye that Never Sleeps: A History of the Pinkerton National Detective Agency*. Bloomington, IN: Indiana University Press, 1982.

Mott, M. H. *History of the Regulators in Indiana*. Indianapolis, IN: Indianapolis Journal Company, 1859.

Nation, Richard Franklin. "Home in the Hoosier Hills: Agriculture, Politics, and Religion in Southern Indiana, 1810–1870." University of Michian, PhD Dissertation, 1995.

Noblitt, Loren W. *Tragic Destiny: the demise of the Reno Gang*. Brownstown, IN: Jackson County Historical Society, 2000.

Nolan, Patrick B. *Vigilantes on the Middle Border: a study of self-appointed law enforcement in the states of the Upper Mississippi from 1840 to 1880*. New York, NY: Garland Publishing, 1987.

Panek, LeRoy Lad. *Before Sherlock Holmes: How Magazines and Newspapers Invented the Detective Story*. Jefferson, NC: McFarland & Company, Inc., 2011.

Parsons, John. *A Tour through Indiana in 1840: The Diary of John Parsons of Petersburgh, Virginia* (edited by Kate Milner Rabb). New York, NY: Robert M. McBride, 1920.

Patterson, Richard. "The Reno Gang." *American History*. Vol. 17, no. 4, June 1982.

Patterson, Richard. *Train Robbery: The Birth, Flowering, and Decline of a Notorious Western Enterprise*. Boulder, CO: Johnson Books, 1981.

Pinkerton, Allan. *History and Evidence of the Passage of Abraham Lincoln from Harrisburg, PA to Washington, D.C.* Pamphlet, 1868.

Pinkerton, Allan. *Thirty Years a Detective*. 1884.

Pinkerton, Allan. *The Works of Allan Pinkerton*. Public Domain. Accessed 2014.

Pinkerton, Frank. *Dyke Darrel the Railroad Detective or The Crime of the Midnight Express*. Public Domain. Accessed 2015.

Reno, John. *The Life of John Reno: The World's First Train Robber written by himself* (edited by Robert W. Shields). Seymour, IN, 1940.

Riffenburgh, Beau. *Pinkerton's Great Detective: The Amazing Life and Times of James McParland*. New York, NY: Viking Penguin, 2013.

Rule, Lucien V. (Rev.), Litt. D., *The Scarlet Mask, A Tale of the Reno Gang* (mss.) bound, thirty chapters. Dictated to a convict at the Old Prison South, Jeffersonville, Indiana, where he was nine years chaplain. From Volland.

Schrink, Jeffrey and Frances. "Southern Indiana Vigilance Committee." *Indiana Folklore: A Reader.* Vol. XI, no. 1, 1978.

Sellers, Charlotte. *Saving Seymour Stories.* Seymour, IN: Seymour Museum, 2007.

Singer, Jane, and John Stewart. *Lincoln's Secret Spy: The Civil Case that Changed the Future of Espionage.* Guilford, CT: Lyons Press, 2015.

Smith, Roger F. *From the Ohio to the Mississippi.* Cincinnati, OH: Mt. Airy Printing Co., 1965.

Stiles, T. J. *Jesse James: Last Rebel of the Civil War.* New York, NY: First Vintage Books Edition, 2002.

Thornbrough, Emma Lou. *Indiana in the Civil War Era, 1850–1880.* Indianapolis, IN: Indiana Historical Society, 1965.

Thornbrough, Gayle, and Dorothy Riker (compilers). *Readings in Indiana History.* Indianapolis, IN: Indiana Historical Bureau, 1956.

Thurston, Robert. *A History of the Growth of the Steam Engine,* Amazon Digital Services, 2011 (originally published in 1878).

Volland, Robert Frederick. "The Reno Gang of Seymour." MA Thesis, Indiana University, 1948. Edited by Robert W. Shields.

Wade, Erik C. "Constituting Whiteness: The National Horse Thief Detective Association and Racial Mores in Indiana, 1850–1930." PhD Dissertation. Purdue University, 2011.

Williams, David Ricardo. *Call in Pinkerton's: American Detectives at Work for Canada.* Toronto, ONT: Dundurn Press, 1998.

Wilson, Isaac A. *Four Years in a Home-Made Hell.* Siloam Springs, AR: The Herald Printing Company, 1894.

Wilson, R. Michael. *Frontier Justice in the Wild West: Bungled, Bizarre, and Fascinating Executions.* Guilford, CT: TwoDot, 2007.

Wolmar, Christian. *The Great Railroad Revolution: The History of Trains in America.* Public Affairs, 2012.

NEWSPAPERS

Brownstown Banner
Chartiton Democrat
Cincinnati Gazette
Cincinnati Enquirer
Indianapolis Sentinal
Iron-Clad Age
Louisville Courier
New Albany Daily Ledger
New Albany Weekly Ledger
New Albany Daily Commercial
The New York Times
The North Missourian
Richmond (Ind.) Radical
Rockford Herald

Seymour Democrat
Seymour Daily Tribune
Seymour Times
Seymour Tribune
Seymour Weekly Times
St. Louis Republican

Notes

Prologue

ix *Bring us the sheriff!:* All text dialogue in italics is fictionalized and is a possible dialogue based on the situation.

Chapter One

2 so would crops.: Conversely, the northern part of the state was settled later because it consisted of primarily rolling prairie land.

2 exceeds that of the land itself.": From Thornbrough, Gayle, and Dorothy Riker (compilers). *Readings in Indiana History.* Indianapolis, IN: Indiana Historical Bureau, 1956.

2 those who became too tired to walk.": Parsons, John. *A Tour through Indiana in 1840: The Diary of John Parsons of Petersburgh, Virginia* (edited by Kate Milner Rabb). New York, NY: Robert M. McBride, 1920, pp. 328–29. Parsons in Terre Haute.

4 It meets Tuesday evenings.": *The Rockford Herald,* February 16, 1856.

6 if not in the whole country.": *Seymour Weekly Times,* February 26, 1876. A centennial edition that includes biographies of many of the town leaders as well as a brief history of Seymour.

7 not but what these latter are essential also.": *The Rockford Herald,* March 1856.

Chapter Two

11 we scarcely knew how to act.": Reno, John. *The Life of John Reno: The World's First Train Robber written by himself* (edited by Robert W. Shields). Seymour, IN. 1940. p. 1.

12 this flogging for weeks afterward.": Reno, p. 2.

13 I think they did not hear me.": Reno, p. 2.

14 on that lonely bank of the Mississippi.": Reno, pp. 4–7.

14 blankets hung up by one of their corners.": Reno, p. 8.

15, "thus ended in this unspectacular manner.": Reno, p.11.

19 noted a disgruntled Pinkerton.: This story is told in dozens of articles and books about Allan Pinkerton. See bibliography.

Chapter Three

27 eagerness of bidders," wrote one historian.: Brant and Fuller. *History of Jackson County Indiana,* Chicago, IL, 1883. Meedy Shields historical information is contained in a biography as well as throughout the information about Seymour.

29 a stagecoach, and a steamboat.: An omnibus was a fixed-rail system in which a streetcar or tram was pulled along rails by horses. Stagecoach operators in cities often made the switch to this system of conveyance. The first omnibus in New York City showed up in 1827.

30 and love change and travel for themselves.": Robert Louis Stevenson, "The Amateur Emigrant," *The Works of Robert Louis Stevenson,* Swanston ed., London: Chatto and Windus, 1911.

31 within a couple of growing seasons.: Faragher, John Mack. *Sugar Creek: Life on the Illinois Prairie.* New Haven, CT: Yale University Press, 1986.

32 "poisoning the morals of the youths of the vicinity,": Postel's tavern burning, *The Seymour Times,* 1859.

33 Barnes' condition is critical.": *Seymour Times,* October 10, 1861.

35 in American legal history," writes legal historian Laurence Friedman.: Lawrence Friedman, *A History of American Law,* 3rd revised edition, New York, NY: Touchstone, 2005, p. 105.

37 along with the fraud and animal cunning.": Friedman, p. 109.

37 and his stationery by one open eye.: This is where the term private eye, which is often used to refer to any private detective, came from.

Chapter Four

40 had to come out and disband the company.": Reno, p.13.

41 the six or eight hours of fierce fighting.": Reno, p. 13.

41 forbidding and squally in 1862 and '63 . . .": Sellers, Charlotte. *Saving Seymour Stories.* Seymour, IN: Seymour Museum, 2007, p. 15.

42 sinewy, apparently in excellent condition.": Sellers, p. 16.

42 sitting in a tent "beastly drunk.": Sellers, pp. 16–17.

42 a resignation was reluctantly sent in.": *Seymour Weekly Times,* February 26, 1876.

43 "caused him to resort to stimulants.": Sellers, p. 18.

43 have been accompaniments since the middle of May.": *Seymour Times,* August 21, 1862.

44 All the Seymour boys are all right.": *Seymour Times,* October 8, 1863.

45 "the slaughter pen in the stockyards of Chicago": National Park Service information, nps.gov/stri/learn/historyculture/slaughterpen.htm, retrieved May 20, 2016.

46 all the produce that farmers can haul to town.": *Seymour Times,* July 2, 1863.

47 had badly injured two of the provost guards.: Reno, pp. 15–16.

47 My father and her constantly quarreled.": Reno, p. 16.

48 the Confederate Army surrendered.: Reno, pp. 16–18.

Chapter Five

52 I will let you know in the morning.'": Goodwin, Doris Kearns. *Team of Rivals: The Political Genius of Abraham Lincoln*. New York, NY: Simon & Schuster, 2005. Goodwin quoting Seward quoting Lincoln.

52 that "Nuts" (Lincoln) had departed safely.: MacKay, James. *Allan Pinkerton: The First Private Eye*. New York, NY: John Wiley & Sons Inc., 1997, pp. 101–5.

53 a great time in Dixie by and by.'": MacKay, p. 103, Pinkerton assasination attempt.

54 by the vainglorious detective [Pinkerton].": MacKay, p. 103.

54 and throw ridicule on his Administration.": Goodwin, p. 312, quotes from George Templeton Strong's diary.

55 I am at your command.": MacKay, pp. 106–9.

55 and well skilled in their business.": MacKay, pp. 106–9.

56 to obtain an interview with the Chief Executive.": Pinkerton, Allan. *The Works of Allan Pinkerton*. Public Domain. Accessed 2014. p. 139.

56 and strains of martial music filled the air.": Pinkerton, p. 138.

57 and ultimately change all of them.: MacKay, p. 92.

58 what had happened and in what order.: In 1882, Mark Twain had a murderer identified by his fingerprints in *Life on the Mississipp*i, but police were slow to adopt the practice of fingerprint analysis.

59 clandestine correspondence with Southern leaders.": Pinkerton, p. 139.

61 halfway between the White House and the Capitol.: Dennis Brady, "President-elect Lincoln arrived to a less-than-monumental Washington," *Washington Post*, Sunday, November 7, 2010.

61 quite disorderly since their arrival.": Diary of Mary Henry. Smithsonian Institution.

63 by the Confederates at the First Battle of Bull Run.: Karen Abbott, *Liar, Temptress, Soldier, Spy*. New York, NY: Harper, 2014. Abbott covers Belle Boyd, Emma Edmonds, Rose O'Neal Greenhow, and Elizabeth van Lew in this wonderful book about women in the Civil War.

63 to continue surveillance until instructed not to.: Pinkerton, "The Spy and the Rebellion."

63 a note on her desk written by Jefferson Davis.: Rose O'Neale Greenhow, *My Imprisonment and the First Year of Abolition Rule at Washington*. London, 1863. pp. 56–57.

64 and was not to be caught at a disadvantage.": Greenhow.

Chapter Six

66 and counterfeiters in the country": Boley, Edwin J. *The Masked Halters*. Seymour, IN: Graessle-Mercer, 1977, p. 53.

68 to all respectable people this must be stopped.": *The Seymour Times*, September 9, 1860.

69 moving to the Reno properties in Rockford.: *Seymour Weekly Times*, February 26, 1876; Volland, Robert Frederick. "The Reno Gang of Seymour." MA Thesis, Indiana University, 1948. Edited by Robert W. Shields, pp. 82–83.

69 perpetrators to speedy and condign punishment.": Boley, pp. 55–56.

70 and assassins that infest this place.": *Seymour Times*, July 27, 1865.

70 to the sick and dying men at the front.: *Seymour Times*, August 3, 1865.

CHAPTER SEVEN

74 by whom they are respectively made payable.": Thomas J. Craughwell. *Stealing Lincoln's Body*. Boston, MA: Belknap Press, 2008, pp. 38–40.

75 based on the future credit of the nation.: Craughwell, pp. 41–42.

77 "a national evil demanding a national remedy.": *The New York Times*, July 30, 1862.

78 Chase let his man do as he pleased.: Craughwell, p. 42.

79 I believe you have the right idea.": Craughwell, p. 44.

79 laundered the gang's money along with counterfeit boodle.: Craughwell, pp. 46–56. The counterfeiting gang surrounding the Renos and working closely with them spread from Cincinnati, OH, to Chicago, IL, to St. Louis, MO.

CHAPTER EIGHT

81 the men called the "calaboose.": Calaboose is a nineteenth-century term for a local jail.

81 to ask them what they were going to do.": Reno, p. 19.

81 and we're going to serve you the same way.'": Reno, p. 20.

82 and honored and loved in his own family.": Sellers, pp. 23–24.

82 setting privies over the stream should be stopped.: Sellers, p. 25.

82 I 'played possum' on them.": Reno, p. 20.

83 would have been found there the next morning.": Reno, pp. 20–21.

83 in the dark as he so rightly deserved.": Reno, p. 21.

84 constituting the mob were drunk . . .": *Seymour Times*, September 13, 1866.

84 criminal laws of their State," had all the powers of constables.: Horse Thief Detection Law, State of Indiana, 1865.

85 critical study of American violence and vigilantism.: Brown, Richard Maxwell. *Strain of Violence: Historical Studies of American Violence and Vigilantism.* New York, NY: Oxford University Press, 1975.

CHAPTER NINE

87 and the creation of almost every luxury that we now enjoy.": Robert Thurston, *A History of the Growth of the Steam Engine*, Amazon Digital Services, 2011 (originally published in 1878).

92 or one-half that amount for either.": *The Indianapolis Daily Journal,* October 8, 1866.

92 reward for the arrest of the thieves.": *The New York Times*, October 8, 1866.

93 one or more of the Reno brothers for the train job.: Pinkerton's account of the Reno Gang and first train robbery.

94 vote for a Democrat you vote for a rebel.": *Seymour Times*, October 4, 1866. One week before election day.

94 communications and poor whisky has made him what he is.": *Seymour Times*, Septermber 27, 1866.

97 a cache between the ceiling and the garret.: Pinkerton's account of the first train robbery.

98 they were heavily plated, and had fair appearance.": *Dickerman's United States Treasurey Counterfeit Detector and Banker's & Merchant's Journal.* John Holler Publisher. Vol. XVIII, no. 1, 1901.

98 skeleton keys, nippers, drills, punches, jacks, clamps, etc.": *The Manufacturer and the Builder,* "On Burglar's Tools," Volume 6, Issue: 5, May 1874, p. 108.

99 They were taken west, probably to St. Louis.": *Seymour Times*, October 11, 1866.

100 presumed to be Adams Express money.: *Seymour Times*, October 11, 1866.

102 into the picture in October 1866: Pinkerton account of first train robbery.

CHAPTER TEN

104 before the vigilance committee came knocking.: Reno, p. 23.

104 slowly and silently toward Brownstown.": *Seymour Times*, April 4, 1867. The Talley and Brooks lynching was written about in all of the regional papers from New Albany to Indianapolis.

104 Brooks and Talley out to the lawn.": Volland, p. 135.

105 to whom or for what purpose we do not know . . .": *Brownstown Banner,* August 28, 1879; Boley, pp. 144–45.

106 bring them to justice through the regular channels.": *The Indianapolis Daily Journal*, April 2, 1867.

106 the criminal law of self-defense must be their justification.": *The Indianapolis Daily Journal*, April 2, 1867.

107 Each class is necessary to the other . . .": *Seymour Times*, April 4, 1867.

107 dirty tricks he would go the way of the others.": *Seymour Times*, April 4, 1867.

107 and we vote him a heap of thanks.": *Seymour Times*, April 4, 1867.

CHAPTER ELEVEN

108 betting" but instead lost every single dollar.: Reno, p. 23.

110 could have held onto it long enough to get there.: *New Albany Weekly Ledger*, Second annual Jackson County Fair sometime in early October 1867.

111 our money soon ran out.": Reno, p. 24.

111 held a revolver on him while Hammond emptied the safe.: *New Albany Weekly Ledger*, October 23, 1867, as taken from the *Chicago Republican*.

113 practices that render any reformation doubtful.": In 1876 Henry M. Beadle wrote *The History of Jackson County and the Express Robberies*, which was later run in installments in *The Seymour Daily Tribune.* This quote about Hammond and Colleran appeared in *The Seymour Daily Tribune*, May 8, 1935.

CHAPTER TWELVE

115 an unenviable notoriety for years past.": *Seymour Times*, September 7, 1865.

115 embraced by the entire Reno family.: Wilson, Isaac A. *Four Years in a Home-Made Hell*. Siloam Springs, AR: The Herald Printing Company. 1894. There may or may not be one copy of this book in a private collection. The quoted sections from Wilson are from Volland.

115 part of town near the new fairgrounds.: Volland, pp. 138–39. Volland adds the note that Isaac and his brother must have also been black, since their father was black, but points out that Isaac never refers to himself that way.

116 Both were immediately rebuilt.: Volland, p. 139.

118 and then into a clearing in the far woods.: A dark lantern is a metal lantern with one glass or clear pane that could be covered by a panel when you required darkness. Think of it as an early flashlight.

119 give southerners some payment for freeing their slaves.: Isaac Wilson as per Volland, pp. 142–43. The order was New Life Sons and Daughters of Columbus, which only appears in Wilson's book. There's no reference to it in the *Cyclopedia of Fraternities* or elsewhere.

119 Four of the number arrested are women.": *Seymour Times*, November 7, 1867.

119 lie down and insert their nails in each other's eyes.": *Seymour Times*, November 14, 1867.

120 some $30 in money found in the drawer.: *Seymour Times*, November 22, 1867.

120 Terms $2.50 a year.": *Seymour Times*, November 29, 1867.

120 along the railroad, as was done in this instance.": *Seymour Times*, December 6, 1867.

121 range from $6 to $8 per head.": *Seymour Times*, December 6, 1867.

121 contemplating eternity or the infinity of space . . .": *Seymour Times*, December 6, 1867.

CHAPTER THIRTEEN

122 grip-sack with baked chicken and bread.": Reno, p. 24.

123 being in the country [sic] treasurer's office.": Reno, p. 25.

123 twenty-two thousand and sixty-five dollars, a nice haul indeed.": Reno, p. 26.

124 feet and left them by the roadside.": Reno, p. 26.

124 appear as much like real drovers as possible.": Reno, p. 27.

125 our room occasionally by way of pastime," Reno wrote.: Reno, p. 27.

125 how successfully I had covered up my tracks.": Reno, p. 28.

125 under the circumstances under which I was arrested.": Reno, p. 28.

126 and meet me. I am worn out.": Boley, p. 180.

126 if this money is not returned!": Reno, p. 29.

127 no difference at all to a mob from Missouri . . .": Reno, p. 30.

127 he acknowledged his guilt and divulged the affair.": *The North Missourian*, December 19, 1867; Boley, pp. 182–84.

128 an experienced workman like him was a short one.": Reno doesn't talk about blowing the safe in his autobiography but he was referred to as a safe-blower in many newspaper accounts, so it's very likely he blew the safe in Gallatin and just didn't mention it.

128 couldn't be induced to blow up a safe.": *Seymour Times*, December 27, 1867.

128 five or ten years at the most.: Reno, p. 30.

129 would be done regardless of the hazards," wrote John.: Reno, p. 31.

129 had the reputation of being men of steel nerves.": Reno, p. 31.

129 compelled to stay and see it out.": Reno, p. 32.

129 "on the list and went in for free.": Reno, p. 32.

129 "good as his word to make the rescue.": Reno, p. 32.

CHAPTER FOURTEEN

130 and materials of the three papers.": *Indianapolis Journal*, March 27, 1868; Boley, pp. 211–12.

130 one year from the 25th day of March, 1868.": *Seymour Times*, April 3, 1868.

130 "He is a good scholar and an excellent writer.": *Seymour Times*, April 3, 1868.

131 Omaha, Nebraska (just over the state line), but not caught.": *Indianapolis Journal*, February 20, 1868.

132 and their detection may be considered extremely doubtful.": *Council Bluffs Weekly Nonpareil*, February 29—March 28, 1868. From Boley, pp. 207–8.

132 being friends with William Pinkerton (Allan's son).: Moffett said he got his information from the Pinkerton Archives. However, all of the Reno Gang material was burned in the Great Chicago Fire of 1871, so I think his information came mainly from William Pinkerton. It is wonderfully colorful and too good not to include.

132 hoped to get a lead on the stolen treasury money.: Moffett, Cleveland. *True Detective Stories: From the Archives of the Pinkertons.* New York, NY: G. W. Dillingham Co., 1893, pp. 56–57. John Reno never mentions the name Pinkerton in his autobiography, perhaps as a way to erase the detectives from his memory and the "shame" at being kidnapped. Reno's *Autobiography* and the dozens of books Allan Pinkerton wrote after retiring from fieldwork resemble each other in their level of detail, which is almost too good to believe. The two men are also the heroes of their own narratives.

133 Frank Reno (although he could not be certain since he had never seen Frank Reno before).: Moffett, pp. 56–58.

134 "We'll see about that," answered Mr. Pinkerton.: Moffett, p. 59.

135 arrested with Rogers were not Reno, Ogle, and Perkins.: *Council Bluffs Weekly Nonpareil*, February 29, 1868.

135 than was taken from the Mills county safe.": *Chariton Democrat*, March 7, 1868.

135 was never a member of the Methodist Church here.": *Council Bluffs Weekly Nonpareil*, February 29, 1868; Boley, p. 206.

136 and fancy goods ever brought to the west, could be found.": *Council Bluffs Weekly Nonpareil*, April 4, 1868; Boley, p. 208.

136 no doubt the result of his dramatic courtroom exit.: Volland, pp. 176–80.

CHAPTER FIFTEEN

138 and another through his hair by his ear," reported the paper.: *Indianapolis Daily Sentinel*, May 26, 1868.

138 injuries from which it is thought he will not recover.": *Indianapolis Daily Sentinel*, May 26, 1868.

138 Adams Express on the Jeffersonville Railroad, Ohio.": *The New York Times*, May 24, 1868.

139 and going down discovered the true state of affairs.": *Seymour Democrat*, May 27, 1868.

139 that and other roads as occasion may offer.": *Seymour Democrat*, May 27, 1868.

142 "Pending this it is not judicious to speculate.": *Fort Wayne Daily Gazette*, October 5, 1868, A Scene in Court—The Tables Turned.

CHAPTER SIXTEEN

145 'all right; let me know when you're ready.'": Flanders quoted in the *Fort Wayne Daily Sentinal*, March 15, 1878, from the *Cincinnati Enquirer*.

150 are glad to see, the citizens are now likely to do.": *Cincinnati Commercial*, dateline Seymour, Ind., July 12, 1868.

154 a Police whistle, buttons, and other trinkets.": *Seymour Democrat*, July 22, 1868.

154 prove that it had ever belonged to them.": *Fort Wayne Daily Sentinal*, March 9, 1878.

CHAPTER SEVENTEEN

159 John Moore was still wearing his hat.: Hearsay from Hon. O. H. Montgomery to Robert W. Shields, his grandson, as recounted by Volland, pp. 206–7.

159 under the circumstances, others might have done even more.": *New Albany Weekly Ledger*, July 29, 1868, p. 4.

159 had black hair, and a dark complexion.: *New Albany Weekly Ledger*, August 5, 1868.

CHAPTER EIGHTEEN

161 "any of his friends the Renos are hanged by vigilantes.": *New Albany Weekly Ledger*, July 29, 1868; Volland, p. 212.

161 William became defiant while "Simeon shook with fear.": *New Albany Weekly Ledger*, Volland, p. 213.

162 they would protect the prisoners under all circumstances.": *New Albany Daily Ledger*, August 1, 1868.

162 he was never arrested before on any charge.": *New Albany Daily Ledger*, August 1, 1868.

164 "Can you blame me, a sister, for standing by my brothers?": *New Albany Daily Ledger*, August 1, 1868.

164 "will be taken to Scott County on September 7 for trial.": *New Albany Weekly Ledger*, August 5, 1868.

167 "If they touch my brothers, God will punish them!": Volland, pp. 223–24; *New Albany Weekly Ledger*, September 16 and 28, 1868.

Chapter Nineteen
171 Bail was set at $60,000.: Boley, pp. 300–310.

171 has figured in some of the boldest burglaries in the States.": *New Albany Weekly Ledger*, August 12, 1868.

171 most efficient burglars and robbers in the country.": *The Louisville Journal*, August 14, 1868.

172 whenever I see fit to do so.": *New Albany Weekly Ledger*, August 20, 1868.

172 except for the "Said Machine and Piano.": Boley, pp. 333-336.

173 Anderson claimed that Pinkerton and Weir lied on the stand.: *New Albany Daily Ledger*, September 15, 1868.

173 prisoners & the justice yesterday decided to hold them. . . .": Boley, p. 339–41. Boley collected copies of these State Department letters concerning the extradition, which had been previously unpublished.

174 and to surrender them to the proper authorities.: Boley, pp. 341–43, Boley's private collection.

174 lives were in danger if they were to be extradited to Indiana.: Boley, pp. 344–47.

175 could not be protected once they reached the state.: Boley, pp. 348–50.

176 that was taking him on a tour of the city.: *New Albany Daily Ledger*, October 17, 1868.

176 which could take up to a week.: Boley, pp. 358-362.

178 "an accident caused by a mistake in signals.": Horan, James D. & Howard Swiggett. "Gold, Guns, and Gallows." *The Pinkerton Story*. New York, NY: G. P. Putnam & Sons, 1951.

Chapter Twenty
180 and he was again pulled up.: *Richmond Indiana Radical*, December 24, 1868, picking up a special from the *Cincinnati Gazette*.

182 at least a half an hour!" The jury was horrified.: Volland, pp. 274–78, from various newspaper accounts.

183 "Oh, my brother! My baby, baby brother!": Volland, pp. 274–78; newspapers made much of the pitiful words of Laura Amanda, which she repeated over and over, wringing her hands as she wept. See *New Albany Daily Ledger*, December 12, 1868.

184 'We don't know anything about it').": *The New York Times*, December 28, 1868.

185 but a promise of terrible meaning.": *The Indianapolis Journal*, December 14, 1868.

186 instead of confiding the secret to a 'superstitious person.'": *New Albany Daily Ledger*, December 26, 1868.

187 only Kentucky does not pretend to be civilized.": *Cincinnati Gazette*, December 13, 1868.

CHAPTER TWENTY-ONE

190 to settle before he retires from the Department of State.": Volland, p. 290; *The Indianapolis Journal*, December 24, 1868.

191 by the very fact of its existence.": Volland, p. 290; *The Indianapolis Journal*, December 24, 1868.

191 introduced into the Senate of the United States.": Volland, p. 293; Senate Bill 705, 40th Congress, 3rd session, introduced by Lyman Trumbull of Illinois.

191 or attacks a jailor is to be fined and jailed.: Volland, p. 295; *Congressional Globe*, Washington, DC, 1869.

CHAPTER TWENTY-TWO

193 and pressing demands of the people to revive the *Times*.": *Seymour Times*, July 22, 1869.

194 If lynch law was ever right, it was right in that case . . .": *Seymour Times*, March 7, 1871.

195 and evident sincerity, which the writer freely concedes.": *Seymour Weekly Times*, February 22, 1876.

CHAPTER TWENTY-THREE

197 my feelings are as sensitive as those of the least guilty.": Reno, p. 36.

198 Reno wrote that these terms were upheld.: Reno, p. 40.

199 pleasure the company of such a pet is to a man in prison.": Reno, pp. 42–44.

199 to restrain them from their liberty.": Reno, p. 44.

199 I would at first think it was him.": Reno, p. 45.

200 to again view the scenes of his boyhood.": *St. Louis Republican*, February 19, 1878.

201 recollection of what I even said or did that day.": Reno, p. 46.

201 But he would soon starve to death in Indiana.": Reno, p. 47.

201 and been good citizens of society today.": Reno, p. 48.

201 and a very ruined reputation.": Reno, p. 48.

202 the most skillful safe-breakers in the United States.": *Indianapolis Journal*, March 9, 1878.

203 the only way to try me was under a tree.": *Indianapolis Journal*, March 9, 1978.

203 the same disfavor as is expressed in Seymour.": *Indianapolis Journal*, March 16, 1878.

203 agricultural life on their farm near town.": *Seymour Times*, August 14, 1880.

203 He got sentenced to three years in prison.: *Brownstown Banner*, April 23, 1885.

204 buried in the old City Cemetery near his three brothers.: There were rumors that John Reno may have had an illegitimate son by Mollie Nagle, his childhood sweetheart from Rockford. But as of now, that's still just a rumor.

CHAPTER TWENTY-FOUR

206 85,000 larch trees imported from Scotland.: In one version of the story, 85,000 young larch trees came into New York harbor on a ship from Scotland in mid-winter.

The man who was hired to arrange for their transportation to Larch Farm stopped for a drink, and by the time he reached the dock, the trees had frozen. Pinkerton ordered 85,000 more trees.

207 and settling on his flowers.: Some say Pinkerton imposed a five-dollar fine on those who broke this rule.

Chapter Twenty-Five

209 two barbers, a photograph gallery, a tannery, and two breweries.": Sellers, p. 32.

210 filled with a perfume anything but delicate.": Sellers, p. 36.

210 John Moore had the tree girdled and then set on fire.: Schrink, Jeffrey and Frances. "Hangman's Crossing." *Indiana Folklore: A Reader.* Vol. XI, no. 1, 1978, p. 96; *Seymour Democrat*, February 9, 1882.

212 *continued until the country is rid of thieves and cut-throats.:* All quotes from Monroe's paper.

Chapter Twenty-Six

213 always smolders just below the surface.": Personal correspondence.

215 something so unattractive as the Reno Brothers.": *Seymour Daily Tribune,* September 23, 1989.

215 response to these threats is to turn it over [to the cemetery commission].": *Seymour Daily Tribune,* September 23, 1989.

216 There's more of it going on than you think.": *Seymour Daily Tribune,* May 21, 2009.

216 because they're there and stupid people do stupid things.": *Seymour Daily Tribune,* May 28, 2009.

Index

Able, Clay, 127

Adams Express Company, 89–90, 138–40, 144, 145, 160, 161
    extradition battle, 173–78
    first train robbery, 87–102
    fourth train robbery, 144–54
    hires Brown to prosecute Reno Gang, 171–72
    Pinkerton advises to try four robbers together, 166
    and Pinkerton Detective Agency, 92, 211
    search for money after Reno brothers' funeral, 185–86
    second train robbery, 109–11
    tries to recover money from robberies, 168

Aetna House, 100

Allen, E. J., 57

Anderson, Charlie, 139–40, 144, 163
    arrested in Windsor, 169, 171
    death by hanging, 180–89
    extradition, 168–78
    prison escape attempt, 175, 176

Baker, Conrad, 174–75, 176–77

Ballinger, John, 125, 126, 127–28, 132

Baltimore, MD, 50–54, 55–56

Baltimore & Ohio (B&O) Railroad, 25, 55–56

banks and banking, 18–19, 73–75

Beadle, Henry M., 113

Beauregard, P.T.G., 59–60, 63–64

Benton, Wilbur, 105

Bicknell, Judge, 99, 100

Biebusch, Frederick, 79

Black Hawk War, 23–24

Boley, Edwin, 105, 215

boodle, 75, 141

bounty jumpers/brokers, 45–46, 47–48

Boyd, Ben, 79, 97, 98

British Band, 23–24

British North America Act, 170

Brooks, John, 101, 103–7
Brown, George W., 55
Brown, Jason B., 94, 101, 112, 171–72
Brown, Richard Maxwell, 85
Brownstown, IN, 96, 99, 100, 104–7, 145–54
Bump, Marshal, 135
Burnside, Ambrose, 66
Butler, Mr., 71

Carter, Ben, 159
Carter, Peter, 115, 116
Carter, Travis, 71, 115–16, 159, 209, 212
Cassidy, Butch, 206, 211
Chartist movement, 15–16
Chase, Salmon P., 74, 78
Chicago, 15, 17–18, 20–21, 140, 205–6
Civil War, 40–49, 60–62, 66–67, 189
Clark, Henry, 179
Clark, Mary R., 82
Clifton, Theodore, 146, 147, 148, 150–54
coins, counterfeit, 97–98
Colleran, Michael, 109, 111, 112, 113, 172
conductors, railroad, 38
coneys, 75, 78
conscription, 43
Council Bluffs, IA, 131, 132–34
counterfeiting, 18–19, 36, 73–79, 97–98, 134, 141, 203

Craig, John, 19–20
currency, 18–19. *See also* counterfeiting
Curtin, John, 177
Cutler, Marian, 101, 103

Daviess County, MO, 125, 127
Davison, A. A., 82, 116–19
Demand Notes, 74, 75
Democratic Party, 85, 94, 120, 194
detective services, 20–21, 57–58. *See also* Pinkerton Detective Agency
Diggs, Nelson, 79
Dixon, Sam, 67
Dunbar, Mr., 109
Dundee, IL, 17–20
Dunham, C. L., 105–6

Egan, John, 93, 94–98, 200
Elliott, Volney, 122–29, 145, 146–50, 150–54
engravers, 76–77, 79
espionage, 59–60, 62–64
express cars, 88–89, 109–11, 137, 146
express companies, 91–92. *See also* Adams Express Company
extradition, 168–78, 191–92

Faraghar, John Mack, 30
fees, states, 36–37
Felker, Samuel, 79, 140–43
Felton, Samuel, 50, 53, 54
Fergus, Robbie, 17–18

Filer, James, 99
fires, 1, 32–33
First Legal Tender Act, 74
Flanders, James, 144–45, 146, 154, 202–3
Fletcher, George, 169
Floyd County, 176, 178
Floyd County Courthouse, 182, 183
Floyd County jail, 160
Foley, Patrick, 177
Ford, John L., 183
forgery. See counterfeiting
freethinkers, 196
Friday, Jack, 169
Friedman, Laurence, 35, 37
Frisby, John, 79
Fullenlove, Sherriff, 139, 161, 177, 180

Gaither, Mr., 109–11
Gallatin, MO, 122–29
Garrett, John, 55
Garrity Gang, 140, 168–69
Glenwood, IA, 133–34, 136
Goss, Giles, 80, 83, 84
Goudy, Elisha, 200, 210
grave robbing, 185
graynotes, 74
Great Chicago Fire, 205–6
Green, George, 71, 82
greenbacks, 74, 75, 77
Greenhow, Rose O'Neal, 59–60, 62–64
Groub, John, 71

Hammond, Walker, 109, 111–12, 113, 114, 172
handcars, railroad, 90–91, 133–34
hangings. See lynchings
Hangman's Crossing, 158–59, 161, 210
Harkins, F. G., 138, 169
Harvey House, 144, 210
Hazen, Larry, 93, 94–98, 200
Henry, Mary, 61
History of the Growth of the Steam Engine (Thurston), 87
Hollinsworth, J. W., 82
Horan, James, 177
horse racing, 80–81, 108
Hudson, George. See Jerrell, Henry
Hulse, Jim, 119
Hunt, Henry, 18–19, 20
Hunter, William, 170, 173

Indian Removal policy, 24
Indianapolis, IN, 34, 40, 114, 125, 160
Ingersoll, Robert Green, 196
Iowa robberies, 131–36

Jackson County, IN, 69, 99
aftermath of Reno brothers' hanging, 192
Agricultural Fair, 99–100, 110
during Civil War, 43–44
Reno Gang in, 86
vigilance committee (See Seymour Vigilance Committee)

James Gang, 91, 206, 210–11, 216
Jeffersonville & Indianapolis
    Railroad, 137–40, 158
Jerrell, Henry, 144, 145, 146–50,
    156, 157–59
Jewett, Judge, 160–64
Johnson, Andrew, 93–94, 131, 174
Johnson, George, 176
Jonas, Nellie, 159
Jones, Samuel A., 162
Jordan, Captain, 62
Judd, Norman, 51, 53, 54

Kane, George P., 51
Keyes, Erasmus D., 62
Kinney, Ben, 119
Kling, Joseph, 159
Know-Nothing party, 6
koniackers, 75

Lamb, Cain D., 115, 116, 119
Lamon, Ward, 52, 54
Lane, Joseph, 62
Larch Farm, 206–8
Larney, John, 139–40
laundered money. *See* money
    laundering
law enforcement, 85. *See also*
    vigilantism
Lawson, Hattie, 64
Lee, Anderson, 182
Legal Tender Note, 74, 75
Levi, Lyle, 161
Lewis, Pryce, 64
Lexington, IN, 161–62, 165–67

Life of John Reno, The (Reno),
    10–11, 46–47, 197, 201
Lincoln, Abraham, 39, 50–56,
    78–79
Love, J. S., 140–43
Love, John, 71
Lozier, Chaplain, 181–82
Ludy, Dan, 135
lynch law, 70, 71
lynchings. *See also* Seymour
    Vigilance Committee
    Anderson, and Frank, Simeon,
      and William Reno, 179–81,
      190–92
    Clifton, Roseberry, and Elliott,
      151–54
    Jerrell, Moore, and Sparks,
      158–59, 161
    Talley and Brooks, 104–7

Mace, George, 80–81, 83, 84
Marshfield robbery, 137–40, 154,
    160, 162, 169
Mattoon, IL, 156–57
McBeth, Sam. *See* Reno, John
McCartney, (John) Peter, 79, 97,
    98
McClellan, George B., 56–57,
    59
McCormick, John, 130
McCulloch, Hugh, 78–79
McGee, Joseph H., 126
McKay, Andy, 201
McKinney, Ben, 157–58
Miller, Elam, 89–90, 100

Mills County Treasury, 133–34, 135

Missouri State Penitentiary, 128, 129, 197–200, 210

Mitchell, Cain, 115, 116, 119

Mitchell, Hiram, 12

Moffett, Cleveland, 132

Mollie Matches, 139–40, 169

Molly Maguires, 206

Monck, Lord, 170, 176

money laundering, 77, 79, 97. *See also* counterfeiting

Monroe, Jasper R., 4–9, 172
  becomes freethinker, 196
  campaign against Reno Gang, 8–9, 71, 85, 211
  during Civil War, 41–45
  death of, 212
  defends Sparks and John Reno, 128
  and Democratic party, 85, 94, 120, 194
  divorces and remarries, 82
  interest in promoting Seymour, 71
  later life, 193–96
  moves to Seymour, 31
  negative impact of Reno Gang on Seymour, 149–50
  Reno brothers' funeral, 184–85
  and Republican party, 85, 120, 194
  returns home after Civil War, 67
  sells Seymour's papers, 130–31
  and Seymour Vigilance Committee, 69–70, 106–7, 119, 196, 212
  starts *Rockford Herald*, 6–8
  starts *Seymour Times*, 8, 31
  writes about lynching of Reno brothers, 194
  writes about Rockford after arson fires, 33
  writes about world's first train robbery, 99

Moore, John, 144–54, 156, 157–59, 210

Morgan, John Hunt, 66–67

Morton, Governor, 66, 112–13

Murfreesboro, Battle of, 44–45

My Imprisonment and the First Year of Abolition Rule in Washington (Greenhow), 64

Nace, George. *See* Mace, George

Nagle, Mollie, 34, 47, 110–11, 114, 125

National Banking Acts, 75

National Detective Agency. *See* Pinkerton Detective Agency

Native Americans, 23–24

Nelson, Jack, 201

Nethliz, Jargo, 183

New Albany jail, 177, 178, 179–81

New Orleans, 3, 13, 23

Newby, Harmon, 115, 116, 118–19

North West Police Agency, 15

Northwest Ordinance of 1787, 34–36

Ogle, Miles, 134, 136
Ohio & Mississippi (O&M)
    Railroad, 22–23, 144–45, 158
    first Reno Gang train robbery,
        87–102
    second train robbery, 108–13
    Shields appointed to board of
        directors of, 24–25
    threats from Reno Gang, 161
Old Rockford. *See* Rockford, IN
O'Neal, Robert, 116
O'Neil, Pat, 168–69
operatives, 51, 58, 64–65, 78, 93,
    206, 207

Pana, IL, 80–86
Pattison, Robert, 119
Perkins, Albert, 134, 136, 163
Perrette, County Commissioner,
    180, 181
pig farming, 2–3
Pinkerton, Allan. *See also*
        Pinkerton Detective Agency
    and Adams Express Company,
        166, 211
    after Reno Gang, 205–8
    anger at delay in prosecuting
        Reno Gang, 172
    attempt to assassinate, 175–76
    as author, 207
    charges Reno brothers with
        conspiracy to commit felony,
        163

Chicago's first detective, 20–21
    during Civil War, 49
    DC espionage rings, 59–60
    death of, 207
    early career, 15–18
    and espionage rings, 63–64
    extradition of Reno Gang
        members, 168–78
    and Felker, 142–43
    fourth Reno Gang train
        robbery, 146–47
    and Greenhow, 63–64
    hired by Stanton, 63
    hires Winscott as informant,
        156–57
    and Jason Brown, 171–72
    and Lincoln, 39, 50–55
    McClellan summons to
        Cincinnati, 56–57
    operatives, 51, 64–65, 93, 206,
        207
    provides detective services to
        several railroad companies,
        101–2
    and railroad crime, 21, 38, 92
    and Reno Gang train robberies,
        101
    Reno Gang's first train robbery,
        91, 93
    retires to Larch Farm, 206–8
    second Reno Gang train
        robbery, 109–11
    starts National Detective
        Agency, 37–39
    starts secret service department,
        57–60

suffers stroke, 205

third Reno Gang train robbery,
 139–40

tracks down counterfeiters,
 18–19

on trail of Reno Gang, 132–33

Pinkerton, Robert, 205, 208

Pinkerton, William, 132–33, 177,
 205, 208

Pinkerton Code, 37–38

Pinkerton Detective Agency,
 37–39, 92. *See also* Pinkerton,
 Allan

beginning of, 57–58

capture Reno brothers, 160

headquarters, 140

loses files in Great Chicago
 Fire, 205–6

operatives (*See* operatives)

successes after Reno Gang, 206

Pinkerton Story, The (Horan), 177

planing mill, 71, 115–16, 209

Pomeroy, Thomas M., 174

pork-packing, 2–3, 120–21

Postel's tavern, 32

queer, 75, 203

Rader House, 67, 95–96, 151, 159

railroads

consequences of Reno Gang
 robberies, 211

and crime, 20–21

development of, 25–27

early travel on, 29–31

laws, 28–29

as Pinkerton's early clients, 38

Reed, Adaline, 32

Reno, Clinton, 10, 32, 46, 86, 172,
 187, 200, 203–4, 210

Reno, Frank, 10, 11, 32, 86, 98,
 133, 144, 163, 203

arrested in Windsor, 169, 171

begins robbing businesses, 67

buried in City Cemetery,
 Seymour, 214

captured by William Pinkerton,
 134–36

during Civil War, 46

connection to Seymour
 robberies, 116–17

death by hanging, 179–89

early life, 12–13

escapes to Windsor, Canada,
 139–40

extradition, 168–78

and Isaac Wilson, 117–19

prison escape attempt, 175,
 176

promises to help John escape
 prison, 129

returns to Rockford after Civil
 War, 66

robbery in Jonesville, 114–15

third train robbery, 139–40

Reno, James, 86

Reno, John, 32, 86. *See also* Reno
 brothers; Reno Gang

arrested, 34, 95–96, 99, 200,
 203–4

autobiography (*See Life of John Reno, The* (Reno))
betting on election, 94–95
as bounty broker, 47–48
as bounty jumper, 46
and Civil War, 40–49, 189
and counterfeiting, 73
death of, 204
early life, 10–13
fails to appear at trial, 100, 101
finds bag of gold, 33–34
first out-of-state robbery, 122–29
first train robbery, 171
and George Mace, 80–81
gets 25-year prison sentence, 128–29
as head of criminal network, 98
horse betting, 108
in Indianapolis, 34, 40, 114
and James Flanders, 202–3
life after prison, 200–204
marries Sarah Reno, 203
and Mollie Nagle, 110–11, 114, 125
in New Orleans, 13–14
only known photograph of, 156–57, 211
pardoned by Missouri governor, 199–200
pets, 198–99
prison years, 197–200
questioned about horse theft, 82–84

returns to Rockford after Civil War, 66
runs away from home, 12–15
shares cell with John Brooks, 103
and Walker Hammond, 111–12
Reno, Julia Ann, 10, 12, 31–32, 33, 80, 99, 172
Reno, Laura Amanda, 10, 32, 128, 172
after brothers' lynching, 183–85, 192
defends her brothers, 160–61, 163–64, 167
marries Elijah Goudy, 210
Reno, Sarah, 183, 203, 214
Reno, Simeon, 10, 32, 66, 86, 144. *See also* Reno brothers; Reno Gang
arrested for train robbery, 95–96, 99
betting on election, 94–95
as bounty jumper, 46
buried in City Cemetery, Seymour, 214
death by hanging, 179–89
first train robbery, 171
as head of criminal network, 98
third train robbery, 139–40
trial, 160–67
Reno, Trick, 33–34, 187
Reno, Wilkinson, 1, 10, 12, 31–32, 86, 93
after Reno brothers' hanging, 192

buys burned out lots in
Rockford, 33
death of, 210
has John arrested for stealing
money, 34
house searched, 96–98
posts bail, 99, 101
Seymour Vigilance Committee
warning, 187
Reno, William, 10, 32, 86, 98, 144
buried in City Cemetery,
Seymour, 214
during Civil War, 46
death by hanging, 179–89
headstone, 215–16
third train robbery, 139–40
trial, 160–67
Reno brothers. *See also* individuals
as bounty jumpers/brokers,
45–46
buried in City Cemetery,
Seymour, 216
and the Civil War, 40–49, 189
and horse racing, 81
and Republican party, 40, 45,
94
reputation, 96–97
wagers on election results, 94
Reno Gang, 66. *See also*
individuals
and Adams Express Company,
211
begins robbing businesses, 67
connections in Rockford, IN,
97

and counterfeiting, 75, 79,
97–98
fallout from New Albany jail
hangings, 190–92
first out-of-state robbery,
122–29
first train robbery, 87–102,
171–72
fourth train robbery, 144–54,
160, 166
jail breaks, 86
Monroe's campaign against,
8–9, 71, 85, 211
negative impact on town of
Seymour, 149–50
Pinkerton on trail of, 132–33
robs Richards' home, 69
second train robbery, 108–13,
172
and Seymour Vigilance
Committee, 151–54
takes advantage of transients
near train stations, 68–69
third train robbery, 137–40, 169
Reno Law, 84
Republican Party, 40, 43, 45, 85,
94, 120, 194
Richards, Mrs. Joel, 69
Rittenhouse, Joe, 201
robberies. *See also* train robberies
in Iowa, 131–36
Reno Gang's out-of-state,
122–29
Rockford, IN, 1–9, 148
arson fires, 32

death of, 29
as hiding place for criminals, 33, 49, 97
Reno Gang headquarters, 67
residents move to Seymour, 32
robberies, 120
Rockford Herald, The, 3, 4, 6–8, 31
Rockford House hotel, 1, 4, 32
Rogers, Michael, 133–34, 135–36
Roseberry, Charlie, 145, 146–50, 150–54

Salt Creek Mob, 116
Sanford, E. S., 101, 139
Scott, John, 104, 112–13, 114, 150–54, 157, 174
Scott, Winfield, 51–52, 54
Scott County, 137
Scott County courthouse, 160–67
Scott County Grand Jury, 171
Scully, John, 64
secret service, 57–60
Secret Service, U. S., 79, 141
Sellers, Charlotte, 213
Semple, Jack, 202
Seward, C. A., 173, 174
Seward, Fred, 51–52, 54
Seward, William, 53, 169–70, 173–74, 190, 191
Seymour, Hezekial C., 24–25
Seymour, IN, 68, 81, 148
  after the Reno Gang, 192, 209–12
  beginnings of, 7–8
  birth of, 22–39

and Civil War, 41–45
lawlessness in, 70
Monroe's interest in promoting, 71
negative impact of Reno Gang on, 149–50
petty crimes in, 71–72
Reno brothers bodies returned to, 184
today, 213–16
Seymour Times, 8, 31
  article about Reno being questioned about horse theft, 84
  during Civil War, 43–44
  Monroe becomes editor again, 193–96
  Monroe's bitter editorials after Civil War, 70
  sold by Monroe, 130–31
  and vigilance committee, 70, 106, 212
  vigilantism, 119
  world's first train robbery, 99
Seymour Vigilance Committee, 70–71, 85, 112, 114, 155–56, 158–59
  after Reno Gang's fourth train robbery, 151–54
  aftermath of Reno brothers' hanging, 192
  first appearance in Jackson County, 103–7
  goes after Simeon and William Reno, 164–67

lynchings, 179–89
and Monroe, 69–71, 196, 212
sheriff tries to discourage, 160
threatens Scott County sheriff,
161
tortures, 115–16, 118–19
warning after Reno brothers'
hangings, 186–88
Shields, Lycurgus, 99
Shields, Meedy, 7–8
acquires land near Rockford,
22–23
on board of directors of O&M
Railroad, 24–25
death of, 81–82
founder of Seymour, IL, 27–28
railroad laws, 28–29
rumors about Rockford fires, 33
shovers, 75–76, 77, 97
6th Massachusetts Infantry, 55
Slagle, George, 82
slavery, 14, 26
Sleight, Louis, 79
Smith, Dan, 127
Smith, George, 18–19, 20
snake shows, 68–69
Sparks, Frank, 118, 125–26, 144,
145, 148
arrest of, 95–96, 99, 157–59
betting on election, 94–95
first Reno Gang train robbery,
171
fourth Reno Gang train
robbery, 146–50, 156
hanging, 158–59
and Jasper Monroe, 128

Spencer, Charles, 163
spies, 59–60, 62–64
Stanton, Edwin, 63, 78
states' rights, 31
Strong, George Templeton, 54
Swigget, Howard, 177

Talley, John, 103–7
Thompson, John, 76
Thornton, Edward, 170, 176,
190–91
Thurston, Robert, 87
time zones, 29
torture, 115–16
train robberies
Reno Gang's first, 87–102, 171
Reno Gang's fourth, 144–54,
160, 166
Reno Gang's second, 108–13,
172
Reno Gang's third, 137–40
transcontinental railroad, 26–27
Trumbull, Lyman, 191
Tucker, Ebenezer, 2
Tyler, Dallas, 204

Union Express Company, 168
U.S. Note, 74

Vidocq, Eugene Francois, 57–58
Vienna, IN, 164–65, 166, 167
vigilance committee. See Seymour
Vigilance Committee
vigilantism, 84–86, 114–21. See
also Seymour Vigilance
Committee

Warne, Kate, 51, 53, 64, 205

Warren, Frank, 170

Washington, DC, 50, 53–56, 59–60, 60–62, 62–64

Webster, Timothy, 51, 54, 55, 57, 64–65, 207

Webster-Ashburton Treaty, 171, 173

Weir, L. C., 170, 172–73, 176

Weir, Robert M., 174

Welsh, Long John, 201

Whedon, Conductor, 137, 138

Wilson, David F., 105

Wilson, Grant, 67, 114–15

Wilson, Henry, 62

Wilson, Isaac, 115, 116–19

Wilson, Lafayette, 115

Wilson, William, 161–62

Windsor, Canada, 139–40, 144, 168–78

Wineman, Phillip, 30

Winscott, Dick, 82, 156–57, 157–58

Wisconsin Marine and Fire and Insurance Company, 18–19, 20

Wood, William P., 78, 79, 141

Woodward, Sam, 107

About the Author

Rachel Dickinson is a writer whose work has appeared in numerous publications including *The Atlantic, Smithsonian.com, Outside, Men's Journal, American Way, Aeon, Salon,* and *Audubon.* She has been awarded two Travel Classics awards, an American Society of Journalists and Authors award for best book, a National Endowment for the Humanities Youth Fellowship, and a coveted Thomas J. Watson Fellowship. The author of *Falconer on the Edge: A Man, His Birds, and the Vanishing Landscape of the American West,* she lives in Freeville, New York.